Teacher's Guide
Step-by-Step

Daily Lessons

Kindergarten
Volume 2

**by Stamey Carter
and
Lyn Wendon,
Originator of Letterland**

Published by **Letterland International Ltd**,
Barton, Cambridge CB23 7AY, UK

Tel: +44 (0) 1223 262 675
Fax: +44 (0) 1223 264 126

www.letterland.com

© Letterland International Ltd 2009.

This edition published 2011.

First published 2009.

Product code: USTGK2

ISBN: 978-1-862095-991

10 9 8 7 6 5 4 3

LETTERLAND is a registered tradmark of Lyn Wendon

The authors assert the moral right to be identified as the authors of this work.

A catalogue record for this book is available from the Library of Congress, Washington, D.C.

A catalogue record for this book is also available from the British Library.

Written by Stamey Carter and Lyn Wendon

Edited by Lyn Wendon and Kate Mennell

Editorial Assistant: Klara Harjung

Adapted and extended from the 2003 edition of the Letterland Teacher's Guide by Gudrun Freese

Illustrated by Kerry Ingham, Kathy Baxendale and Geri Livingston

Photographs by Steve Lumb and Janine Hosegood

Design by Ken Vail Graphic Design, Cambridge, UK

Cover design by Letterland International Ltd

Printed and bound in Singapore

Acknowledgments
The first author wishes to thank his mentors Darrell Morris and Rebecca Felton for their generous and wise teaching and guidance over many years.

The authors and publishers would like to thank teachers and administrators in western North Carolina and in Blountstown, Florida for piloting this Letterland edition and for their valuable input and encouragement. A very special thanks to Vickie Norris for her invaluable contributions and suggestions but most of all for her contagious enthusiasm, her sense of "making it fun," and her constant concern for children who struggle with reading.

Special thanks are also due to the following schools for sharing their excellent classroom practices reflected in the photographs in this Teacher's Guide: Bishops Hill Primary School, Taunton, Somerset, England; Hardin Park Elementary School, Boone, North Carolina; Tolworth Infant & Junior School, Twickenham, Surrey, England, and to all the teachers who have made learning about Letterland so much fun for the children in their classrooms.

"Children learn best when they are enjoying themselves." Lyn Wendon

Contents

Introduction

To recap on the Introduction in Volume One of this Teacher's Guide, Letterland has for over 35 years led children all over the world on a delightful, engaging path to reading and writing. As more and more research accumulates on reading acquisition and how the young human brain learns, the intuitions and understandings of Letterland's originator, Lyn Wendon, continue to prove their value. This new expanded edition maintains these Letterland merits and provides even more day-by-day support for teachers to help all children become eager readers.

Letterland teaching methodology aligns closely with the findings of the National Reading Panel on the most effective ways to teach phonemic awareness and phonics.

National Reading Panel Statements

The motivational power of associating letters with <u>interesting characters</u> or hand motions and incorporating this into activities that are fun is important for promoting young children's learning.

(NPR, 2000, p 2: 125)

In a study by Ehri, Deffner, and Wilce (1984), children were shown letters drawn to assume the shape of objects... s drawn as a snake, h drawn as a house (with a chimney)...Children...taught in this way learned them better than children who were taught letters ... with pictures unrelated to the letter shapes...Application of this principle can be found in Letterland (Wendon, 1992)...

(NPR, 2000, p 2: 125)

Systematic, <u>synthetic phonics</u> instruction had a positive and significant effect on disabled readers.... low-achieving students ... [and] low socioeconomic status (SES) children...

(NPR Summary Report, 2000, p 11)

It is also critical for teachers to understand that systematic phonics instruction can be provided in an entertaining, vibrant, and creative manner.

(NPR Summary Report, 2000, p 11)

In Letterland...

Children meet friendly characters like Dippy Duck and learn Action Tricks to go with their sounds.

Children not only learn sounds from the Letterlanders but learn correct letter formation from songs relating handwriting strokes to the characters body parts.

Letterland gives priority to all-through-the-word blending and segmenting of sounds in a cumulative teaching order to ensure a firm phonic foundation for all further word study.

/m/ /a/ /t/, mat

With Live Reading and Spelling, songs, art work, drama, games and other fun activities, children happily soak up phonic knowledge and use it to become confident readers.

Step-by-Step for Kindergarten, Volumes 1 & 2

This Volume 2 completes the important Letterland Word Building Section 2 begun in Volume 1. In the following Sections 3-7, it then provides new teaching strategies, extends children's application of letter sound skills, and presents new phonic information with child-friendly Letterland fables, songs, games and more. All seven Sections are summarised below. Both Volumes also include detailed Intervention programs.

SECTION 1 — **Phonemic Awareness Fast Track** *Step-by-Step for Kindergarten,* Volume 1 uses a playful game format to give all children a 'nodding acquaintance' of the lower case **a-z** letter shapes and sounds in a brief 18-25 days at the start of the first term. This Fast Track start has a beneficial impact on all the rest of the school year.

SECTION 2

Volume 1 — **Word Building** The bulk of the teaching in this Section 2 is in Volume 1 (Lessons 19-87), and is completed here in Volume 2 (Lessons 88-107). Lessons 19-107 provide an in-depth study of the lower case and capital letters' shapes and sounds, each one delivered in a language-rich story setting, together with songs, games, riddles and role-playing of letter behavior. Right from the 6th letter on, every new sound taught is put to immediate use in word building to consolidate phonic knowledge. Children also learn from alliterative sentences which they echo-read with the teacher.

Volume 2 — The focus here is on listening to the target sound repeatedly occurring in their mouths as they speak. A separate strand in *My Letterland Reading Booklet* gradually brings in key sight words through echo-reading and repetition in choral reading. Teachers can time the introduction of this separate Sight Word strand to suit their class's needs.

SECTION 3 — **Onsets and Rimes** In this Section, children consolidate and apply their phonic knowledge to words using the read-by-analogy strategy. "If I can read **cat**, then I can read **hat**, **sat**, and **bat**." They also build sentences in fun, interactive activities that lead toward reading five new *Take-Home Readers*. Fluency with reading simple decodable words is the focus.

SECTION 4 — **Consonant Blends** Twenty all-new songs help you present the consonant blends along with interactive stories and games to engage children in this new level of reading and spelling words.

SECTION 5 — **The Vowel Men and Silent Magic e** Your children will love dramatizing the story of the Silent Magic **e** –"with the power to make the Vowel Men appear." In the process they will learn to decode hundreds of new words and continue to build basic skills in reading and writing.

SECTION 6 — **Vowel Men Out Walking** Decoding skills are extended to more and more words with seven pairs of vowel letters (e.g. **ai, ee, oa**) in which "the first Vowel Man says his name, but his friend won't do the same." Further activities in drama, music and art help children consolidate these new phonic facts and practice reading words and text fluently.

SECTION 7 — **The Vowel Stealers** The challenging **r**-controlled vowel sounds are made fascinating and manageable by stories of the Robot brothers who capture the vowels and carry them off in their net bags. Children learn to catch these **r**obbers at their tricks and thereby correctly sound out and master scores of new words.

Lesson Plan Structure (Volumes 1 & 2)

Sections & lesson number

1: Phonemic Awareness Fast Track (1–18)

- An effective way to meet or review the **a–z** Letterland characters and learn their letter sounds
- Develops awareness of initial sounds in words
- Lessons 1-18 to cover in 18 to 25 days

2: a–z Word Building (19–107)

- Focus on each **a–z** letter in more detail including handwriting, capital and lowercase
- Build words beginning with the first six letters
- Introduce **long vowels** while keeping the focus of word building on short vowels
- Introduce common consonant digraphs:
  ch ck sh th <u>th</u> ng
- Introduces basic irregular words along with decodable words in reproducible story booklets

3: Onsets and Rimes (108–137)

- Activities for using analogy to read and spell words
- 15 short vowel word families to develop automatic word recognition with word cards
- Word building and sentence building activities
- More decodable booklets

4: Consonant Blends (138–148)

- 11 lessons for teaching consonant blends
  bl cl fl gl pl sl
  br cr dr fr gr pr tr
  sc sk sp st sm sn sw

5: Long Vowels and Magic e (149–162)

- 11 lessons for teaching little words ending in long vowels and words with Magic **e**:
  he me she, no go so, my fly try, etc.
  a-e e-e i-e o-e u-e

6: Vowel Men Out Walking (163–172)

- 12 lessons for teaching long vowel pairs:
  ai ay ee ea ie oa ue

7: The Vowel Stealers: r-controlled vowels (173–180)

- 12 lessons for teaching **r**-controlled vowels:
  ar er ir or ur

Assessment Outcomes

- Say the 26 **a–z** Letterland character names
- Say the letter sounds **a–z** in response to the plain letter
- Sort words according to initial sounds
- Sequence three spoken letter sounds

Letter Sounds (a–z, ch, ck, sh, th, ng)

- Say the letter sound in response to the plain letter with accuracy and fluency
- Write letter(s) in response to sound
- Match upper and lowercase letters (**Aa–Zz**)

Words

- Blend CVC words accurately and fluently
- Segment and spell CVC words
- Read a selection of high-frequency words

- Decode words on the basis of analogy with rhyming words
- Decode words more efficiently by 'chunking' simple rimes (**e.g. c-at, h-at**)
- Read decodable words and a selection of high-frequency words in sentences and stories
- Spell CVC words

- Blend and Segment CCVC words
- Read additional high-frequency words

- Read and spell little words with long vowels at the end
- Blend and segment words with Magic **e** pattern
- Read additional high-frequency words

- Blend and segment CVVC words
- Read additional high-frequency words

- Blend and segment words with **r**-controlled pattern
- Read additional high-frequency words

Section 2

a-z Word Building

(continued)

Lessons 88-107

Jumping Jim's Sound

Review

- **PCCs ă, b, ĕ, g, ĭ, j, m, ŏ, s, s=z, y, t, u, ck** Use the 'Quick Dash' (see Volume 1, page 233).

Jumping Jim, his sound, action and song

✔ **Preparation and materials**
- *BPCC:* **j** plus Review *PCCs*
- *Alphabet Songs* CD, # 11
  Option: Project lyrics, *TG CD 2*
- *Letterland ABC Book,* p 24 or
  Living ABC Software
- *Vocabulary Cards* for **j**
- Classroom labels
- *A-Z Copymaster,* **j**

✔ **Small group/independent**
- **j** to picture-code, *TG CD 2*

p 25

- **Jumping Jim** It's listen-and-think time again. There are several boys in Letterland I could be thinking of right now. This one is just a little older than you are. He has dark hair and he is very fit. He has a favorite **j**acket that you will usually see him wearing. And he is very good at doing something very difficult…. and that is **j**uggling! Sometimes he even **j**uggles with **j**am **j**ars! **"Jumping Jim."** Show his *BPCC* and explain, Jumping Jim is very talented at **j**uggling. He can even **j**uggle four balls so fast that you can only ever see one of them. He can also do something **j**ust amazing! He can **j**ump while he **j**uggles! Can you point in the direction he is **j**umping? What is that direction? **"The Reading Direction."**

- **Show his plain letter** to remind everyone how Jumping Jim looks in words. Ask the children where his shoes would go, his juggling ball and his head, etc. Turn the card over to confirm their answers.

- **Sound** Show the plain letter again and rediscover his letter sound using the Sounds Trick (Vol. 1, page 221): Jumping Jim, /**j**/. Teach his Action Trick (Vol. 1, page 227).

- **Song** Sing Jumping Jim's *Alphabet Song.* Show the picture side of his *BPCC* when you sing his name and the plain side for his sound and action. (Or use the *Software.*)

- **Letter Name and Sound** People who don't know about Letterland call this letter a '**j**' (jay). We will learn more about that letter name later, but right now we want to remember the most important thing about Jumping Jim, and that is his sound. It's a quick sound that **j**umps quickly right out of your mouth. You have to keep your mouth almost closed while you say it, /**j**/. Say it with me, /**j**/. Let's say it three times, like we are juggling with Jim, /**j**/ /**j**/ /**j**/.

Phonemic awareness and language development

Listen

- **ABC book** Read about Jumping Jim (or use the *Software*). Emphasize his sound and explore the picture together.

- **Vocabulary Cards** Show the three pictures and the big words on the backs and use your classroom labels (e.g. **jigsaw puzzles, jars, jackets**) to draw attention to Jumping Jim's sound.

- **Ask questions and discuss** What kind of shoes does Jumping Jim wear, boots? Or **j**ogging shoes? What would you expect Jumping Jim to spread on his toast: butter and honey? or **j**uicy **j**elly? Who can tell me Jumping Jim's three favorite months of the year? Does anyone have a birthday month that begins with Jumping Jim's sound?

Games

- **Jumping Jim's Jokes** After asking each question below, have the class say /**j**/ to remind them to use Jim's sound to help them think of the answer. Children may not get many answers, but they will like going through them again to see how many they do get on a second or third try. They may also like to memorize a few riddles to ask parents, siblings, or friends.

    What makes Jumping Jim laugh? **jolly jokes**

    What made Jumping Jim jump out of the ocean? **jellyfish**

    How does Jumping Jim like to travel? **by jumbo jet**

    To what countries in Asia would Jumping Jim like to journey? **Japan, Java**

    What does Jumping Jim like on his toast? **jelly, jam**

    What does Jumping Jim like best about Halloween? **jack-o-lanterns**

    What does Jumping Jim like to drive? **a jeep**

    What are Jumping Jim's favorite playground activities? **jumping rope, jungle gym**

    Where would Jumping Jim go to see wild animals? **jungle**

    What is Jumping Jim's favorite big cat? **jaguar**

- **Jumping Jim's Tongue Twister** Can anyone say Jumping Jim's tongue twister fast three times in a row without twisting it?

    Don't giggle when you juggle,
    or jiggle when you giggle.

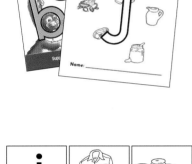

- **A-Z Copymaster** Discuss the pictures and then model finger tracing, saying Jumping Jim's *Handwriting Verse* as your trace:

    Just draw down Jim, bending his knees,
    Then add the one ball that everyone sees.

    Observe and help as needed with their tracing and rainbow writing while everyone fills the room with /**j**/ /**j**/ /**j**/ sounds.

Small group/independent activities

- **Picture-coding** (**Ind**) Model picture-coding Jumping Jim and give out large plain **j**'s.

- **Pocket chart/table reading** (**SG**) Build the words below for children to rollercoaster the sounds and read. Ask for volunteers to try decoding a word on their own either before or after the group does, depending on the child's confidence. (For details, see *Pocket Chart Reading*, Vol. 1, page 239.)

    PCCs: ă, b, ĕ, g, ĭ, j, m, ŏ, s, s=z, t, ŭ, ck

    Words: jet, jets, jot, job, jog, jug, jugs, Jim, jam, Jack

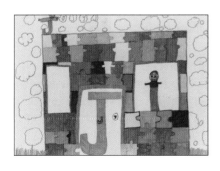

- **Beginning Sounds and Handwriting** Add **j** words to *Beginning Sound Picture* sorting for those who need this practice, and do handwriting with letters introduced so far in this section. (See Appendices, page 240 for Small Group Beginning Sound Games for each new letter, available for any children who may still need support in this basic skill.)

- **Software** Children will continue to benefit from using the *Software* with new letters and any other letters that need more practice.

Jumping Jim's Letter Shapes

Preparation and materials

✔ **Preparation and materials**
- *BPCCs*: **J**, **j** plus Review *PCCs*
- *Handwriting Songs* CD, # 11 or *Living ABC Software*
- Jumping Jim name card, *TG CD 1*
- *Sentence Copymaster*, p 11

✔ **Small group/independent**
- **J j** to picture-code *TG CD 1*
- *My Letterland Reading Booklet*, p 32, *TG CD 1*
- *Workbook 3*, pp 18-19
- *A-Z Copymasters* **j** and **J**
- Individual letter sets
- Handwriting: Select from *Early Years Handwriting Copymaster*, pp 10, 28 *ELT Handwriting*, pp 6-7

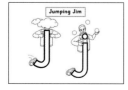

Review

- **Word Stretching Warm Up** What can all of these things do? Say the first word, children repeat. One child says each sound. All repeat the segmented sound. (Mystery answer: **Fly**.)

    Words: **bee (b-ee), kite (k-i-te), jet (j-e-t), bat (b-a-t)**

- **PCCs ă, b, c, ĕ, f, g, ĭ, j, k, l, l, y, j, n ŏ, t, ŭ, ck, ll, ff** Play 'Guess Who?' (Vol. 1, page 234) with all *PCCs* listed. Use 'Handwriting Review' here with whole class or during small groups (page 242).

Letter shapes: J and j

- **BPCC** Finger-trace the **j** on the picture side as you say Jumping Jim's *Handwriting Verse*. Repeat it with the plain side:

    Just draw down Jim, bending his knees.
    Then add the one ball which everyone sees.

- **Writing lowercase j** Draw a huge **j** on the board. Sing or chant Jumping Jim's *Handwriting Verse* while children slowly air-trace the letter.

- **Capital J** First show the **j** *BPCC* picture side. As you explain the Capital Letter Trick, reveal the **J** *BPCC* picture side. In many words you'll see Jumping Jim **j**umping below the line, but whenever he gets a chance to start an important word, he is so pleased that he does a big **j**ump, right up on to the line and his head disappears in the clouds! Then we can't even see any of his **j**uggling balls.

- **Show the Jumping Jim name card** Review the Character Name Trick. How can you tell whose name this is?

Sentence Copymaster

- Project the sentence or write it on the board and share the picture. The children listen for words with initial /**j**/ sounds as you read it. Have them finger-trace the large hollow **j**. Reread the sentence with children echo-reading and listening for the /**j**/ sounds in their own speech. Have them circle each **J** and **j**, rainbow write inside the large **j**, and color the page.

Small group/independent activities

- **Picture-coding (Ind)** Model picture-coding of **J** and **j** and have children picture-code their own **J j**.

- **My Letterland Reading Booklet (SG/Ind)** page 30. Look up, it's Jumping Jim. Read this new page *to*, then *with* the children. Talk about why we might have to look up to see all of Jim (**"he jumps so high"**) and what else we would see if we looked up at him (**"one juggling ball"**). Reread the previous pages together. Then have partners reread to each other as you observe, and have individuals point and repeat the words to you. Children can illustrate the page at any time.

- **A-Z Copymaster (SG)** Show children how to trace the capital letter **J**. Have them finger trace, rainbow write, and add pictures beginning with /**j**/.

- **Spelling with letter sets (SG)** Follow the procedure listed under the Teacher Strategies—Spelling with *Letterland Word Builders* (Vol. 1, page 242), with the whole class, or with the children organized into small groups.

  Note: Children do not need Capital letters, but when they all spell a name aloud they should say "Capital" first, i.e. **"Capital J, e, f, f, Jeff."** Children use blank tiles for letters that are in the same word more than once if they have no duplicate letters.

  Letters needed: a, b, c, e, f, f, g, i, j, k, l, l, j, n, o, t, u

  Words for children to spell: bell, jet, Ben, Jeff, job, Jack, jug, Jill

- **Workbook 3 (SG/Ind)** As you guide students in completing these pages, have them trace the picture-coded Jumping Jim on page 18 with their fingers before writing their own letters.

- **Optional** Share the *Alphabet Name Verse* for **j** now, or later (*TG CD 2*).

Assessments for Lessons 61-89 are found on pages 44-52 of this volume.

Lesson 90: Day 1

Red Robot's Sound

Preparation and materials
- *BPCC*: **r** plus Review *PCCs*
- *Alphabet Songs* CD, # 19
  Option: Project lyrics, *TG CD 2*
- *Letterland ABC Book*, pp 40-41
  or *Living ABC Software*
- *Vocabulary Cards* for **r**
- Classroom labels
- *A-Z Copymaster*, **r**, p22

Small group/independent
- **r** to picture-code, *TG CD 2*

Red Robot's Alphabet Song

Red Ro-bot, Red Ro-bot.
See how he runs.
See how he runs.

He rrreally makes
a growling sound.

He's always heard,
but he's never found.

Have you ever seen
such a rascal around!
'Rrr..., rrr..., rrr...'.

Review

- **PCCs ă, b, d, ĕ, g, ĭ, n, ŏ, p, r, ŭ, ch, ng** Review Letterlanders and sounds as needed. Repeat, asking for sounds only. Repeat even faster.

Red Robot, his sound, action and song

- **Red Robot** I'm thinking right now of someone in Letterland who would love to get into a **r**ocket and **r**oar off into Space. If I told you he would be even happier if the **r**ocket he **r**oared off in was **r**ed, would you be able to figure out who we'll be learning more about today? **"Red Robot!"** You are so **rrr**ight! Use the *BPCC* to **r**emind everyone what this **r**ollerskating **r**ascal looks like when he is in Letterland. Red Robot can **r**un fast without his **r**oller skates. But with his **r**oller skates on, he can **r**eally **r**ace along at an incredible speed. That makes him one of the fastest **r**acers in Letterland! Which way is he **r**ollerskating? What is that direction? **"The Reading Direction."** Show his plain letter and ask where his roller skates would go, his robber's sack, his arm, and his hand, etc. Turn the card over to confirm their answers.

- **Sound** Show Red Robot's plain letter (*BPCC*) again, and rediscover his letter sound using the Sounds Trick: Red Robot, /**rrr**/. Teach his Action Trick.

- **Song** Sing Red Robot's *Alphabet Song*. Show the picture side of his *BPCC* when you sing his name, and the plain letter for his sound and action.

- **Letter Name and Sound** People who don't know about Letterland call this letter an '**r**' (are), but right now we want to remember the most important thing about Red Robot; his sound. It's like a growling sound, or a sound like his robot motor running.

p 41

We can keep his sound running like that, but we have to keep our mouth almost closed to do it. Say it with me, "/rrr/." Let's say it three times, like we are hearing that motor running as we race along with Red Robot, "/rrr/ /rrr/ /rrr/."

Phonemic awareness and language development

Listen

● **ABC book** Read about Red Robot (or use the *Software*). Emphasize his sound and explore the picture together.

● **Vocabulary Cards** Use both sides and your classroom labels (e.g. **reading center, rules, ruler, recycle**) to draw attention to Red Robot's sound.

● **Ask questions and discuss** Red Robot is a troublemaker in Letterland because he has a habit of **r**unning off with things that begin with his /**rrr**/ sound, even when they don't belong to him! Now listen carefully because I am going to say some names of things. If you think Red Robot would **rrr**un off with them, make his sound /**rrr**/ and do his action. If you think he would not **r**un off with the thing, respond with thumbs down. **Rrr**ready? **R**ocks, **r**ings, spoons, **r**eading books, money, **r**ice cakes with **r**aisins, puzzles, **r**ecipes, **r**are **r**eptiles, cell phones, cameras, **r**ed **r**ockets. Praise words: **R**ight, **r**emarkable.

● **Alliteration Game** Suggest categories such as the ones below and have children come up with the words. Write words on the board. Let the children help count the number of words in each category.

Alliteration Game for Red Robot

<u>Animals</u>	<u>Things That Go</u>	<u>Foods</u>	<u>He does well at</u>	<u>Favorite music</u>
rooster, rabbit, rat, rattlesnake, raven, reindeer, rhinoceros, reptile, robin	racers, racing car, raft, railroad, road, rocket, roller skates	raisins, rice, ravioli <u>Where does he eat?</u> a restaurant by the river	rhyming, riddles, roller skating, racing, reading, being a rascal, roaming around	rock 'n' roll <u>His hideaway is</u> on Red Rock Range, right by some rapids in a rocky river

---

● **A-Z Copymaster** (**SG**) Discuss the pictures and then model finger tracing, saying Red Robot's *Handwriting Verse* as your trace:

> Run down Red Robot's body. Go up to his arm and his hand.
> Then watch out for this robot roaming round Letterland.

Observe and help as needed with their tracing and rainbow writing while everyone fills the room with /**r**/ /**r**/ /**r**/ sounds.

Small group/independent activities

● **Picture-coding** (**Ind**) Model picture-coding Red Robot and give out large plain **r**'s.

● **Word Building: Pocket chart/table reading** (**SG**) For details see *Spelling with Letterland Word Builders* (Vol. 1, page 239.) Build the words below for children to arm-blend. Ask for volunteers to try decoding a word on their own either before or after the group does, depending on the child's confidence.

    PCCs: ă, b, d, ĕ, ĭ, n, ŏ, p, r, ŭ, ch, ng

    Words: red, rod, rid, rib, rub, chip, chap, rap, ran, rang, ring

● **Beginning Sounds and Handwriting** Add **r** words to *Beginning Sound Picture* sorting for those who need this practice, and do handwriting with letters studied so far in this section. (See page 240 for a special **r** game.)

- **Software** Children will continue to benefit from using the Software with new letters and any other letters that need more practice.

Red Robot's Letter Shapes

Preparation and materials
- *BPCCs*: **R**, **r** plus Review *PCCs*
- *Handwriting Songs* CD, # 19, on *TG CD 2*, or *Living ABC Software*
- Red Robot name card, *TG CD 2*
- *Sentence Copymaster*, p 19

Small group/independent
- **R r** to picture-code, *TG CD 2*
- *My Letterland Reading Booklet*,
- p 33, *TG CD 2*
- Copies of Spelling Boxes, *TG CD 2*
- *Workbook 4*, pp 2-3
- *A-Z Copymasters*, **r** and **R**
- Handwriting: Select from *EY Handwriting Copymaster*, pp 18, 42 *ELT Handwriting*, pp 38-39

Red Robot rolls to a big red rocket.

Red Robot is running away.

33

Review

- **PCCs ă, b, d, ĕ, g, ĭ, n, ŏ, p, r, ŭ, ck, ng** Play 'Guess Who' with all *PCCs* listed. Use the 'Handwriting Review' with whole class or small groups (page 242).

Letter shapes: R and r

- **Word Stretching Warm Up** All these words are ways to do what? Say the first word, children repeat. One child says each sound, all repeat. (Mystery answer: **Move**.)
  Words: **run (r-u-n), roll (r-o-ll), ride (r-i-de), race (r-a-ce)**
- **BPCC** Finger-trace the **r** on the picture side as you say Red Robot's *Handwriting Verse* (on CD or *Software*). Repeat it with the plain side.
- **Writing lowercase r** Draw a huge **r** on the board. Sing or chant Red Robot's *Handwriting Verse* while children slowly air-trace the letter. (on CD or *Software*)
- **Capital R** First show the lowercase *BPCC* picture side. As you explain the Capital Letter Trick, reveal the capital *BPCC* picture side. Whenever Red Robot starts somebody's name or a sentence, he takes a deep breath, changes his shape a lot, and grows much taller. You can tell from this that he is a **r**eal **r**ascal, because the **r**eason he changes his shape so often is to try to make it harder for you to **rrr**ecognize him when you're **rrr**eading!
- **Show the Red Robot Name card** Review the Character Name Trick: How can you tell whose name this is? By the **rrr**epeat of the capital **R**'s, **rrr**ight?

Sentence Copymaster
- Project and share the picture and have children finger trace the large hollow **r**. Choral-read the sentence together, all listening for five /**rrr**/ sounds. Have them circle each **R** and **r**, rainbow write inside the large **r**, and color the page. Circulate to observe correct '**rrr**ainbow writing', finger pointing, and repeating the words.

Small group/independent activities

- **Picture-coding (Ind)** Model picture-coding of **R** and **r** and have children picture-code their own **R r**.
- **My Letterland Reading Booklet (SG/Ind)** page 30. Read this new page *to*, then *with* the children. Talk about why Red Robot is running away, or who he is running from. Choral-read the previous pages together. Then have partners '**rrr**eread' the familiar words from memory to each other as you observe, and have individuals point and repeat the words to you. Children can illustrate the page at any time.

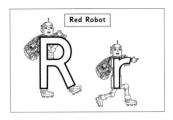

Red Robot

- **A-Z Copymaster (SG)** Show children how to trace the capital letter **R**. Have them finger trace, rainbow write, and add pictures beginning with /r/.
- **Spelling Boxes (SG)** See Spelling Boxes (*TG CD 2*)
  Words for children to spell: Set 1: **run, rag, rock** Set 2: **that, ring, rub**
- **Workbook 3 (SG/Ind)** As you guide the children in completing these pages, have them finger-trace the picture-coded robot on page 2 before writing their own letters.
- **Handwriting** Select from handwriting options listed in the materials box.
- **Optional** Share the *Alphabet Names Verse* for **r** now or later. (*TG CD 2*)

Lesson 92: Day 1

Quarrelsome Queen's Sound

Preparation and materials
- Make or locate a crown and a small umbrella for introducing the Queen and for Live Spelling
- *BPCCs*: **q** plus **u** (plain side only)
- *PCCs*: Review
- *Alphabet Songs* CD, #18 Option: **Project lyrics**, *TG CD 2*
- *Letterland ABC book*, p 28 or *Living ABC Software*
- *Vocabulary Cards* for **q**
- Classroom labels
- *A-Z Copymaster*, **q**

Small group/independent
- **q** to picture-code, *TG CD 2*

PCC

BPCC's

Review

- PCCs **ă, ĭ, s, s=z, t, ck, qu, ll** Use the 'Quick Dash' (Vol. 1, page 233).

Quarrelsome Queen, her sound, action and song

- **Quarrelsome Queen** It's lisetn-and-think time again. Some Letterlanders just won't do things the way the rest of them do, and I am thinking of one of them. What's worse, this Letterlander is a very important person. So she isn't setting a very good example by the way she behaves. Here are two more clues: She has beautiful long hair, and she wears a crown. Who is it? **"Quarrelsome Queen!"** Use the **q** BPCC to remind everyone what this **qu**ick and **qu**arrelsome **qu**een looks like when she is in Letterland. Do you know what **quarreling** means? It means fussing and arguing with other people. Letterland's **Qu**een is very **qu**ick to **qu**arrel with anyone. She is so **qu**arrelsome that she won't even face in the Reading Direction! No wonder people call her **Qu**arrelsome **Qu**een! Let's point in the Reading Direction with one hand. Now with your other hand, point in the direction the **qu**een is facing. It's the wrong way, isn't it? What a **Qu**een! Can you say her name again?

- **The Royal Umbrella** Show the picture side of the **qu** PCC and the picture side of the **q** BPCC. (There is no **qu** BPCC.) There is something else about the **Qu**arrelsome **Qu**een that makes her different. The **qu**een is extremely proud of her long, beautiful hair. Show the picture side of the **qu** card. She always takes her royal umbrella with her wherever she goes, to protect her hair from the rain and the sun. Turn to the plain side of your **q** BPCC and add your **u** BPCC, plain side. So whenever we see **Qu**arrelsome **Qu**een's letter in words we will see her **u**mbrella letter right beside her, close to her long, beautiful hair. With the plain **qu** PCC ask the children to point to where the queen's hair would be, and her crown, her face. Use the **qu** PCC picture side to confirm their answers. Explain that her royal umbrella looks like the one in the *Letterland ABC* book. If YOU want to avoid a **qu**arrel with **Qu**arrelsome **Qu**een when you write her letter in a word, make sure you don't forget to add her umbrella letter right next to her every time!

- **Sound** Continue using the **q** and **u** BPCCs. Show her plain letter BPCC again and rediscover her letter sound using the Sounds Trick: Quarrelsome Queen, /**qu**/. Teach Quarrelsome Queen's Action Trick.

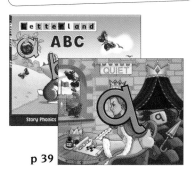

Quarrelsome Queen's Alphabet Song

Quarrelsome Queen says
'qu...' in words,
'qu...' in words,
'qu...' in words.

Quarrelsome Queen says
'qu...' in words.

She must have
her umbrella.

- **Song** Sing Quarrelsome Queen's *Alphabet Song*. Show the picture side of her **q** *BPCC* when you sing her name, and the plain side for her sound and action. (Or use the *Software*.)

- **Letter Name** People who don't know about Letterland call this letter a '**q**' (cue). We will be using that name sometimes, too, but right now we want to remember the most important thing about Quarrelsome Queen, and that is her sound. We need to open our mouths only a little bit when we say her quick sound. Say it with me, /**qu**/. Now let's do her Action, and say her sound three times, **qu**ickly. "/**qu**/ /**qu**/ /**qu**/."

Phonemic awareness and language development

Listen

- **ABC book** Read about Quarrelsome Queen (or use the *Software*). Emphasize her sound and explore the picture together. Ask who else faces the wrong way in words, and look briefly at Golden Girl's picture. Remind everyone that in her case it is not because she is quarrelsome, but because she gets giddy in her garden swing. You may also like to discuss Zig Zag Zebra, the only other Letterlander who looks the other way in words, and why.

- **Vocabulary Cards** Go over the pictures and the big words on the backs. Keep these cards handy to remind students of their meanings when they sound out these words in Live Reading. Use your classroom label (e.g. "**Quiet Corner**" or perhaps just "**Quiet!**" by your reading center or book area) to draw attention to Quarrelsome Queen's sound.

- **Ask questions and discuss** Quarrelsome Queen is very quick to quarrel. She has at least 9 quarrels a day which may explain why her letter looks like the number 9. If you think my question to you would make her quarrel, frown and say "quarrel." If you think she would not quarrel, say "quiet" and smile.

  - Would she quarrel if you told her that her hair was messy? "**Quarrel!**"
  - What if you told her to turn around and face the reading direction? "**Quarrel!**"
  - What if you told her that her hair was the most beautiful hair in Letterland? "**Quiet.**"
  - What if you asked to borrow her umbrella? "**Quarrel!**"
  - What if you called her a number 9? "**Quarrel!**"
  - What if you called her a very lovely queen? "**Quiet.**"

- Praise word: Quite right!

- **A-Z Copymaster** Discuss the pictures and then model finger tracing, saying Quarrelsome Queen's *Handwriting Verse* as your trace:

  Quickly go round the Queen's cross face.
  Then comb her beautiful hair into place.

Observe and help as needed with their tracing and rainbow writing while everyone fills the room with /**qu**/ /**qu**/ /**qu**/ sounds.

Games

- **Interview the Queen** Let the children make up their own **q**uestions for the Queen and you play the role of **q**ueen and answer their **q**uestions as you think she might.

- **Queenly Questions** Use these today and review on a subsequent day.
  - What is Quarrelsome Queen's favorite US coin? **quarter**
  - What does one of her favorite pets keep saying? **quack-quack**

p 39

- What player does she like to watch on an American football team? **quarterback**
- What size is Quarrelsome Queen's bed? **queen-size**
- What covers her bed? **queen-size quilt**
- What is Quarrelsome Queen afraid of falling into? **quicksand**

Live Reading

- Refer to Volume 1, page 237 for details on Live Reading, if needed. Two children should hold the **qu** *PCC*. The first child could wear the crown and face the opposite way from the reading direction holding her half of the *PCC* at her side. The other child helps to hold the **qu** and holds the umbrella. Other children in words should face forward but turned slightly in the reading direction.

  PCCs: ă, ĭ, l, s, s=z, t, ck, qu, ll

  Words: **quit, quits, quick, quack, quill, quills, quilt**

Small group/independent activities

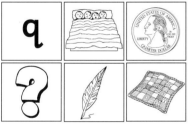

- **Picture-coding** (**Ind**) Model picture-coding **qu** and give out large plain **qu**'s.
- **Pocket chart/table reading** (**SG**) For children who would benefit from the repetition of these rather challenging words, repeat the words used above in Live Reading, this time making the words on the table.
- **Beginning Sounds and Handwriting** Add words that begin with Quarrelsome Queen's sound to your *Beginning Sound Picture* sorting activities (for those who need this practice) and do handwriting with letters introduced so far in 'Section 2: **a-z** Word Building.' (See page 240 for a special **qu** game.)

Quarrelsome Queen's Letter Shapes

✔ **Preparation and materials**
- *BPCCs:* **Q**, **q** plus Review *PCCs*
- *Handwriting Songs CD*, # 18 or *Living ABC Software*
- Quarrelsome Queen's name card, *TG CD 2*
- *Sentence Copymaster*, p 18

✔ **Small group/independent**
- **Q q** to picture-code, *TG CD 2*
- *My Letterland Reading Booklet*, p 34, *TG CD 2*
- *Workbook 4*, pp 4-5
- Handwriting: Select from *A-Z Copymasters*, **Q**, **q** *EY Handwriting Copymasters*, pp 17, 41 *ELT Handwriting*, pp 34-35

Quarrelsome Queen

Quarrelsome Queen quickly makes quilts.

Circle Quarrelsome Queen's letters in the sentence, then find the things that include her sound.

Qu
qu

Review

- **Word Stretching Warm Up** Where do you see all these things? Say the first word. Children repeat it. Have one child say each sound. All repeat the segmented word. (Mystery answer: **In the sky**.)

  Words: **bird (b-ir-d), blue (b-l-ue), star (s-t-ar), cloud (c-l-ou-d), moon (m-oo-n), sun (s-u-n)**

- **PCCs ă, e, ĭ, h, ŏ, p, t, ŭ, ck, ff, ll, qu, ss**. Play 'Guess Who' (Vol. 1, page 234) with all *PCCs* listed. Use the 'Handwriting Review' (page 242) with the whole class or small groups.

Letter shapes: Q and q

- **BPCC** Finger-trace the **q** on the picture side as you say Quarrelsome Queen's *Handwriting Verse*. Repeat it with the plain side:

  Quickly go around the Queen's cross face.
  Then comb her beautiful hair into place.

- **Writing lowercase q** Draw a huge **q** on the board. Sing or chant Quarrelsome Queen's *Handwriting Verse* while children slowly air-trace the letter. (*Handwriting Songs CD* or *Software*)

- **Capital Q** First show the **q** *BPCC* picture side. As you explain the queen's Capital Letter Trick, reveal the **Q** *BPCC* picture side. Whenever Quarrelsome Queen starts a name or a sentence, she does it from her Quiet Room. (This is also where she goes to recover from all her quarreling.) Show the Quarrelsome Queen name card. Review the Character Name Trick. How can you tell whose name this is?

Sentence Copymaster

- Project the Quarrelsome Queen page, and have children finger-trace the large, hollow **q**. Read the sentence. Have children echo-read it with you, listening for the four /**qu**/ sounds in their own speech. Have them circle each **Qu** and **qu**, rainbow write in the large **q**, and color the page. Circulate to observe correct **q** tracing and finger-point reading.

Small group/independent activities

- **Picture-coding (Ind)** Model picture-coding of **Qu** and **qu** and have children picture-code their own large plain **Qu qu**.

- **My Letterland Reading Booklet (SG/Ind)** page 32. This quilt is for Quarrelsome Queen. Read the new sentence together and choral-read a few previous pages. Then let partners review them and draw while you observe, checking finger-pointing, and specific words.

- **Workbook 4 (SG/Ind)** Guide students as they finger-trace, write, and complete the pages.

- **Spelling with letter sets (SG)** Build the words below as in Vol. 1, page 242.

  Letters to be used: **a, c, e, f, f, h, i, k, l, l, o, p, q, s, s, t, u**

  Words to spell: **quit, quick, pick, pill, quill, hiss, puff, pass, pet, pot**

Quarrelsome Queen and her Quiet Room

- **A-Z Copymaster (SG)** Show children how to trace the capital letter **Q**. Have them finger trace, rainbow write, and add pictures beginning with /**qu**/.
- **Handwriting, Intervention, Software** Continue these activities based on the children's needs.
- **Optional:** Introduce the *Alphabet Name Verse* for the **'q'** (*TG CD 2*) now or later.

Lesson 94: Day 1

Vicky Violet's Sound

Review

- PCCs **a, b, c, ĕ, f, l, ĭ, j, m, n, s, t, v, ll, x** Use the 'Quick Dash'.

Vicky Violet, her sound, action and song

- **Vicky Violet** In listen-and-think time today we are going to learn more about one of two young girls in Letterland. She has a favorite color that is also the name of a flower. When you hear **v**iolin music you might think of her, or when you hear the rumbling of a **v**olcano. She loves to run the **v**acuum in her house, because her **v**acuum makes a **vvv**room sound. Who is it? **"Vicky Violet!"** Use the **v** BPCC to remind everyone what this **v**ery lovely girl and her **v**ase of **v**iolets look like when she is in Letterland. Show her plain letter and ask the children where her **v**iolet flowers would go and where she stands beside it. Turn the card over to confirm their answers. Showing the picture side say, There is something else in Vicky's vase besides the violets. Something they need. What is it? **"Water."** V**v**very good! Now what would happen if we turned her over? Rotate the card slowly to an upside down position. The water and violets would spill out! Turn to show the plain side. Show it upside down. So if we see Vicky Violet turned this way, what should we do? Why?

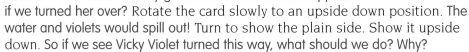

- **Sound** Show her plain letter (*BPCC*) again and rediscover her letter sound using the Sounds Trick: Vicky Violet, /**vvv**/. Teach Vicky Violet's Action Trick.
- **Song** Sing Vicky Violet's *Alphabet Song*. Show the picture side of her *PCC* when you sing her name and the plain side for her sound and action. (Or use the *Software*.)
- **Letter Name** People who don't know about Letterland call this letter a **'v'** (vee). We will be using that name later on, too, but right now we want to remember the most important thing about Vicky Violet, and that is her sound. Say it with me, /**vvv**/. Can you feel your top teeth touching your bottom lip and your voice making it vibrate? It is a sound that we can stretch out. And when we do, sometimes it tickles. Let's say Vicky's sound and hold it until we run out of breath, "/**vvvvvvv.../.**"

Preparation and materials
- *BPCCs:* **v** plus Review *PCCs*
- *Alphabet Songs* CD, # 23
- Option: Project lyrics, *TG CD 2*
- *Letterland ABC Book*, p 48 or *Living ABC Software*
- *Vocabulary Cards* for **v**
- Classroom labels
- *A-Z Copymaster*, **v**

Small group/independent
- **v** to picture-code, *TG CD 2*

Vicky Violet's Alphabet Song

Vicky's Vase of Vi-o-lets.
Lovely Vase of Vi-o-lets.

The sound they make in words is 'v v v...'.
The sound they make in words is 'v v v...'.

Vicky's Vase of Vi-o-lets.
Lovely Vase of Vi-o-lets.

p 49

Phonemic awareness and language development

Listen

- **ABC book** Read about Vicky Violet (or use the *Software.*) Emphasize her sound and explore the picture together.

- **Vocabulary Cards** Go over the pictures and the big words on the backs to draw attention to Vicky Violet's sound.

- **Ask questions and discuss** Where in Letterland would you go to find **v**ery lovely **v**iolets like the ones in **V**icky's **v**ase... the Letterland Library or **V**olcano **V**alley? What is a very healthy group of foods beginning with /**vv**/...? "**Vegetables.**" Why are **v**egetables so healthy for us? "**They have Vitamins.**" Can you name the five **v**owels? What is Vicky's favorite flavor of ice-cream? Strawberry, chocolate or **v**anilla? Praise words: **Very, v**ery good.

Game

- **Make-a-vase** Call out the words below. Tell the children if the word begins with Vicky Violet's sound, they should "make-a-vase," (do her **V**-shaped action) and say her sound. If the word does not, put thumbs down silently. Call on individuals to do some words. If unsure, have the child say, **"Vicky Violet, vvv..."**, and then the word to help the child listen for the **v**-sound.

  Words: **v**alley, **v**iolin, candy, **v**isitor, picture, **v**iolets, **v**oice, **v**est, sidewalk, ladder, **v**ibrations, **v**egetables, balloon, **v**an, vel**v**et, flowers, children, **v**ote, shadow, **v**et, **v**illage, yesterday, **v**olcano, **v**anish.

- **A-Z Copymaster** Discuss the pictures and then model finger tracing, saying Vicky Violet's *Handwriting Verse* as you trace:

  Very neatly, start at the top.
  Draw down your vase, then up and stop.

  Observe and help as needed with their tracing and rainbow writing while everyone fills the room with /**v**/ /**v**/ /**v**/ sounds.

Small group/independent activities

- **Picture-coding (Ind)** Model picture-coding Vicky Violet and give out large plain **v**'s.

- **Pocket chart/table reading (SG)** Build the words below for children to arm-blend the sounds and read. Ask for volunteers to try decoding a word on their own either before or after the group does, depending on the child's confidence. See *Pocket Chart Reading* (Vol. 1, page 239)

  PCCs: **ă, b, c, ĕ, f, l, ĭ, j, m, n, s, t, v, ll, x**

  Words: **can, van, man, mat, met, vet, vets, jet, let, tell, bell, fell, fill, fix**

- **Beginning Sounds and Handwriting** Provide beginning sound activities and handwriting practice for children with new letters and review letters based on their needs. (See page 240 for a special **v** game.)

- **Software** Children will continue to benefit from using the Software with new letters and other letters that need more practice.

Vicky Violet's Letter Shapes

Preparation and materials
- BPCCs: **V**, **v** plus Review *PCCs*
- *Handwriting Songs* CD # 23, or *Living ABC Software*
- Vicky Violet's name card, *TG CD 2*
- *Sentence Copymaster*, p 23

Small group/independent
- Large **V v** to picture-code, *TG CD 2*
- *My Letterland Reading Booklet*, p 35, *TG CD 2*
- *Workbook 4*, pp 6-7
- Handwriting: Select from *A-Z Copymasters*, **V**, **v** *EY Handwriting Copymaster*, pp 22, 46 *ELT Handwriting*, pp 42-43

Review

- **Word Stretching Warm Up** Where might all of these animals live? Say the first word, children repeat. One child says each sound, all repeat. (Mystery answer: **A farm**.)
- **Words**: **goose (g-oo-se), duck (d-u-ck), horse (h-or-se), cow (c-ow), pig (p-i-g)**
- **PCCs ă, b, ĕ, g, l, n, ŏ, t, ŭ, v, ck** Play 'Guess Who' (Vol. 1, page 234) with all *PCCs* listed. Use the 'Handwriting Review' with the whole class or small groups (page 242).

Letter shapes: V and v

- **BPCC** Finger-trace the **v** on the picture side as you say Vicky Violet's *Handwriting Verse* again. Repeat it with the plain side.
- **Writing lowercase v** Draw a huge **v** on the board. Sing or chant Vicky Violet's *Handwriting Song* while children slowly air-trace the letter. (*Handwriting Songs* CD or *Software*.)
- **Capital V** First show the **v** *BPCC* picture side. As you explain the Capital Letter Trick, reveal the **V** *BPCC* picture side. Whenever Vicky Violet starts a name or a sentence, she uses a very valuable, very big vase. Review the Character Name Trick. How can you tell whose name this is?

Sentence Copymaster

- Project the Vicky Violet page and share the picture. Have children finger-trace the large hollow **v**. Read the sentence. Have the children echo-read it with you, listening for the four /**vvv**/ sounds in their own speech. They circle each **V** and **v**, rainbow write inside **v**, and color the page. Circulate to observe correct rainbow writing, finger pointing, and 'reading' from memory.

Small group/independent activities

- **Picture-coding (Ind)** Model picture-coding **V** and **v**. Children picture-code their own large plain **V v**.
- **My Letterland Reading Booklet (SG/Ind)** page 35. Vicky Violet went to visit a volcano. Choral-read the new sentence together and one or two previous pages. Let partners reread while you observe, check finger-pointing, and specific words.
- **Workbook 4 (SG/Ind)** Guide children as they finger-trace, write, and complete the pages.
- **A-Z Copymaster (SG)** Show children how to trace the capital letter **V**. Have them finger trace, rainbow write, and add pictures beginning with /**v**/.
- **Handwriting** Choose from the handwriting options listed in the materials box above.

- **Spelling with Letter Sets** Guide the children in orally segmenting and then building these words:

  Letters: a, b, e, g, l, n, o, t, u, v

  Words: beg, bet, vet, let, net, not, nut, van

- **Optional** Share the *Alphabet Names Verse* for **v** (*TG CD 2*).

Lesson 96

ve Words

Preparation and materials
✓ • *PCC:* **ve** plus Review
✓ **Small group/independent**
  • **ve** to picture-code, *TG CD 2*
  • Copies of Spelling Boxes, *TG CD 2*

Review

- **PCCs ă, d, ĕ, g, h, ĭ, l, n, p, t, v** Use 'Quick Dash' (Vol. 1, page 233).

Vase Prop **e**

- **Pocket Chart**

  PCCs: ă, ĕ, g, h, ĭ, l, n, p, t, v, ve

  Words: lip, live, give, have, van, vet

- We've learned a lot about Vicky and her Vase of Violets. Today we are going to learn about something new that happens when the Vase of Violets is just about to tip over on the end of a word. What would happen if the Vase tipped over? **"The water and violets would pour out."**

- Make the word **lip**. Have the class arm-blend the sounds and read.

- Have everyone point to their lips.

- Say, Now, we want to make the word **live**. Like, I **live** on Maple Street. **Live**. You say it. **"Live."**

- Let's stretch out **live** and see what letters we need to change to turn **lip** into **live**. **"lllliiivvvv. lll –iii –vvv."**

- What letters do we need to change? **"Peter Puppy has to go, and Vicky Violet with her vase should take his place."**

- Okay. Change cards to make **liv**. Now, look at the vase of violets. Do you see how it rests on a tiny little point? If a wind came along, that vase just might tip right over. And guess what, in Letterland the wind always blows in the Reading Direction!

- Let's all turn our heads in the Reading Direction and blow like the wind. As children blow, tip the **v** card so it is lying in on its side.

- Oh, that's not right! Luckily, Mr. E is always trying to be helpful, so he has made a special **e** to help out. Place the **ve** PCC after **li** to form **live**. He calls this little red **e** a 'Vase Prop **e**', because it props up the Vase whenever it comes at the end of a word. And the Vase Prop **e** doesn't make any sound at all! It is silent.

- Let's rollercoaster this word. Remember, the **e** is silent. It doesn't make a sound.

- Question children at various points in the lessons: Where does the **e** go? Why? What does the **e** say?

- Have children help decide how to make the words **give** and **have** on the pocket chart and let them explain the need for the Vase Prop **e**.

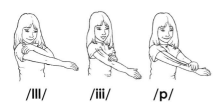

/lll/   /iii/   /p/

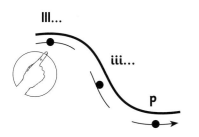

/lll/   /iii/   /vvv/

g i **ve**

h a **ve**

- Make the words **van** and **vet** to show how the Vase is safe when there are other letters beside it to keep it from being blown over. The danger is always at the end of words.

Live Spelling

- Follow the usual steps (Vol. 1, page 238.) When spelling a word with **v**, try the **v** (single letter) card first. Let the class pretend to try to blow it over. Of course, only the **v**'s on the end of the word will be affected by the wind. The child with the **v** card will enjoy pretending to being tipped over, and will need a child holding the **ve** card to join him, replacing the **v** card.

    PCCs: ă, d, ĕ, g, h, ĭ, l, n, t, v, ve

    Words: van, hat, have, had, hid, lid, live, give, vet

Small group/independent activities

- **Picture-coding** Model picture-coding **ve** and provide a large plain **ve** for each child to code. Children may want to write other words with **ve** around the large **ve**.
- **Spelling Boxes** Show the class that final **ve** goes in a single box. Call out these words: Set 1—**van, give, have** Set 2—**vet, live, sing**
- **Intervention** Continue daily practice with children who have not mastered Section 1 and 2 skills.

Lesson 97

Oscar's Bothersome Little Brother

✔ **Preparation and materials**
- *PCC:* **Oscar's Bothersome Little Brother** plus Review

✔ **Small group/independent**
- Copies of Spelling Boxes, *TG CD 2*
- Write these words, one per page for picture-coding: **love, have, done, give, live, come, some**

Review

- **PCCs** ă, c, d, ĕ, ē, g, h, ĭ, l, m, n, s, t, v, ve Play 'Guess Who' (Vol. 1, page 234) with all *PCCs* listed. Use the 'Handwriting Review' with the whole class or small groups (page 242).

Pocket Chart

PCCs: c, d, e (Mr. E plain side), ĭ, l, m, n, s, v, ve, Oscar's Little Brother

Words: live, love, come, some, done

Review Vase Prop e

- Make **live** in the pocket chart using the plain letter sides including the **ve** *PCC*. Point to each letter and ask children to say the sound that the letter makes. As they give the sounds turn the cards over to the picture side.
- Having established that the **e** is silent, ask a child to explain why the **e** is there.
- Review the term 'Vase Prop **e**'.

/lll/...
/ŭŭŭ/...

.../v/

Introduce Oscar's Bothersome Little Brother

- Show *PCC* for Oscar's Bothersome Little Brother. Tell his story something like this, Can you guess whose little brother this is...? Yes, this is Oscar's Bothersome Little Brother. Can you say his name with me? **"Oscar's Bothersome Little Brother."** If you see his letter in a word (turn to the plain side), it looks just like Oscar and Mr. O. Turn back to the picture side. Isn't he really cute and sweet? But there is a reason that he is called 'Bothersome'. That means he bothers you or causes you problems. It is because he is just a baby and he hasn't learned to say /ŏŏŏ/ like his big brother Oscar. Little Brother just says /ŭŭŭ/. Say his sound with me, /ŭŭŭŭŭ/.

- Does his sound remind you of anyone else's sound? Yes, he sounds like Uppy Umbrella. So, the thing that is bothersome is that when we hear /ŭŭŭ/ we don't know whether to write the word with Uppy Umbrella's letter or Oscar's Bothersome Little Brother's letter.

- Replace the **i** on the pocket chart with Little Brother on the picture side. Tell the children, Sometimes when we see an **o** in a word we can't tell if it will be Oscar, Mr. O, or Oscar's Bothersome ...? **"Little Brother."** But today we can see Little Brother so we know he will say...? "/ŭŭŭ/."

- Have the children arm-blend the word **love**. Then make up a sentence with the word about Little Brother, e.g. "We all love Little Brother even though he is bothersome."

Silent **e**

- Show the plain **e** side of the Mr. E card. Sometimes this letter appears at the end of words when they don't even need a Vase Prop. It will be silent. That means it doesn't make any sound at all. So if I ask you to be silent what would you do? Let's try that. Everybody make a little noise until I say 'Silent'. Good job. Now this time let's make a little noise, but when I hold up the silent **e** card, everyone be silent. (Try this a few times). And if I ask you what the silent **e** sound is, you would say... (Guide children to be silent when you ask this question.) This is one question that can be answered by saying nothing at all!

some

cotton

glove

- Make **come, some, done** in turn on the pocket. Use the plain side of the Mr. E *PCC* for the silent **e**. Have children arm-blend each word and use these Oscar's Little Brother words in a sentence about him.

Sentences on the Board

- Write these sentences on the board: "Oscar Orange loves his little brother. Oscar gives him some _____." Read the sentences to the children as you point to the words. Read them with the children a few times. Have children suggest various words taht could go in the blank. Have several children take turns pointing to the words as the class reads.

- Write several words on the board with Little Brother's /ŭ/ sound, e.g. **Monday, month, son, dove, glove, done, undone, cotton, come, some, brother, other**. Let them picture-code these words on the board. Let other children put a slash through the silent **e**'s, or erase and rewrite the **e** in dashes.

Live Spelling

● Follow the steps for Live Spelling (Vol. 1, page 238) Have the silent **e** line up when needed. When the **/vvv/** sound is heard have the child with the **v** get in place and decide if the Vase Prop **e** is needed. If it is needed, have the child with the **v** put it aside and help the **ve** child hold the **ve** card instead.

> **PCCs:** ă, c, d, ĕ, ē, g, h, ĭ, l, m, n, s, t, v, ve, o (Little Brother)
>
> **Words:** come, some, give, van, have, done, love. vet

Small group/independent activities

● **Picture-coding** Model picture-coding Oscar's Bothersome Little Brother and the other letters in the word **love**. Give each child a page with one of the above words written large on the page to picture-code. Use some of these to make a display of Vase Prop **e** words and Oscar's Little Brother words.

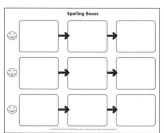

● **Word Building: Spelling Boxes** Show the class that the final **ve** goes in a single box and that silent **e** goes in the box with the letter before it (e.g. **c-o-me**). Call out these words: Set 1—**give, love, come**
Set 2—**van, live, some**

● **Intervention** Continue daily practice with children who have not mastered Section 1 and 2 skills.

> **Lesson 98**

Review j, q, r, and v

● See Review

✔ **Preparation and materials**
- See Review
- *Alphabet Songs* and *Handwriting Songs* CD # 11, 18, 19, 23 (lyrics on *TG CD 2*)
- *ABC Book,* p 24, 38, 40, 48
- *Beginning Sound Pictures* for **j, q, r, v**, *TG CD 2*
- Character Name cards for **j, q, r,** and **v** *TG CD 2*
- Copies of *Decodable Booklet,* *TG CD 2*
Cptional:
- *Action Songs* CD or *ABC Adventures* Software
- Prepare Eyes Shut

✔ **Small group/independent**
- Write sentences from 'The Queen is Sad' Decodable booklet on sentence strips
- *My Letterland Reading Booklet*
- Cption: *My First Reading Flashcards*

Review

● **Capital Big PCCs A, A, E, t, t, J, O, O, Q, R, ʊ, ʊ, V, VE Big PCCs j, q, r, v PCCs o** Little Brother, **qu, ve.** Use the 'Quick Dash' (Vol. 1, page 233).

Jumping Jim, Quarrelsome Queen, Red Robot, and Vicky Violet

● **Sounds** Review characters and sounds. If time allows, sing along with the *Alphabet Songs* CD (or *Software*) for all four letters. Or you could just chant the lyrics together. Children do the actions when they come to the sounds. Have one child hold up the Character Name Card whenever they hear it. Have another child hold up the plain letter side of the *BPCC* when they come to the Letterlander's sound.

● **Shapes** To review handwriting, write a large **j, q, r,** and **v** on the board and have children air-trace the letter as they say or sing the words of each *Handwriting Song*. (CD or *Software*.)

● **Capitals** Review capital letters by having children find each capital letter on the *Class Train Frieze* and let other children explain the story logic for the **J, Q, R,** and **V** Capital Letter Tricks. (Or play the Capitals Game, see Volume 1, pages 67-68.)

The Queen is sad!

A Letterland Take-Home Reader Lesson 98

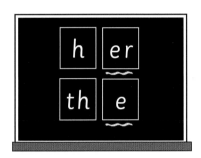

h | er
th | e

the

Red Robot gives her lots of rocks.

Quarrelsome Queen is still sad.

Jumping Jim gives her lots of jam.

But Quarrelsome Queen is still sad.

- **ABC book** Show the **j** page to the children for about 20 seconds. Then see how many words they can name which begin with the character's sound. Do the same with **q**, **r**, and **v**.

   Variation Use the *Living ABC Software* for **j**, **q**, **r**, and **v** story sections.

Decodable Booklet: 'The Queen is Sad'

- **The Queen is Sad** You may prefer to project or enlarge a copy of this story on the first day and then make copies for rereading on subsequent days.

Introduce the booklet

Suggested steps for sharing this booklet: 'The Queen is Sad'.

- Review the book, discussing the title and pictures, but *save the final page as a surprise.*
- Have children name what each character brings to try to cheer up the queen.

Tricky Words

- Tell children that there are two *Tricky Words* in this story that you want to show them before they read it. The *Tricky Words* are **her** (review) and **the**.
- Draw two *Sounds Boxes* on the board for **her** and two for **the**.
- Ask for the first sound (**h**) and last sound (**r**) and write them in.
- Add the **e** and point out to children that in **her**, we do not hear Eddy Elephant's sound or Mr. E's name in the middle of this word. Explain that in Letterland, when any letter seems to be making a sound that it doesn't usually make, to show it we draw a wiggly line underneath it.
- Next introduce **the** and use it in a sentence or two. Have children say the word. Ask children to listen for the first sound and decide on the letters for the first box. Remind them about the **the** in **the thunder** story, if need be. (See Vol 1, page 171.)
- Most of the time the vowel in the word **the** is pronounced as a *schwa* sound (basically the same sound as Uppy Umbrella's short vowel sound.) Write the letter **e** in the second box. Does it need a wiggly line under it? Yes, because it is not making its usual sound. Add a wiggly line. You could also picture-code the **th** in this extremely high usage word.
- Now read both words with the class a few times as you point.

Reading the booklet

- Read the first two pages, modeling how a child might carefully decode the sentence.
- Then reread the page with the class.
- Let a volunteer or a pair of volunteers read the next page aloud.
- Reread the page with the whole class.
- Read each subsequent page as above.
- Before showing the final page, ask, What do you think Oscar Orange came with? How do you think the Queen will react?
- Discuss why the Queen was glad in the end.

Reading for fluency

- Reread the book with the whole class in a more fluent fashion.
- Reread the book with half the class reading one sentence (What the character brought) and the other half reading the next (the queen's reaction).

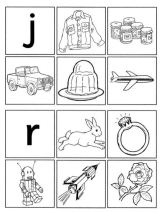

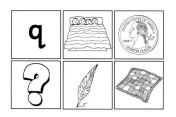

Eyes Shut Riddle Game

Red Robot gives her lots of rocks.

Quarrelsome Queen is still sad.

Jumping Jim gives her lots of jam.

But Quarrelsome Queen is still sad.

Vicky Violet gives her lots of violets.

Still the Queen is sad. Oscar Orange comes with...

...his Bothersome Little Brother and the Queen is glad!

● Practice reading later in small groups and send home when mastered. Keep at least one copy in your classroom library.

Picture Sorting

● **Beginning Sound Pictures** Sort pictures beginning with the **j, q, r, v** sounds on a pocket chart with the whole class. (See 'Sort it Out', Vol 1, page 254.)

Optional Activities

● **Action Songs** For an active, fun way to involve children with Letterland characters and sounds, use the *Action Songs CD* or the same songs on the *ABC Adventures* Software. Sing the songs for **j, q, r, v,** and any other letters you wish to review.

● **Eyes Shut Riddle Game** Play this game as described in the Appendices, page 243. Add riddles for **j, q r,** and **v** to the box at this time.

  j – I just love to travel by **j**eep or by **j**et. Who am I?

  q – I spend three **qu**arters of my time **qu**arrelling. Who am I?

  r – I **rrr**un off with other people's **rrr**adios and **rrr**ollerskates. Who am I?

  v – We have lovely **vvv**elvet petals and **vvv**elvet leaves. Who looks after us?

● Use your box of riddles anytime for a quick review of letter sounds, or as an occasional time filler. Some children may be able to read the older more familiar riddles for you.

Small group/independent activities

● **Decodable Booklet (SG/Ind)** Reread 'The Queen is Sad' as a group and then let partners finger-point as they read to each other. Monitor the finger-pointing and point to specific words in the text for children to identify. If children need more practice with the booklet, save the copies for small group reading until mastered. Then send home for reading to parents, keeping a few copies in your classroom library.

● **Follow up to Decodable Booklet (SG/Ind)** Write the sentences from the booklet on sentence strips. Children rebuild the story on the pocket chart. One child could read sentences from the book. The other has to put the sentences in order. Both check it together and then switch roles and begin again. Children could also try to put the sentences in order without looking at the booklet. After placing all the sentences, they can use the book to check.

● **Picture Sorting (SG)** For children who need more practice, do more sorting with the *Beginning Sound Pictures*.

● **Handwriting** Choose from the handwriting materials for **j, q, r,** and **v** listed on pages 4 , 11, 7 and 14 respectively.

● **My Letterland Reading Booklet (SG/Ind)** There is no new page for this lesson, so it is a good time to review the previous pages with small group choral reading or partner reading.

● **For more practice matching capital and lowercase** see Volume 1, pages 68-69.

Walter Walrus's Sound

Preparation and materials

- *BPCC:* **w** plus Review *PCCs*
- *Alphabet Songs* CD, # 24
- Option: Project lyrics *TG CD 2*
- *Letterland ABC Book*, p 50 or *Living ABC Software*
- *Vocabulary Cards* for **w**
- Classroom labels
- *A-Z Copymaster,* **w**

✔ **Small group/independent**
- **w** to picture-code *TG CD 2*

Reading Direction

Walter Walrus's Alphabet Song

Wwwww...,
what's that we hear?

Is Walter Walrus near?

'Wwww...', wow, that's him!

You may get wet, I fear!

Review

- PCCs **ă, b, ĕ, g, ĭ, n, t, w, ll, ng, th** Use 'Quick Dash' (Vol. 1, page 233).

Walter Walrus, his sound, action and song

- **Walter Walrus** Today I'm thinking of a Letterland animal. It's an animal that loves to swim. It has little ears, but you can't see them. When it swims it wiggles its tail and its whiskers in the water. Could it be Dippy Duck? Why not? (No whiskers). So, who is it? **"Walter Walrus."** Show the **w** *BPCC* to remind everyone what this **w**et and **w**ily **w**alrus looks like when he is in Letterland. Walter Walrus loves to **w**ave and splash his flippers in his **w**ater **w**ells and get his Letterland friends all **w**et. Now if you look at his tail behind him and check which way his eyes are looking, you can tell what direction he is ready to **w**addle along in. What is that direction? **"The Reading Direction."**

- **Show his plain letter** and ask the children where his flippers go and his head. Turn the card over to confirm their answers. Show the plain side again and ask, Where does the water in his wells go? Slowly rotate the card upside down and ask, What would happen to the water if his letter was turned upside down? **"It would all run out."** Yes, and his letter would look just like Munching Mike's Mom's letter. Turn the card right side up. But you can always tell the difference, because Walter Walrus's letter always has those two places for his water wells. What is this **w**allowing **w**alrus's name again? **"Walter Walrus."**

- **Sound** Show his plain letter (*BPCC*) again and rediscover his letter sound using the Sounds Trick: Walter Walrus, /**www**/. Teach the class Walter Walrus's Action Trick.

- **Song** Sing Walter Walrus's *Alphabet Song*. Show the picture side of his *BPCC* when you sing his name and the plain side for his sound and action. (Or use the *Software*.)

- **Letter Name** People who don't know about Letterland call this letter a '**w**' (double-you). We will be using that name later, but right now we want to remember the most important thing about Walter Walrus, and that is his sound. You need to keep your mouth almost closed to make it correctly. Say it with me, /**w**/.

Phonemic awareness and language development

Listen

- **ABC book** Read about Walter Walrus (or use the *Software*). Emphasize his sound and explore the picture together.

- **Vocabulary Cards** Show the pictures and the big words on the backs. Also use your classroom labels (e.g. **window, water, wash, Wednesday**) to draw attention to Walter Walrus's sound.

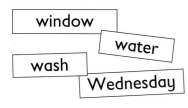

- **Ask questions and discuss.** Walter Walrus is one of two main troublemakers in Letterland. He often causes trouble for letters next to him in a **w**ord by splashing **w**ater on them from his two **w**ells. The problem is he **www**ants to make trouble, so **we** are going to have to **www**atch out for him, because he can cause trouble for us as **w**ell! How do you think Walter Walrus moves in the Reading Direction? Does he slither and slide along or does he **w**addle? Do you think **W**alter would rather **w**ade in the **w**ater, or march in the mud? Praise words: Wonderful! What a winner! Well done! You win! You've won! **W**ow!

Games

- **Walter's Waddling Game** Tell children that they are going to act out some action words that begin with Walter Walrus's sound in this game. Let's form a circle and try some of the actions. First let's **walk**. Have everyone walk around in a circle clockwise. When I call out **Wait**, everyone must stop. Work out with the children how they will do the next action words.

    Actions while moving: **waddle** (like a walrus), **wobble** (more stiffly like a penguin), **wade** (lift feet high like walking slowly in water).

- After a few movements, call **Wait!** Everyone stops and faces the center of the circle. Explain: We are going to do the next actions standing still, but in this game only do the action if the word begins with Walter's **/www/** sound. If it doesn't, just stand still.

- Actions while standing: **wiggle**, spin, blow, **wash**, reach, **watch**, **wink**, pull, cry, **wave**, jump, run, **wag**. Call on someone to tell which other Letterlander they can hear starting each alternate word.

- After the two or three standing actions, call another movement word so everyone moves around in a circle again until you call **Wait**. Then call out more standing actions.

- Continue alternating between moving and standing actions as long as it seems fun and time permits.

- **A-Z Copymaster** Discuss the pictures and then model finger tracing, saying Walter Walrus's *Handwriting Verse* as your trace:

    When you draw the Walrus wells,
    with wild and wavy water,
    whizz down and up and then....
    whizz down and up again.

Observe and help as needed with their tracing and rainbow writing while everyone fills the room with "/**w**/ /**w**/ /**w**/" sounds.

Small group/independent activities

- **Picture-coding (Ind)** Model picture-coding Walter Walrus and give out large, plain **w**'s to picture-code.

- **Pocket chart/table reading (SG)** Build the words below for children to arm-blend the sounds and read. Ask for volunteers to try decoding a word on their own either before or after the group does, depending on the child's confidence.

    PCCs: **ă, b, ĕ, g, ĭ, n, t, w, ll, ng, th**

    New words: **wag, wig, wet, web, well, will, win, with, wing**

- **Beginning Sounds and Handwriting** Add **w** words to *Beginning Sound Picture* sorting for those who need this practice, and do handwriting with the letters studied so far in this Section. (For a special **w** game, see page 241.)

Walter Walrus's Letter Shapes

Preparation and materials

- *BPCCs:* **W, w** plus Review *PCCs*
- *Handwriting Songs* CD, # 24 or *Living ABC Software*
- Walter Walrus Name card, *TG CD 2*
- *Sentence Copymaster,* p 24

Small group/independent

- **W w** to picture-code, *TG CD 2*
- *My Letterland Reading Booklet,* p 36, *TG CD 2*
- *Workbook 4,* pp 8-9
- *A-Z Copymasters* **W** and **w**
- Handwriting: Select from *EY Handwriting Copymaster,* pp 23, 47 *ELT Handwriting* pp 48-49

Walter Walrus is wet in the water.

Go away, Walter Walrus! I am getting wet!

Review

- **Word Stretching Warm Up** Who can do all these things? Say the first word, then ask the children to repeat. One child says each sound, then all repeat. (Mystery answer: **A dog, or puppy.**)

    Words: **run (r-u-n), jump (j-u-m-p), pant (p-a-n-t), wag (w-a-g), bark (b-ar-k)**

- **PCCs ă, b, ĕ, g, ĭ, n, s, t, w, ll, ng, th** Play 'Guess Who' (Vol. 1, page 234) with all *PCCs* listed. Use the 'Handwriting Review' with the whole class or small groups (page 242).

Letter shapes: W and w

- **BPCC** Finger-trace the **w** on the picture side as you say Walter Walrus's *Handwriting Verse*. Repeat it with the plain side:

    When you draw the Walrus wells with wild and wavy water,
    whizz down and up and then whizz down and up again.

- **Writing lowercase w** Draw a huge **w** on the board. Sing or chant Walter Walrus's *Handwriting Verse* while children slowly air-trace the letter. (*TG CD 2,* or *Software*)

- **Capital W** First show the picture side of the **w** *BPCC*. As you explain Walter Walrus's Capital Letter Trick, reveal the picture side of the **W** *BPCC*. Whenever Walter Walrus starts a name or a sentence, he takes a deep breath and gets bigger. His water wells get much bigger and deeper, as well!

- **Show the Walter Walrus Name card.** Review the Character Name Trick: How can you tell whose name this is?

Sentence Copymaster

- Project the Walter Walrus page and share the picture. Have children finger-trace the large hollow **w** on their copies. Choral-read the sentence together, all listening for the four /**www**/ sounds in it. The children circle each **W** and **w**, rainbow write in the large **w**, and color the page. Circulate to observe correct handwriting strokes, finger-pointing and repeating the words.

Small group/independent activities

- **Picture-coding (Ind)** Model picture-coding of **W** and **w**, and have children picture-code their own **W w**.

- **My Letterland Reading Booklet (SG/Ind)** page 36. Go away Walter Walrus! I am getting wet! Read the new sentence together and several of the previous pages. Ask a few children to describe what they are going to draw in their picture to go with the caption. Then let partners reread while you observe, check finger pointing, and specific words.

- **Spelling Boxes (SG)** See Spelling with *Letterland Spelling Boxes* (Vol 1, page 243)
    Words: Set 1: **wag; wing, web** Set 2: **with, song, well**

- **A-Z Copymaster (SG)** Show children how to trace the capital letter **W**. Have them finger-trace, rainbow write, and add pictures beginning with /**w**/.

- **Workbook 4 (SG/Ind)** Guide students as they finger-trace, write, and complete the pages.
- **Handwriting** Select from handwriting options listed in the materials box.
- **Software** Children will continue to benefit from using the software with new letters and letters that still need more practice.
- **Intervention** Continue to help all children master needed skills based on Letterland assessments as well as other sources of information.
- **Optional** Introduce the *Alphabet Name Verse* for **w** (*TG CD 2*).
- **Stories to explain wh** For any child who is curious to know the **wh** stories (for **when**, **who**, etc.) ahead of time, they are set out in the Letterland *Beyond ABC Book*.

Preparation and materials ✔
- *BPCC:* **x** plus Review *PCCs*
- *Alphabet Songs* CD, # 25
- Option: *Project lyrics, TG CD 2*
- *Letterland ABC Book,* p 52 or *Living ABC Software*
- *Vocabulary Cards* for **x**
- Classroom labels
- *A-Z Copymaster,* **x**

Small group/independent ✔
- **x** to picture-code, *TG CD 2*

Fix-it Max's Alphabet Song

Now let's whisper, whisper 'k-ss', whisper, whisper 'k-ss'.

Now let's whisper, whisper 'k-ss', whisper, whisper 'k-ss'.

With a 'k-ss', 'k-ss' here and a 'k-ss', 'k-ss' there; here a 'k-ss', there a 'k-ss', everywhere a 'k-ss', 'k-ss'.

Now let's whisper, whisper 'k-ss', whisper, whisper 'k-ss'.

Lesson 101: Day 1

Fix-it Max's Sound

Review

- PCCs **ă, b, c, d, ĕ, f, i, k, m, n, ŏ, s, ŭ, x** Use the 'Quick Dash'.

Fix-it Max, his sound, action and song

- **Fix-it Max** It's Listen-and-think time again. The Letterlander I want to tell you more about today is not a grown-up. It's one of the children in Letterland who goes to the Letterland school. People really like this child, because he can be very helpful. He might be seen holding a hammer; but it is not Noisy Nick. You might want to go to see him if you broke a toy. Who is it? **"Fix-it Max."** Use his *BPCC* to remind everyone what this excellent fixer and his letter look like in Letterland. Now you can see Max's name right here on his cap and we can see he is the only one in Letterland whose name doesn't start with his sound. Max makes his sound at the end of his name. So we read his name in what direction? **"The Reading Direction."** Yes, and we come to his sound right at the end, Ma**x**. Show his plain letter and ask the children where his hands go and his legs go. Turn the card over to confirm their answers.

- **Sound** Show his plain letter *BPCC* again and rediscover his letter sound (at the end of his name) using the Sounds Trick: Fix-it Max, /**x**/. Teach Fix-it Max's Action Trick (*TG CD 1* page 227).

- **Song** Sing Fix-it Max's *Alphabet Song*. Show the picture side of his *PCC* when you sing his name and the plain letter with his sound and action. (*TG CD 2* or use the *Software*.)

- **Letter Name** People who don't know about Letterland call this letter an '**x**' (eks). We will learn more about that name later, but right now we want to remember the most important thing about Fix-it Max, and that is his sound. His sound is a quiet, quick sound, made by whispering /**k**/ and /**s**/ together fast. Whisper it with me, /**ks**/. Let's whisper it three times. It could be the sound made by Max sawing a piece of wood: "/**ks**/ /**ks**/ /**ks**/." People use his letter sometimes to write a **kiss**, too. Maybe that is why his sound is also like saying the word 'kiss' in a whisper.

Page 53

Phonemic awareness and language development

Listen

- **ABC book** Read about Fix-it Max (or use the Software). Emphasize his sound and explore the picture together.

- **Vocabulary Cards** Show the pictures and the big words on the backs, and use your classroom labels (e.g. **exit**, **toy box**) to draw attention to Fix-it Max's sound.

- **Ask questions and discuss** Do you think Max ever whispers his **/ks/** sound at the beginning of a word? No, he never does. (In the word 'x-ray', people use his letter name, 'eks', which has an /ĕ/ sound first. In the word for the musical instrument 'xylophone,' he takes a quick snooze and says /**zzz**/.) How old do you think Fix-it Max is, five, six, or seven? Do you think he would like his milk plain, or would he like to mi**x** in some chocolate? Ma**x** makes his **/ks/** sound in only a few words because he is always so busy fi**x**ing things for other people. Kicking King and Sammy Snake know about this, so they often do the job of making his sound for him in words like boo**ks** and wee**ks**. Sometimes Clever Cat helps, too, in words like ro**cks**, and bri**cks**.

Games

- **Questions about Fix-it Max** Ask these questions and guide students to choose words with Max's **/x/** sound. Briefly explain any word meanings that are unfamiliar.

    Does Fix-it Max like to play the piano, or **fix** broken things?

    What does Fix-it Max carry his lunch in? a **box**? or a bag?

    What is Fix-it Max's favorite animal? a cow? or a **fox**?

    When you cook, do you use Fix-it Max's sound in the word bake? or **mix**?

    To get a quick message to Talking Tess, would Max send her an email? or a **fax**?

    Max fixed an important sign over a door. Can you guess what it said? **EXIT**

    What type of horn does Fix-it Max like to play? a trumpet or a **sax** (-ophone)

    What does Fix-it Max say when he finishes fixing something? "What's **next**?"

- **A-Z Copymaster** (**SG**) Discuss the pictures and then model finger tracing, saying Fix-it Max's *Handwriting Verse* as your trace:

    Fix two sticks to look like this.
    That's how to draw a little kiss.

Observe and help as needed with their tracing and rainbow writing while everyone fills the room with "**/ks/ /ks/ /ks/**" sounds.

Small group/independent activities

- **Picture-coding** (**Ind**) Model picture-coding Fix-it Max and give out large plain **x**'s to picture-code.

- **Reading with letter sets** (**SG**) Call on individuals to arm-blend and read some of the words, followed by the whole group doing the same.

    Letters: **ă, b, f, ĭ, m, ŏ, s, x**

    Words: **Max, fax, fix, mix, six, box, fox**

- **Beginning Sounds and Handwriting** Practice new letters and review other letters according to your children's needs. (For a special **x** game, see page 241.)

Fix-it Max's Letter Shapes

✔ Preparation and materials
- *BPCCs:* **X, x** plus Review *PCCs*
- *Handwriting Songs* CD, # 25 or *Living ABC Software*
- *Fix-it Max name card, TG CD 2*
- *A-Z Copymaster,* **x**

✔ Small group/independent
- **X x** to picture-code, *TG CD 2*
- *My Letterland Reading Booklet,* p 37, *TG CD 2*
- *Workbook 4,* pp 10-11
- *A-Z Copymasters* **X** and **x**
- Handwriting: Select from Individual letter sets; *EYH Copymaster,* pp 24, 47; *ELT Handwriting,* pp 50-51

Fix-it Max

Fix-it Max can see a fox in a box.

Circle all Fix-it Max's letters in the sentence, then find the things that end with his sound.

Review

- **Word Stretching Warm Up** Where could you find all these things? Say the first word, children repeat. One child says each sound, then all repeat. (Mystery answer: **In a house**.)

  Words: rug (r-u-g), lamp (l-a-m-p), couch (c-ou-ch), bed (b-e-d), tub (t-u-b)

- **PCCs ă, b, c, f, ĭ, k, m, s, t, x, th** Play 'Guess Who?' (Vol. 1, page 234) with all *PCCs* listed. Use the 'Handwriting Review' with the whole class or small groups (page 242).

Letter shapes: X and x

- **BPCC** Finger-trace the **x** on the picture side as you say Fix-it Max's *Handwriting Verse*. Repeat it with the plain side:

  Fix two sticks to look like this.
  That's how to draw a little kiss.

- **Writing lowercase x** Draw a huge **x** on the board. Sing or chant Fix-it Max's *Handwriting Verse* while children slowly air-trace the letter. (CD or *Software*)

- **Capital X** First show the picture side of the **x** *BPCC*. As you explain Fix-it Max's Capital Letter Trick, reveal the picture side of the **X** *BPCC*. To make his capital letter, Max takes a deep breath and grows bigger, and so does his letter!

- **Show the Fix-it Max Name card** Review the Character Name Trick: This one is different from the other Letterlander's names. How is it different? (His letter comes at the end.)

Sentence Copymaster

- Project Fix-it Max's page and share the picture. Have children finger-trace the large hollow **x**. Read the sentence. Reread it with the children echo-reading, all listening for the four /**x**/ sounds in their own speech. Have them circle all of Fix-it Max's letters, rainbow write in the large **x**, and color the page. Circulate to observe correct tracing and finger-point reading of the words.

Small group/independent activities

- **Picture-coding (Ind)** Model picture-coding of **X** and **x** and have children picture-code their own **X x**.

- **My Letterland Reading Booklet (SG)** page 37. Fix-it Max can fix it. Read the new sentence together and several previous pages. Ask the children what they are going to draw for Fix-it Max to work on. Then let partners reread while you observe, check finger-pointing, and specific words.

- **Spelling with letter sets (SG)** For instructions, see Vol 1, page 242.)

  Letters: a, c, f, h, i, k, m, n, s, t, x

  Words: tack, tax, fix, six, mix, math, thanks

- **Workbook 4 (SG/Ind)** Guide the children as they finger-trace, write, and complete the pages.
- **A-Z Copymaster (SG)** Show children how to trace the capital letter **X**. Have them finger-trace, rainbow write, and add pictures beginning with /**x**/.
- **Handwriting** Select from handwriting options listed in the materials box.
- **Software and Intervention** Continue to fine tune these activities to meet individual needs.
- **Optional** Share the *Alphabet Names Verse* for **x** (*TG CD 2*) now or later.

Lesson 103: Day 1

Yellow Yo-yo Man's Sound

Review

- **PCCs ă, ĕ, d, h, m, s, t, ŭ, y, ch, ck, ll, th** Use the 'Quick Dash'.

Yellow Yo-yo Man, his sound, action and song

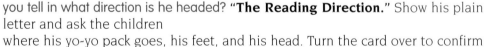

- **Yellow Yo-yo Man** Are you ready for listen-and-think again? I'm looking forward to telling you more about one of the men you have already met in Letterland, but first you need to discover who it will be. Here are some clues. He has dark hair, and he loves being around children. He is also very clever with his hands. He can even yank the toys he sells so they climb up a string! Who is it? **"Yellow Yo-yo Man!"** Use the *BPCC* to remind everyone what this friendly yo-yo seller looks like. With his pack of **y**o-**y**o's on his back, can you tell in what direction is he headed? **"The Reading Direction."** Show his plain letter and ask the children where his yo-yo pack goes, his feet, and his head. Turn the card over to confirm their answers.

- **Sound** Show his plain letter *BPCC* again and rediscover his letter sound using the Sounds Trick: Yellow Yo-yo Man, /**y y y**/. Teach Yellow Yo-yo Man's Action Trick.

- **Song** Sing Yellow Yo-yo Man's *Alphabet Song*. Show the picture side of his *BPCC* when you sing his name and the plain side for his sound and action. (Or use the *Software*.)

- **Letter Name** People who don't know about Letterland call this letter a '**y**' (why). We will learn more about that name later, but right now we want to remember the most important thing about Yellow Yo-yo Man, and that is... **"his sound."** You can keep his sound going but you have to keep your mouth almost closed as you say it. Say it with me, /**yyy**/. (Make sure nobody lets their jaw drop at the end, distorting his sound to /**yuh**/.)

Preparation and materials
- *BPCC*: **y** plus Review *PCCs*
- *Alphabet Songs* CD, # 26
- Option: **Project lyrics**, *TG CD 2*
- *Letterland ABC Book*, p 54 or *Living ABC Software*
- *Vocabulary Cards* for **y**
- Classroom labels
- *A-Z Copymaster*, **y**

Small group/independent
- **y** to picture-code, *TG CD 2*

Yellow Yo-yo Man's Alphabet Song

Yo-yo Man says
'y y y...' in words.

Yes sir, yes sir,
'y y y...' in words.

Yellow yo-yos he will sell,
and work for other men
as well.

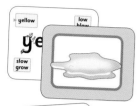

Phonemic awareness and language development

Listen

- **ABC book** Read about Yellow Yo-yo Man (or use the *Software*). Emphasize his sound and explore the picture together.

- **Vocabulary Cards** Show the pictures and the big words on the backs and use your classroom labels (e.g. **yellow**) to draw attention to Yellow Yo-yo Man's sound.

- **Ask questions and discuss** You can hear the Yellow Yo-yo Man's /**yyy**/ sound in words like **y**ellow, **y**ou, and **y**oung. Not many words need Yellow Yo-yo Man's sound, so he only has a few chances to get out there and earn his living selling **y**o-yos. That is why sometimes Yellow Yo-yo Man works for Mr. I, in words like **my**, **by**, and **try**. There is another Vowel Man that Yo-yo Man does jobs for too, but only at the ends of words. Can you hear him saying 'e' for Mr. E at the ends of names like Am**y**, Jenn**y**, Mick**y**? But today we want to think mostly about the Yo-yo Man making his *own* sound, /**yyy**/, at the *beginning* of words so we can play our next game.

Games

- **'Who's Got the Yo-yo?' Game** Let the children pass a yo-yo around while you turn away. After a few moments turn back and all say, **"Yo-yo, yo-yo, who's got the yo-yo?"** The child holding the yo-yo answers the first question as if he or she were Yellow Yo-yo Man. Repeat passing the yo-yo for the next child's turn.

  1. Yo-yo Man, what is your favorite color? **yellow**
  2. Yo-yo Man, what do you do when you get sleepy? **yawn**
  3. Which answer to a question do you like best: **yes** or no?
  4. Was the day before today **yesterday**, or tomorrow?
  5. Do you sell yo-yo's in the summer, or all through the **year**?
  6. Are you an old man, or a **young** man?
  7. Which do you like best **yogurt**, or ice-cream?
  8. Does your dog bark, or **yelp**?
  9. Do you like to show people how to yank your yo-yos in the **yard**, or in the house?
  10. When you are excited, do you keep your mouth shut, or **yell** 'Yippee!'

- **A-Z Copymaster** (**SG**) Discuss the pictures and then model finger tracing, saying Yellow Yo-yo Man's *Handwriting Verse* as your trace:

  You first make the yo-yo sack on the Yo-yo Man's back,
  and then go down to his toes so he can sell his yo-yos.

  Observe and help as needed with their tracing and rainbow writing while everyone fills the room with "/**y**/ /**y**/ /**y**/" sounds.

Small group/independent activities

- **Picture-coding** (**Ind**) Model picture-coding **y** and give out large plain **y**'s to code.

- **Pocket chart/table reading** (See Vol 1, page 239.) Form the words below for children to sound out. They use arm-blending as needed. Ask for volunteers to try decoding a word on their own either before, or after the group does.

  PCCs: ă, ĕ, h, m, s=z, t, ŭ, y, ch, ck, ll, <u>th</u>
  Words: yell, yams, ham, hat, that, much, muck, yuck

- **Beginning Sounds and Handwriting** Add **y** pictures to *Beginning Sound Picture* sorting, and do handwriting with letters introduced so far in this section. (For a special **y** game, see page 241.)

Yellow Yo-yo Man's Letter Shapes

Preparation and materials
- *BPCCs:* **Y, y** plus Review *PCCs*
- *Handwriting Songs* CD, # 26 or *Living ABC Software*
- Yellow Yo-yo Man's name card, *TG CD 2*
- *Sentence Copymaster*, p 26

Small group/independent
- **Y y** to picture-code, *TG CD 2*
- *My Letterland Reading Booklet*, p 38, *TG CD 2*
- *Workbook 4*, pp 12-13
- Copies of Spelling Boxes (*TG CD 2*)
- *A-Z Copymasters*, **Y** and **y**
- Handwriting: Select from *EYH Copymaster*, pp 25, 48 *ELT Handwriting*, pp 24-25

Yellow Yo-yo Man

Yo-yo Man has yo-yos for sale.

Circle all Yo-yo Man's letters in the sentence, then find the things that begin with his sound.

Y y

Review

- **Word Stretching Warm Up** What do all these words tell us about? Say the first word, children repeat. One child says each sound, all repeat. (Mystery answer: **A cat**.)

   Words: **nose (n-o-se), tail (t-ai-l), fur (f-ur), paws (p-aw-s), purr (p-urr)**

- **PCCs ă, ĕ, d, h, m, s, t, ŭ, y, ch, ck, ll, th** Play 'Guess Who?' (Vol 1, page 234) with all *PCCs* listed. Use the 'Handwriting Review' with the whole class or small groups (page 242).

Letter shapes: Y and y

- **BPCC** Finger-trace the **y** on the picture side as you say Yellow Yo-yo Man's *Handwriting Verse*. Repeat it with the plain side:

   You first make the yo-yo sack on the Yo-yo Man's back,

   and then go down to his toes so he can sell his yo-yos.

- **Writing lowercase y** Draw a huge **y** on the board. Sing or chant Yellow Yo-yo Man's *Handwriting Verse* while children slowly air-trace the letter. (CD or *Software*.) The verse will apply to whichever **y**-shape you prefer.

- **Capital Y** First show the picture side of the **y** *BPCC*. As you explain Yellow Yo-yo Man's Capital Letter Trick, reveal the picture side of the **Y** *BPCC*. Whenever Yellow Yo-yo Man starts a name or a sentence, he quickly empties out some of his yo-yos (which are heavy) so that he can step lightly up onto the line to show how important that word is. Make lines on the board and write lowercase **y** and capital **Y** to show the difference.

- **Show the Yellow Yo-yo Man name card** Review the Character Name Trick: How can you tell whose name this is?

Sentence Copymaster
- Project the Yo-yo Man page and read the sentence. Reread it with the children echo-reading, all listening for the four /yyy/ sounds. The children circle each **Y** and **y** on their copies, finger-trace and rainbow-write in the large **y**, and color the page. Circulate to observe correct rainbow writing, and the children finger-pointing while repeating the words.

Small group/independent activities

- **Picture-coding (Ind)** Model picture-coding **Y** and **y** and have children picture-code their own **Y y**. Explain that both straight and curved **y**-shapes are correct.

- **My Letterland Reading Booklet (SG/Ind)** page 36. Is it you, Yellow Yo-yo Man? Yes, it is. Choral-read the new sentence together and several of the previous pages. Then let partners go over the familiar words and draw while you observe, check finger-pointing, and specific words.

- **Spelling Boxes (Ind)**

   Words for children to spell: Set 1: **yell, yes, chin**

   Set 2: **path, shock, rug**

- **Workbook 4 (SG/Ind)** Guide children as they finger-trace, and complete the pages.
- **A-Z Copymaster (SG)** Show children how to trace the capital letter **Y**. Have them finger-trace, rainbow write, and add pictures beginning with /**y**/.
- **Handwriting** Select from handwriting options listed in the materials box.
- **Software** Children will continue to benefit from using the software with new letters and other letters that need more practice.
- **Optional** Share the *Alphabet Name Verse* for **y** (*TG CD 2*).

Lesson 105: Day 1

Zig Zag Zebra's Sound

Preparation and materials
- *BPCC*: **z** plus Review *PCCs*
- *Alphabet Songs* CD, # 27
- Option: Project lyrics, *TG CD 2*
- *Letterland ABC Book*, p 56 or *Living ABC Software*
- *Vocabulary Cards* for **z**
- *A-Z Copymaster*, **z**
- Class Train Frieze

Small group/independent
- **z** to picture-code, *TG CD 2*
- You will need to make an extra **z** *PCC* (or borrow from another set)

Zig Zag Zebra's Alphabet Song

Zig Zag Zebra is very shy, saying 'zzz...' while zipping by.

Zebras often seem to be shy, But we'll never really know why.

Review

- **PCCs ă, b, ĕ, f, g, ĭ, j, ŏ, p, s, t, ŭ, x, y, z** Use the 'Quick Dash'.

Zig Zag Zebra, her sound, action and song

- **Zig Zag Zebra** It's listen-and-think time again. Are you ready? Let's think about the Letterland animals again. The animal I'm going to tell you more about today is one of them, a very sweet one, with big black eyes and a soft, velvety nose. Here are two more clues: You might just see some black and white stripes as she **zzz**ooms by because she can run like the wind. We don't see this Letterlander in many words because she is very shy. Who is it? **"Zig Zag Zebra!"** Use the *BPCC* and the *Class Train Frieze* to remind everybody what this **z**ipping and **z**ooming **z**ebra looks like when she is in Letterland. Yes! There she is at the very end of the alphabet! Can you see how she is looking back at all her Letterland friends? She never faces in the Reading Direction because she is so shy. Can anyone tell us who else doesn't face in the Reading Direction and why? (Golden Girl and Quarrelsome Queen.)

- **Show Zig Zag Zebra's plain letter** and ask the children where her nose would be, her mane, her tail, and her legs. Turn the card over to confirm their answers.

- **Sound** Show her plain letter *BPCC* again and rediscover her letter sound using the *Sounds Trick*: Zig Zag Zebra, /**zzz**/. Teach Zig Zag Zebra's Action Trick.

- **Song** Sing Zig Zag Zebra's *Alphabet Song*. Show the picture side of her *PCC* when you sing her name, and the plain letter for her sound and action. (Or use the *Software*.)

- **Letter Name** People who don't know about Letterland call this letter a 'z' (zee). We will be using that name later on, too, but right now we want to remember the most important thing about Zig Zag Zebra, and that is...? **"Her sound."** Say it with me, /**zzz**/. It is a sound that we can stretch out. Let's say it as if she is **z**ipping by /**zzzzzzzzz...**/.

Phonemic awareness and language development

Listen

- **ABC book** Read about **Zig Zag Zebra** (or use the *Software*). Emphasize her sound and explore the picture together.

- **Vocabulary Cards** Go over the pictures and the big words on the backs to draw attention to Zig Zag Zebra's sound.

- **Ask questions and discuss** We know, now, that Zig Zag Zebra is very quiet and shy, so you won't see her letter in a lot of words. In fact, one reason Sammy Snake often makes her **/zzz/** sound for her, is that Zig Zag Zebra is often too shy to say it herself. Even though she is shy, all her Letterland friends know she is friendly and they are very glad when she does appear in words like **z**oo, **z**ebra, and **z**ipper.

- **More about Zig Zag Zebra** Use the ideas below to guide a discussion of other words that begin with **z**. You will be building vocabulary and knowledge as well as learning about the last alphabet letter.

  - Make a **zig zag** pattern on the board and tell students that this is how Zig Zag Zebra runs. Let students practice walking in a zig zag pattern. Tell them that quite a few animals run this way because it makes them hard to catch.

  - Make a **zero** (0) on the board and see if anyone knows this number. Tell them that this is Zig Zag Zebra's favorite number.

  - Write the school's **Zip Code** on the board and explained what this is used for. You could decide together what Zig Zag Zebra's Zip Code might be. Maybe it's 00000!

  - Ask the class if anyone has eaten **zucchini**. Tell them that this vegetable is Zig Zag Zebra's favorite food.

  - If time allows, let children search for words in their books that have Zig Zag Zebra's letter in them. They won't find many, proving how shy she is.

  - Zig Zag Zebra moves so fast she makes a zooming sound. Have the children stretch out this word and say it with gusto; **ZZZ**OOOM!

- **A-Z Copymaster** Discuss the pictures and then model finger tracing, saying Zig Zag Zebra's *Handwriting Verse* as your trace:

  > Zip along Zig Zag's nose. Stroke her neck...,
  > Stroke her back...ZZZoom! Away she goes.

  Observe and help as needed with their tracing and rainbow writing while everyone fills the room with "**/z/ /z/ /z/**" sounds.

Small group/independent activities

- **Picture-coding (Ind)** Model picture coding **z** and give out large plain **z**'s to code.

- **Word Building: Pocket chart/table reading** (See Vol 1, page 239.) Ask for volunteers to try decoding a word on their own either before or after the group does, depending on the child's confidence. Tell children that Zig Zag Zebra has a shy friend called Zoe Zebra, so they will find that a few words end with both of them, just as other words end with Best Friends on the End (**ff, ll, ss**).

  PCCs: ă, b, ĕ, f, g, ĭ, ŏ, s, ŭ, x, y, z, z

  Words: zip, zig, zag, buzz, fuzz, fox, yes

- **Beginning Sounds, Handwriting, Intervention** Continue these vital activities based on children's needs. (For a special **z** game, see page 131.)

Zig Zag Zebra's Letter Shapes

Zig Zag Zebra zooms past the zoo.

Circle all Zig Zag Zebra's letters in the sentence, then find the things that begin with her sound.

Review

- **Word Stretching Warm Up** What do we do with these things? Say the first word, children repeat. One child says each sound, all repeat. (Mystery answer: **Wear them!**)

   Words: **sock (s-o-ck), shoe (sh-oe), shirt (sh-ir-t), coat (c-oa-t), hat (h-a-t), glove (g-l-o-ve)**

- **PCCs ă, b, ĕ, f, g, h, ĭ, l, ŏ, p, s, ŭ, y, z** Play 'Guess Who?' with all *PCCs* listed. Use the 'Handwriting Review' with the whole class or small groups.

Letter shapes: Z and z

- **BPCC** Finger-trace the **z** on the picture side as you say Zig Zag Zebra's *Handwriting Verse.* Repeat it with the plain side.

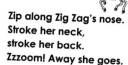

Zig Zag Zebra

**Zip along Zig Zag's nose.
Stroke her neck,
stroke her back.
Zzzoom! Away she goes.**

- **Writing lowercase z** Draw a huge **z** on the board. Sing or chant Zig Zag Zebra's *Handwriting Verse* while children slowly air-trace the letter. (CD or *Software*)

- **Capital Z** First show the **z** *BPCC* picture side. Explain the Capital Letter Trick (Vol 1, page 223) and reveal the **Z** *BPCC* picture side. To overcomes her shyness long enough to start a name or a sentence, Zig Zag Zebra takes a deep breath and gets bigger so everyone will see that the word she is in is important!

- **Show the Zig Zag Zebra name card** Review the Character Name Trick (Vol 1, page 225.) How can you tell whose name this is?

Sentence Copymaster

- Project the Zig Zag Zebra page or write the sentence on the board and share the picture. The children listen for words with initial /**zzz**/ sounds as you read: **Zig Zag Zebra zooms past the zoo.** Reread it while they count the five /**zzz**/ words on their fingers. Children circle **z**'s; trace, rainbow write, and color.

Small group/independent activities

- **Picture-coding (Ind)** Model picture-coding of **Z** and **z** and have children picture-code their own large plain **Z z.**

- **My Letterland Reading Booklet (SG/Ind)** page 35. Come and play, Zig Zag Zebra! Read the new sentence together and several previous pages. Then let partners reread while you observe, check finger-pointing, and specific words.

- **Spelling with letter sets (SG)** If your sets have no duplicate **z, s, l** and **f** use blank tiles or paper rectangles with letters added. Guide building the words.

   Letters: **a, e, f, f, h, i, l, l, p, s, s, u, y, z.**

   Words: **zip, zap, fuzz, fuss, puff, hiss, hill, yell,**

- **Workbook 4 (SG/Ind)** Guide children as they finger-trace and write the pages.

- **A-Z Copymaster (SG)** Show children how to trace the capital letter **Z.** Have them finger-trace, rainbow write, and add pictures beginning with /**z**/.

Review w, x y, and z

Preparation and materials

- You will need a small box to hide the *Beginning Sound Pictures* in, to play the game below. You may like to decorate the box with question marks.
- See Review
- *Alphabet Songs* and *Handwriting Songs* CD, # 24, 25, 26, 27, or *Software*
- *ABC Book,* p 50, 52, 54, 56
- *Beginning Sound Pictures* for **w, x, y, z**, *TG CD* 2
- Name cards for Walter Walrus, Fix-it Max, Yo-yo Man, and Zig Zag Zebra, *TG CD* 2
- Prepare copies of 'What is in the Box' booklet, *TG CD* 2
- Optional: *Action Songs* CD or *ABC Adventures* Software
- Prepare Eyes Shut Riddle Game

Small group/independent

- Write sentences from 'What is in the Box?' Decodable booklet on sentence strips
- *My Letterland Reading Booklet*

What is in the box?

A Letterland Take-Home Reader Lesson 107

Review

- **Capital Big PCCs W, X, Y, Z**
- **PCCs o** (Oscar's Little Brother), **w, x, y, z, qu, ve** Use the 'Handwriting Review' for Capital Letters.

Walter Walrus, Fix-it Max, Yo-yo Man, and Zig Zag Zebra

- **Sounds** If time permits, review characters and sounds by singing along with the *Alphabet Songs CD* (or *Software*) for all four letters. Or just say the words in chorus. Distribute the 4 Name cards and 4 *BPCCs* to 8 children. Have a child hold up the Character Name card whenever you sing or say the name, and another child hold up the *plain* letter side of the *BPCC* when you come to the sound. Other children do the actions as they sing the sounds.

- **Shapes** To review handwriting, write a large **w, x, y** and **z** on the board and have children air-trace the letter as they say or sing the words of each handwriting song. (CD or *Software.*)

- **Capitals** Review capital letters by having some children find each capital letter on the *Class Train Frieze,* and let others explain the story logic for the **W, X, Y**, and **Z** Capital Letter Tricks.

- **ABC book** Show the **w** page to the children for about 20 seconds. Then see how many words they can name that begin with the character's sound. Do the same with the page for each review letter.

  Variation: Use the *Living ABC Software* for **w, x, y**, and **z** story sections.

Decodable Booklet: 'What is in the Box?'

- **What is in the Box?** You may like to project or enlarge a copy of this story on the first day and then make copies for rereading on subsequent days. (*TG CD* 2)

Introduce the booklet

Suggested steps for sharing this booklet:

- Preview the book by discussing the title and pictures, but save the final page as a surprise.
- Remind the children that Golden Girl likes guessing games. She has brought a surprise box for the other Letterlanders to "Guess What is in the Box?"
- Let children make guesses about what is in the box.
- Point out to children the use of initials to show who is talking, WW for Walter Walrus, etc, except for Max whose short name is written out.

Tricky Words

Explain that there are two *Tricky Words* in this story that you want to show them before they read. The *Tricky Words* are **what** and **guess**.

- Draw 3 sound boxes on the board for each word.
- Elicit from the children the first sound in **what**. If they say /**w**/, write in the **wh** and tell them the sound is spelled with these two letters in some words, and they will learn later why the Hat Man is silent in this word. Meanwhile,

write **h** as a dotted letter to show it is silent here, and add a wiggly line underneath it.

- Elicit the last sound in **what** and write in the **t**.

- Ask what sound they hear in the middle, /ŭ/. Affirm that /ŭ/ is right but that an **a** goes in this word. Since that isn't Annie Apple's usual sound let's show it with a wiggly line.

- Elicit the sounds in **guess** in a similar way, showing them that the **u** is the only tricky part of this word, and it can be written as dots to show it is silent.

- Read the words with the class a few times as you point.

Reading the booklet

Read the first two pages, modeling how to decode the sentence. Next, reread the first two pages with the class. Let a volunteer or a pair of volunteers read the next page (page 4) aloud. Reread page 4 with the whole class. Read each page in the same way. Before showing the final page, ask the class: What do you think is in the box?

Reading for fluency

Reread the book with the whole class (or later in small groups) with children reading the parts of the characters. Let the same children read their parts again to gain fluency, then assign new roles and reread. Discuss why each character made their particular guess. Practice reading later in small groups for a day or two until children can read them comfortably, and then send home to share with the family. Keep at least one copy in your classroom library.

Beginning Sound Game

- **Guess What is in the Box?** Use *Beginning Sound Pictures* with the **w, x, y, z** sounds. Place them in the box in a random order. Look in the box at the first picture, i.e. **zoo**. Say something like, This picture begins with Zig Zag Zebra's sound. It is a place you can go and visit. If you went to visit there, you might see Zig Zag Zebra and other zebras. Children guess the word. Show picture to confirm. After you model a few pictures, let children volunteer to give clues (with your support as needed). This could also be a small group game.

Optional activities

- **Action Songs** For an active, fun way to involve children with Letterland characters and sounds, use the *Action Songs CD*, or the same songs on the *ABC Adventures Software*. Sing the songs for **w, x, y, z** and any other letters you wish to review.

- **Eyes Shut Riddle Game** Play this game according to instructions on page 243. Add these riddles for **w, x, y,** and **z** to the box at this time.

   w—I like to **w**allow in **w**arm **w**ater. Who am I?

   x—I have a bo**x** of tools so I can fi**x** things. Who am I?

   y—One day I hope to buy a **y**ellow **y**acht. Who am I?

   z – I love **z**ooming round and round the Letterland **Z**oo. Who am I?

- Use your box of riddles anytime for a quick review of letter sounds.

Eyes Shut Riddle Game

Small group/independent activities

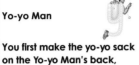

Fix-it Max

Fix two sticks
to look like this.
That's how to draw
a little kiss.

Yo-yo Man

You first make the yo-yo sack
on the Yo-yo Man's back,
and then go down to his toes
so he can sell his yo-yos.

Fix-It Max and Yo-Yo Man's *Handwriting Songs*, available on the *TG CD 2*

- **Decodable Booklet** (**SG/Ind**) Reread "What is in the Box?" as a group. Then let partners finger-point as they read to each other. Monitor the finger-pointing and point to specific words in the text for children to identify. If children need more practice with the booklet to read comfortably, save the copies for more small group reading on subsequent days.

- **Follow up to Decodable Booklet** (**SG/Ind**) Write the sentences from the "What is in the Box" booklet on sentence strips for children to work with in small groups or independently (see page 242 for more details).

- **Picture Sorting** (**SG**) For children who need more practice, do sorting with the *Beginning Sound Pictures* (TG CD 2). (See 'Sort It Out', Vol. 1, page 254.)

- **Handwriting** Choose from the handwriting materials for **w, x, y,** and **z** listed on pages 31, 34, 37, and 40.

- **My Letterland Reading Booklets** (**SG/Ind**) There is no new page for this lesson, so it is a good time to review the previous pages with small group choral reading, or partner reading.

Let's Celebrate a-z!

At this point you have not only completed Section Two of this *Teacher's Guide*, but more importantly you have thoroughly taught the entire alphabet. Why not celebrate this event—with a special day or a special lesson, or just a few review activities? Here are a few suggestions. Also ask the children to make suggestions.

- **Letterland Feast** Arrange for foods or snacks with each letter of the alphabet, i.e., **a**pple slices, **b**lueberries, **c**ranberry **c**ookies, **d**onuts, **e**ggs, **f**igs, etc.

- **Dress Up Day** Each child dresses up as a different Letterlander. Be sure to take lots of photos.

- **Favorite Letterlander** Have everyone pick their favorite Letterlander and collect words with the initial sound to write and/or illustrate along with the character. Children can write a sentence telling about the Letterlander. Then have a special time to share the results.

- **Alphabet Book** Have the children make pages for a class ABC book with drawings or magazine cut-outs.

- **Sing-a-long** Have a Letterland singing time. Let children request favorite songs. Use Actions and name cards for *Alphabet Songs* and air-tracing for *Handwriting Songs*.

- **Read-a-round** Divide class into groups of three to six children. Use copies of the reproducible booklets you have read before and the *Letterland Vowel Readers: Red Series*. each group passes around a different book. Each child reads a page. Then groups can exchange bookos adn go again.

- **Eyes Shut Riddles** Pass out the *PCCs* for **a-z**. Call out a riddle and have the child with the corresponding *PCC* hold it up and call out the Letterlander's name.

- **Traditional Alphabet Names** Give each child one verse of the *Alphabet Names Verses* (TG CD 2) to memorise, or practice reading fluently. Then present all 26 verses to another class, or in an Assembly (with or without simple costumes).

Assessment for Lessons 61-89

This set of assessments includes the eight subtests previously used but with a focus on recent content. In addition, there is a new subtest of Spelling. You will want to refer to Volume 1, pages 91-92 for a discussion of scheduling and at-risk children. In this volume, the instructions for Assessments 1-9 are found on pages 46-47. The pages that the student reads from can be copied from pages 50-52 (for Assessments 6 and 7 see *TG CD*) or they can be read by the child directly from your *Teacher's Guide*. (If so, you may want to copy the teacher instructions to have handy while you test).

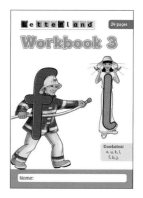

- **Review** The Letterland Workbook 3, pp 18-24, provides a review of the letters and skills assessed here. These are productive activities you can give to other children while you do these individual assessments.

- **Selecting Assessments for Each Child** To help you use your time efficiently, we have suggested below which assessments would most like to be appropriate for particular children based on their relative success in literacy activities up to this point. They are not meant to give hard and fast labels to any children, but simply to help you plan who will be tested on what.

  Children who reached the goal of 40 sounds in 60 seconds on Assessment 7 Letter Sound Fluency during previous esting do not need to repeat this assessment.

    Higher Achieving Children: Assessments 7, 8, 9

    Average Achieving Children: Assessments 4, 6, 7, 8, 9

    Lower Achieving Children: Assessments 1, 2, 3, 4, 6, 9 (If the goal for #1 is met, give #7. If the goal for #4 is met, give #8)

    Note: Asssessments 3, 6, and 9 can be given in a group setting. Other assessments are given individually.

- **Goals** A goal score for each assessment is given in parentheses on the score sheet and in the table below. If a child does not meet the goals on certain assessments he or she should be given the more basic assessment in that area listed in Table A below.

Table A. Additional Tests if Goals Not Met

If the goal is not met on Assessment #_	...administer Assessment #_ (if not already given)
1. Letter Sounds	Character Names Assessment (Volume 1, page 37)
5. Segmentation Accuracy	2. Beginning Sounds in Words
7. Letter Sound Fluency	1. Letter Sounds
8. Word Reading Fluency	4. Word Reading Accuracy
9. Spelling	5. Segmentation Accuracy

- **Using Assessment Information** If a large percentage of your class is not meeting a certain goal, you will probably want to review the whole class in that area and give more attention to it as you move into new lessons.

- If a few individuals are not reaching the goals, emphasis should be given to these skills in small group and special intervention instruction (see Volume 1, pages 192-218). It is a good idea to monitor children in the areas they have shown weakness by retesting them at intervals from bi-weekly to monthly. This monitoring will allow you to see if progress is being made or not. Then, if needed, support those children with more intensive instruction can be provided.

Table B. Assessment Information

No.	Title	For Whom?	No. of Items (Goal)	Teacher Instruction Page	Scoring Page	Student Page
1	Letter Sounds from Lessons 61-89	**Low** (Child who has not shown mastery of a-z letter sounds)	**15** (13)	46	48	50
2	Beginning Sounds in Words	**Low** (Child who has not shown mastery of beginning sounds)	**11** (9)	46	48	none
3	Write Letter in Response to Sound	**Low**	**15** (13)	46	48	writing paper
4	Word Reading Accuracy	**Low, Average**	**10** (8)	46	49	50
5	Segmentation Accuracy	Only children who do not reach goal on #9 Spelling	**21** (18)	47	49	none
6	Matching Capital and Lowercase	**Low, Average**	**5** (5)	47	49	*TG CD*
7	Letter Sound Fluency	**Average, High** (If goal not reached give #1 also)	(40 sounds in 60 secs)	47	49	*TG CD* form B, C, or D
8	Word Reading Fluency	**Average, High** (If goal not reached, give #4 if not already given)	(10 words in 60 secs)	47	49	51
New Assessments (not included in Assessments for Lessons 43-60)						
9	Spelling	**Low, Average, High** (If goal not met, give #5)	**8** (6)	39	49	writing paper

Additional Assessments and Helpful Forms

These are available on the *Teacher's Guide CD 2*.

- **Class Record Sheet:** Section 2 Assessments. Use this form to compile scores and match students with similar needs.

- **Beginning Sounds in Words** This includes all the basic letter sounds with 3 choices of words for each sound to allow for multiple and frequent administrations.

- **Word Recognition Fluency Assessment (All Basic Sounds), Forms A, B, C, D** This is similar to Assessment 8. Assessment 8 for Lessons 61-89 includes only letter sounds covered in these lessons or previously. This Fluency test from the Teacher's Guide CD includes all basic sounds and includes four alternate forms. Giving this Assessment to your higher students on several occasions across the school year will help you document the progress of these children.

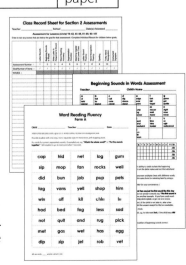

Teacher Instructions for Assessments

1 Letter Sounds (page 50)

Sample Item: Use blank paper to cover the first line of letters on the student copy. Point to the **t**. Tell me the sound this letter makes in words. If the child gives the letter name or says, '**Talking Tess,**' affirm the answer and say, This letter says /**t**/ in words. Now you say that sound.

Test Items: Point to each letter. Now tell me the sound this letter makes in words. If the child gives the letter name or the Letterlander, say, Yes, and what's the sound? If the child still does not give the sound, go to the next letter. Make a checkmark for each correct sound. If incorrect, leave blank or write in the child's answer. For letters **u** and **th**, after the child gives one response, ask, What other sound can this letter (these letters) make in words? Goal: 13 of 15 sounds correct.

2 Beginning Sounds in Words (page 48)

I am going to say a word and you listen and see if you can tell me the first sound. You can use your rubber-band stretching if you like. I want you to say the word and then say just the very first sound. Let's try one. Say **lock**. Wait for response. Now what's the first sound? If the child gives the correct phoneme, go to the next word. If the child gives an incorrect sound or says more than a phoneme, e.g. /**lo**/, mark the item as incorrect and say, Let's stretch **lock** together and then say just the start with our rubber-band just going a tiny little way. Use your hands and encourage the child to join you, **lllooock** /**l**/. Now, you try the next word. Say **fall**, and then say just the start. Encourage the child to stretch the word if it seems useful, but do not give any additional help. Make a check mark if correct. Write down incorrect answers or mark with a **0**. If the child cannot give the sound, but can tell you the correct Letterlander or letter name, you may want to note this. If the child adds **–uh** to a sound, ask for just the first part. If **–uh** is repeated, write what the child said (e.g. "**buh**") and do not count as correct. Goal: 9 of 11 sounds.

3 Write Letter in Response to Sound (Group test, page 48)

Materials: Use the writing materials that the children are used to.

Now, I am going to say a sound, and you are going to write the letter or two letters that make that sound. I'll do the first one. The sound is /**sss**/. It sounds like I'm getting ready to say, "Ssssssammy Sssnake". I'll write his letter. Write an **s** on the board as an example. Call out each sound and have the children write. For /**k**/, you may tell the children to write three different ways that /**k**/ can be written in words. For digraphs (e.g. **ch, th**), you may tell the children that they may need two letters for one sound. Do not give further help except to encourage and praise effort. Count the letter correct if it would be recognizable by you if you did not know what sound had been given. Leave blank if no letter is attempted. Accept capital or lower case. Goal: 13 of 15 sounds correctly written correctly.

4 Word Reading Accuracy (page 50)

Point to the word **leg** and ask, What is this word? If the child gives letter names or sounds or character names say, Can you use your arm rollercoaster to blend the sounds into a word? If the child is still unable to correctly give the word, model putting the sounds on your arm and blending to get the word, **leg**. Have the child repeat this process with you for **leg**. Count **leg** as incorrect and ask the child to Try the next one, as you point to **gum**. Make a checkmark for each correct whole word in the blank. If no word is given, leave the space blank. If an incorrect word is given, write it in the blank. If the child gives sounds only, you may suggest one time for each word that the child 'blend it' or use your usual classroom terminology, e.g. Put it on your rollercoaster. After about 5 seconds' hesitation on a word, move on to the next one. Goal: 8 of 10 words read correctly.

5 Segmentation Accuracy (page 49)

This is a listening and oral segmentation task. Say the word (do not show it). Ask the child to tell you all the sounds in the word. Sample words: **bat**, /**b**/ /**ă**/ /**t**/; **had**; /**h**/ /**ă**/ /**t**/. You may model 'rubber-band word-stretching' with the example words and have the child repeat the segmenting with you. After the examples, provide no further help. Make a check mark for each correct sound spoken separately. Write any errors as well. Goal: 18 of 21 sounds correct.

6 Matching Capital and Lowercase (TG CD 2)

Copy the student page from the *TG CD 2*. Point to the **b** and ask the child to point to the capital for this letter in the other column. Draw a line from Bouncy Ben's letter to his Capital letter. Now match each one with its capital letter by drawing lines to join them. Goal: 5 of 5 matches.

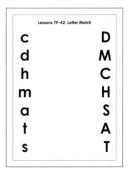

7 Letter Sound Fluency (Form A, Vol 1, page 137; or Form B, C, or D, TG CD 2)

To save paper, you may want to place the score sheet in a plastic sheet protector. Make a slash over any missed letters and a bracket to show the last sound within the 60-second time limit.

Say, I want you to point to these letters and say the sounds, going across this way and then on to the next row and so on. Go as fast as you can without missing sounds. If you don't know one, you can say 'skip' and go on.

Point to the first letter. Before we begin, tell me the sound of this first one. If correct, praise and go to the directions in the next paragraph. If incorrect, say, The sound of this one is ___. Now you say the sound. Count the first letter as an error.

Remember you are going to point to the letters and say the sounds going this way… Begin.

Time for 60 seconds. Mark the end point, and say, "Stop." Record total correct sounds. Also, record any sounds missed. Goal: 40 correct sounds in 60 seconds.

8 Word Reading Fluency (page 51; or Form A, B, C, or D, TG CD 2)

To save paper, you may want to place the score sheet in a plastic sheet protector, and make a slash over any missed words, and a bracket to show the last word within the time limit.

Say, I want you to read these words going across this way, and then on to the next row, and so on. We will stop after one minute, so you probably won't have time to read all of them. You can sound them out or put them on your arm rollercoaster or if you know one right off, go ahead and say it. Go as fast as you can without missing words. If you don't know one you can say 'skip' and go on to the next one.

Remember you are going to start with this word (pointing to the word to the right of the sample) and go this way…. Begin.

If the child says the word in segments, e.g., /**i**/ - /**n**/, but does not follow with the blended word, say What's the whole word? or Put the sounds together. Tell student to go to next word after 5 seconds.

Time for 60 seconds. Mark end point and say, Stop. Record total correct words. Give no credit for saying sounds in a segmented fashion such as /**p**/ - /**i**/ - /**n**/ unless the child then says the whole word, "**pin**." Goal: 10 words correct in 60 seconds.

9 Spelling (page 49)

This assessment can be done with the whole class or in small groups. Provide children with writing materials that they are familiar with. Call out each word and have children repeat it. Use a sentence with the word if needed and then say the word again. Children write the words. Encourage them to try to listen for the sounds and to use their rubber-band-stretching on their own. Goal: 6 of 8 words spelled correctly.

Assessment Record for Lessons 61-89

Child _____

Teacher _____ **Date** _____

(Goal scores for each subtest in parentheses)

1 Letter Sounds (Student reads from page 50)

t	**e**		**u**		**k**	**l**	**f**
(Sample)	____	____	____	____	____	____	____
	/ĕ/	/ē/	/ŭ/	/ū/			

sh	**ch**	**th**		**ck**	**ng**	**ll**	**ff**
____	____	____	____	____	____	____	____
		/th/	/th/				

_____ /15 sounds (13)

2 Beginning Sounds in Words

lock	**fall**	**under**	**edge**	**kite**	**eagle**	**uniform**
____	____	____	____	____	____	____

shop	**cheek**	**thin**	**that**
____	____	____	____

_____ /11 sounds (9)

3 Write Letter in Response to Sound

/f/	/b/	/l/	/k/			/ĕ/	/ŭ/	/sh/
____	____	____	____	____	____	____	____	____
			c	k	ck			

/ē/	/ch/	/th/	/ū/	/th/	/ng/
____	____	____	____	____	____

_____ /15 sounds (13)

4 Word Reading Accuracy (Student reads from page 50)

leg	gum	fish	king	duck	chop	thin	that
____	____	____	____	____	____	____	____

puff	tell
____	____

____ /10 words (8)

5 Segmentation Accuracy

less	shell	kit	those	king	fun	hug
_ _ _	_ _ _	_ _ _	_ _ _	_ _ _	_ _ _	_ _ _

____ /21 sounds (18)

6 Match Capital and Lowercase (Student copy, TG CD 2)

Ff	Kk	Ll	Uu	Ee
____	____	____	____	____

____ 5 matches (5)

7 Letter Sound Fluency Use Form A (Vol 1, page 137) or Form B, C, or D (TG CD 2)

60 seconds: ____ letters correct (Goal: 40)

Letter Sound or Letter Name Check				Form B
c	i	e	j	q
t	m	a	d	x
l	b	u	h	r
w	s	o	k	z
y	n	g	v	p
f	d	n	u	l
j	q	c	w	m
r	i	y	o	e
v	f	s	z	b
h	t			

8 Word Reading Fluency (Use page 51: includes only letter studied thus far in Section 2, or Form A, B, C, or D, TG CD 2)

60 seconds: ____ words correct (Goal: 10)

Word Reading Fluency Form A

cap	hid	net	log	gum
sip	mop	fan	rocks	well
did	bun	job	pup	pets
tag	vans	yell	shop	him
win	off	kit	chin	in
had	bed	fog	less	sad
not	quit	and	rug	pick
met	gas	wet	has	egg
dip	zip	jet	rob	vet

9 Spelling

let	shed	luck	chop	thick
____	____	____	____	____

that	fin	sink
____	____	____

____ /8 words (6)

Student Page: Assessments 1 and 4

1 Letter Sounds

t e u k l

f sh ch th ck

ng ll ff

4 Word Reading Accuracy

leg gum fish king

duck chop thin

that puff tell

8 Word Reading Fluency
Lessons 61-89

Child _____

Teacher _____ **Date** _____

Time for 60 seconds with a goal of 10 words correct.

No credit for correct segmented sounds. If sounded out say, "What's the whole word?" or "Put the sounds together." Tell student to go to next word after 5 seconds.

cup	neck	hug	let	chop
ship	jug	lip	pan	thick
jet	lap	jog	log	duck
shell	them	king	pig	sock
that	ducks	fell	fan	hill
dot	fun	kick	tell	mad
pups	tuck	not	get	fills
nets	sing	long	can	mud
less	met	pans	dock	lick

60 seconds: _____ words correct (10)

cup	neck	hug	let	chop
ship	jug	lip	pan	thick
jet	lap	jog	log	duck
shell	them	king	pig	sock
that	ducks	fell	fan	hill
dot	fun	kick	tell	mad
pups	tuck	not	get	fills
nets	sing	long	can	mud
less	met	pans	dock	lick

Assessment for Lessons 90-107

These nine assessments are similar to previous assessments in Section 2 but with a focus on recently learned material. You may want to refer to Volume 1, pages 91-92 for a discussion of scheduling and at-risk children. In this volume, the instructions for Assessments 1-9 are found on pages 46-47. The pages that the student reads from can be copied from pages 57 and 59 (for Assessments 6 and 7 see *TG CD 2*), or they can be read by the child directly from your *Teacher's Guide* (in which case you may want to copy the teacher instructions to have handy while you test).

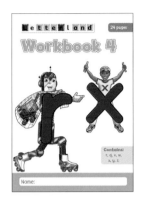

- **Review** *Letterland Workbook 4*, pp 18-24, provides a review of the letters and skills assessed here. These pages provide productive activities you can give to other children while you do these individual assessments.

- **Selecting Assessments for Each Child** To help you use your time efficiently, we have suggested below which assessments would most like to be appropriate for particular children based on their relative success in literacy activities up to this point. They are not meant to give hard and fast labels to any children, but simply to help you plan who will be tested on what.

  Children who reached the goal of 40 seconds in 60 seconds on Assessment 7 Letter Sound Fluency during testing do not need to repeat this assessment.

    Higher Achieving Children: Assessments 7, 8, 9

    Average Achieving Children: Assessments 4, 6, 7, 8, 9

    Lower Achieving Children: Assessments 1, 2, 3, 4, 6, 9 (If the goal for #1 is met, give #7. If the goal for #4 is met, give #8)

    Note: Asssessments 3, 6, and 9 can be given in a group setting.

- **Goals** A goal score for each assessment is given in parentheses on the score sheet and in the table below. If a child does not meet the goals on certain assessments he or she should be given the more basic assessment in that area listed in Table A below.

Table A. Additional Tests if Goals Not Met

If the goal is not met on Assessment #_	...administer Assessment #_ (if not already given)
1. Letter Sounds	Character Names Assessment (Volume 1, page 37)
5. Segmentation Accuracy	2. Beginning Sounds in Words
7. Letter Sound Fluency	1. Letter Sounds
8. Word Reading Fluency	4. Word Reading Accuracy
9. Spelling	5. Segmentation Accuracy

- **Using Assessment Information** If a large percentage of your class is not meeting a certain goal, you will probably want to review the whole class in that area and give more attention to it in as you move into new lessons.

- If a few individuals are not reaching the goals, emphasis should be given to these skills in small group and special intervention instruction (see Vol 1, pages 192-218). It is a good idea to monitor children in the areas of weakness by retesting them at intervals from bi-weekly to monthly. This will allow you to see whether or not futher intensive instruction needs to be provided.

Table B. Assessment Information

No.	Title	For Whom?	No. of Items (Goal)	Teacher Instruction Page	Scoring Page	Student Page
1	Letter Sounds from Lessons 90-107	**Low** (Child who has not shown mastery of a-z letter sounds)	**12** (11)	46	55	57
2	Beginning Sounds in Words	**Low** (Child who has not shown mastery of beginning sounds)	**8** (7)	46	55	none
3	Write Letter in Response to Sound	**Low** (Individual or group)	**11** (9)	46	55	writing paper
4	Word Reading Accuracy	**Low, Average**	**10** (8)	46	55	57
5	Segmentation Accuracy	Only children who do not reach goal on #9 Spelling	**21** (17)	47	56	none
6	Matching Capital and Lowercase	**Low, Average, High** (Individual or group)	**7** (6)	47	56	*TG CD 2*
7	Letter Sound Fluency	**Average, High** (If goal not reached give #1 also)	(40 sounds in 60 secs)	47	56	*TG CD 2* form B, C, or D
8	Word Reading Fluency	**Average, High** (If goal not reached, give #4 if not already given)	(10 words in 60 secs)	47	58	59
9	Spelling	**Low, Average, High** (If goal not met, give #5) (Individual or group)	**9** (7)	47	56	writing paper

Additional Assessments and Helpful Forms

These are available on the *Teacher's Guide CD 2*.

- **Class Record Sheet:** Section 2 Assessments. This form is used to record scores and match students with similar needs.

- **Beginning Sounds in Words** Includes all the basic letter sounds with 3 choices of words for each sound to allow for multiple and frequent administrations.

- **Word Reading Fluency Assessment (All Basic Sounds), Forms A, B, C, D** This is similar to Assessment 8. Assessment 8 for Lessons 90-107 includes only letter sounds covered in these lessons or previously. The Fluency test from the *Teacher's Guide CD 2* includes all basic sounds and includes four alternate forms. Giving this Assessment to your higher students on several occasions across the school year will help you document the progress of these children.

Assessment Record for Lessons 90-107

Child _____

Teacher _____ **Date** _____

(Goal scores for each subtest in parentheses)

1 Letter Sounds (Student reads from page 49.)

j	r	v	qu	ve	o
____	____	____	____	____	____

/ŏ/   /ō/   /o/ (Oscar's Little Brother)

z	x	y	w
____	____	____	____

_____ /12 sounds (11)

2 Beginning Sounds in Words

road	van	best	quick	zoo	joke	yam	wood
____	____	____	____	____	____	____	____

_____ /8 sounds (7)

3 Write Letter in Response to Sound

/j/	/b/	/qu/	/ŭ/		/w/	/r/	/x/
____	____	____	____		____	____	____

u   o

/z/	/y/	/v/
____	____	____

_____ /11 sounds (9)

4 Word Reading Accuracy (Student reads from page 57)

big	red	quit	jet	van
____	____	____	____	____

love	wag	six	yes	zip
____	____	____	____	____

_____ /10 words (8)

5 Segmentation Accuracy

job	wax	rib	quack	vet	love	yell	
_ _ _	_ _ _	_ _ _	_ _ _	_ _ _	_ _ _	_ _ _	_____ /21 sounds (18)

6 Match Capital and Lowercase (Student copy, TG CD 2)

Rr	Qq	Vv	Ww	Xx	Yy	Zz	
_____	_____	_____	_____	_____	_____	_____	_____ /7 matches (6)

7 Letter Sound Fluency

Use Form A (Vol 1., page 137) or Form B, C, or D (*TG CD* 2)

60 seconds: _____ letters correct (Goal: 40)

8 Word Reading Fluency (Use page 58 (includes only letter sounds taught thus far), or Form A, B, C, or D (TG CD 2)

60 seconds: _____ words correct (Goal: 10)

9 Spelling

rush	jog	quick	van	give	well
_____	_____	_____	_____	_____	_____

yes	six	zip	
_____	_____	_____	_____ /9 words (7)

Student Page: Assessments 1 and 4

1 Letter Sounds

j   r   v   qu

ve   o   z   x

y   w

4 Word Reading Accuracy

big   red   quit   jet

van   love   wag   six

yes   zip

8 Word Reading Fluency
Lessons 90-107

Child _____

Teacher _____ Date _____

Time for 60 seconds with a goal of 10 words correct.

No credit for correct segmented sounds. If sounded out say, "What's the whole word?" or "Put the sounds together." Tell student to go to next word after 5 seconds.

lap	jet	van	box	yes
pin	tax	wag	vet	thin
give	wet	quack	fox	zip
cup	rip	yet	log	wing
sock	luck	ran	chin	can
mix	deck	yell	win	jug
mat	come	well	love	chip
thick	rub	quick	song	jam
ten	quit	six	red	live
pack	back	run	rid	jog

60 seconds: _____ words correct (10)

lap	jet	van	box	yes
pin	tax	wag	vet	thin
give	wet	quack	fox	zip
cup	rip	yet	log	wing
sock	luck	ran	chin	can
mix	deck	yell	win	jug
mat	come	well	love	chip
thick	rub	quick	song	jam
ten	quit	six	red	live
pack	back	run	rid	jog

Section 3

Onsets and Rimes

 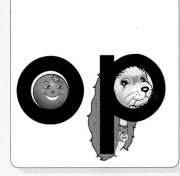

Lessons 108–137

Onsets and Rimes

With 30 lessons **Section 3: Onsets and Rimes** builds on children's knowledge of letter sounds and the skills of segmenting and blending from Section 2. In this new section, children learn to read words by analogy, using the onset (the **c** in cat) and the rime (the **at** in cat) to read words with ease and fluency. The activities make extensive of use of *Word Cards* (from the *Teacher's Guide CD*) for picture-word matching, sorting words, and playing games. Children will also practice reading, building and writing sentences in lively, interactive activities.

- As in the previous section, each daily lesson includes whole group activities, small group activities and some independent activities. Teachers who primarily teach in only one of these settings, i.e. whole group, can adapt the small group activities to the whole group setting to provide the needed instruction and practice.

- Beginning with Section 3, daily lessons are grouped into learning Units. In this section there are five Units as listed here:

    Unit 1: Lessons 108-115 Word families with short **a**

    Unit 2: Lessons 116-121 Word families with short **i**

    Unit 3: Lessons 122-127 Word families with short **o**

    Unit 4: Lessons 128-132 Word families with short **u**

    Unit 5: Lessons 133-137 Word families with short **e**

- The reason for the sequence of short vowels in these units (**a, i, o, u, e**) is to separate the short **e** from the two vowel sounds it is most easily confused with, short **a** and short **i**.

Learning Outcomes and Assessments

Outcomes	Assessments (See pages 132-135)
• Recognize CVC words accurately.	1.Word Reading Accuracy
• Recognize 16 high-frequency words accurately,	2. Reading Tricky Words
• Read CVC words at a rate of at least 10 words correct per minute (wcpm).	3. Word Reading Fluency
• Spell CVC words correctly.	4. Spelling Decodable Words
• Spell 16 high-frequency words correctly.	5. Spelling Tricky Words
• Write simple sentences with a capital letter for the first word and a period at the end.	6. Sentence Dictation

Tricky Words

- Children are taught to read and spell the following 16 Tricky Words in this Section:

is	on	me	see	this	to	in	I
the	no	you	for	she	now	he	was

New Materials from the Teacher's Guide CD

- For each Unit in this section and Sections 4-7, there are new reproducible cards on the *Teacher's Guide CD*. You can copy these onto heavy paper and perhaps laminate them and cut them into individual word and picture cards. The various cards are described here:

- ***Rhyming Pictures*** are used to practice the concept of rhyme, for matching with *Word Cards*, and for illustrating the sentences that children build with the *Word Cards*.

- ***Rime Cards*** are used with ***Picture Code Cards*** in Live Reading and Spelling, for building words on the pocket chart, and for sorting *Word Cards* by rhyming 'family.'

- ***Word Cards*** are used in several ways including sorting by rhyming family, building and changing sentences, and playing games to build accurate and fluent word reading.

  The three types of cards above are all numbered according to the Unit in which they are used. They can be stored together in a plastic bag for each Unit. The bags of cards will fit nicely in a container the size of a shoe box.

- ***Tricky Word Cards*** are used to learn to read and spell high-frequency words including many with irregular spellings. They are used frequently in sentence building activities. The *Tricky Word Cards* are not numbered because they are used in multiple units. You may want to keep them in alphabetical order in the front of the box that you use for the other cards.

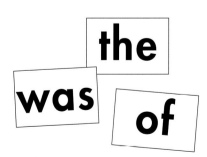

New Activities

- **Live Reading and Spelling** which children previously used in Section 2, are given a new twist here as children read and spell words using Onsets and Rimes.

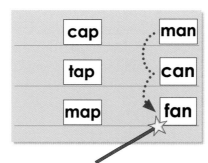

- **Word and Picture Match** Children work on rhyming and word recognition by matching pictures and words and practicing fluent reading of words with game-like activities.

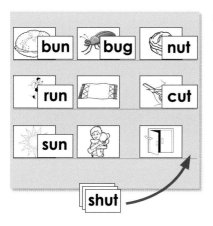

- **Word Sorting** Children sort words visually and by sound. They sort with cards and by writing. They sort with pictures and without pictures.

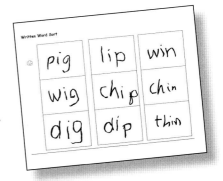

- **Sentence Building and Writing** With the interactive learning tasks, children learn to comprehend and compose sentences. They work on spelling and writing skills in carefully sequenced and scaffolded activities.

- **Decodable Take-Home Booklets** Each Unit builds word and sentence reading skills that culminate in an engaging Take-Home Booklet that puts those skills to use. Children work on comprehension as well by reconstructing or reorganizing the stories with sentence strips.

Unit 1 Word Families with ă

Unit 1: Lesson 108

Rhyming with –at

Review

- **PCCs ă, b, c, f, h, m, r, s, t** Use the 'Quick Dash' (Vol 1, page 233).

Rhyming Chant for -at

- Practice saying the chant together.
- Let children use red to picture-code Annie Apple in **am, bat, cat,** and **that** (but not the **a** in **saying** which features Mr A).
- Underline the **-at** words.
- Ask the children which two Letterlanders make their sounds together in each of the rhyming words.
- You may like to quickly picture-code Talking Tess at the end of each rhyming word.
- Let the children think of more words that rhyme with **at, bat, cat** and **that**. (**pat, mat. sat, fat, flat, rat**).

Hello, I'm Annie Apple.
I am happy saying a in at.
I am happy saying a in bat.
I am happy saying a in cat,
and lots of words like that.

Rhyming Pictures

In the following review of rhyming, students will choose the 1 word that doesn't rhyme with the other 3 words from a set of 4 *Rhyming Pictures*.

- Display these four pictures on the pocket chart (**cat, bat, pig, hat**).
- All name the pictures together.
- Children repeat them and decide which word doesn't rhyme.
- Choose a child to put the pig picture in the 'trash can.'
- All say the 3 words that *do* rhyme again twice.
- Ask frequently, Why do these words go together? Answer: **"They rhyme."**
- Follow the above steps with the two other sets of pictures (**man, pan, fan, dog**) and (**cap, sun, nap, map**).

Live Spelling and Reading

Live Spell the –at words depicted on cards
- Display the 4 *Rhyming Picture Cards* at the left.
- Give out the *PCCs* listed under 'Review.'
- Lead students in rubber-band stretching the first word: **căăăăăăt**.

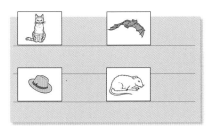

- Children decide on the letters needed to spell the word, and the children with those cards line up to Live Spell it.
- Other children arm-blend the word to check for correct spelling: /c/ /ă/ /t/, cat.
- Ask children to stretch the next word (**bat**) and decide which child needs to sit down and who needs to be at the beginning of the word.
- After Live Spelling 2 more words (**hat, rat**), ask, What two Letterlanders did we use in each and every word today? "**Annie Apple and Talking Tess.**"

Live Read with the Rime Card -at

- Have two children holding **a** and **t** *PCCs* stand together to form **at**.
- Have the class sound out **at** with arm-blending.
- Annie Apple and Talking Tess are in lots of words as we've seen. They are together so much that we have a special card showing both letters on one card. It's called a *Rime Card*.
- Give the two children the *Rime Card* in exchange for their *PCC* cards. Display the *PCCs* nearby. The two children hold the *Rime Card* together.
- Ask everyone, What does this say? "**at**"

Teach Onset and Rime Arm-blending

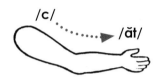

- Line up one child holding the **c** PCC and the children holding **at** to build **cat**.
- Show children how to arm-blend using onset and rime. First say /**c**/ as you touch your shoulder. Then brush quickly down your forearm as you say **at**.
- Have children practice this new method of arm-blending with the word **cat** several times.

Match Word Cards with Picture Cards

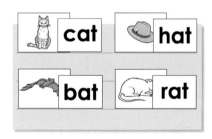

- Show the **cat** *Word Card* and place it on the pocket chart next to the picture of the **cat**.
- Line students up for Live Reading the words **bat, hat**, and **rat**, and practice the Onset and Rime arm-blending of these words.
- After each word is formed for Live Reading, show students the *Word Card* and let someone place the word next to the matching picture.

Read the Words Cards with Picture Cards, then without

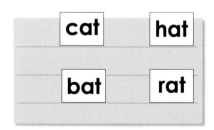

- Point to each *Word Card* on the pocket chart as the class reads them.
- Remove the pictures and have the children read the *Word Cards*.
- Pick up the *Word Cards* and present them as flash cards, to the whole class first. Then let some children try reading the words on their own.
- If a child is unsure of a word, model how to use Onset and Rime arm-blending to sound it out.

Vocabulary Cards and rhyming

- Show students the front and backs of the *Vocabulary Cards*, **cat** and **hat**.
- Point out that the big word in the middle and the words in the corners all have **-at** as the last part of the word.
- Practice reading all the words on the cards with the children.
- Ask for volunteers to try reading a few of the words.
- Leave the cards out for independent exploration with a few other decodable *Vocabulary Cards* (those with the thin blue frame around the picture). Suggest that pairs of children explore reading the words when your schedule allows.

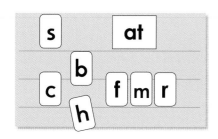

Small group/independent activities

- **Independent Picture-coding** Provide copies of the large, plain **at** and display **ă** and **t** PCCs. Children picture-code and illustrate with pictures of rhyming words.
- **Pocket chart/table reading** Make words using the **at** *Rime Card*. Have the children use Onset and Rime type arm-blending.

  PCCs: **b, c, f, h, m, r, s** plus **Rime Card: at**

  Words: **bat, cat, fat, hat, mat, rat, sat**

- **Pictures and Words** Use the *Rhyming Pictures* and *Word Cards* from today's lesson. Let the children match pictures and words, then remove pictures and read the words again.
- **Concentration Game** Lay the *Rhyming Pictures* and *Word Cards* on the table printed side down. Have the children take turns. A player turns over one picture and one word. If they match, the player 'keeps' the pair. If the word and picture do not match, the player returns the cards to their original place, and the next player takes a turn.

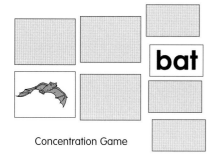

Concentration Game

First Sentence Practice

Materials
- *PCCs: see Review*
- *Rime Card:* **at**, *TG CD 2*
- Unit 1 *Word Cards:* **hat, sat, fat, mat, cat, bat**, *TG CD 2*
- *Tricky Word Cards:* **The, is**, *TG CD 2*

Preparation
- Print copies of 'Lesson 109 Sentence Practice,' *TG CD 2*

Small group/independent
- *Rhyming Pictures:* **cat, bat, rat, hat**, *TG CD 2*

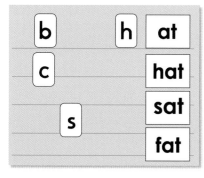

Review

- PCCs **ă, b, c, f, h, m, r, s, t**   Rime Card: **at** Play 'Guess Who?' or use 'Handwriting Review' in whole group or small groups (page 242).

Word Building

  Rime Card: **at**

  PCCs: **ă, b, c, f, h, m, r, s, t**

  Word Cards: **hat, sat, fat, mat, cat, bat**

Begin with the 'at' card, make and arm-blend 'hat'
- Display the **at** *Rime Card*. Have children read it.
- Place the **h** PCC in front to make **hat**.
- Demonstrate Onset/Rime arm-blending. Face the children and place your left hand on your right shoulder and say the onset. Slide your hand down your forearm and say the rime: hhhh-at, hat.
- Ask children to arm-blend **hat** in the same way.

Read the Word Card, build a new word
- Display the *Word Card* for **hat** and ask children to read it.
- Follow the same steps with each word. First build the word with onset and rime. Then place the *Word Cards* under the previous word.
- Everyone reads all the *Word Cards,* as you point each time a new one is added.

Reread the words faster each time

- Point to each word as the class reads, going slowly.
- Repeat reading the words a few times, a bit faster each time.
- Point to the words in random order and everyone reread.

Sentence Building

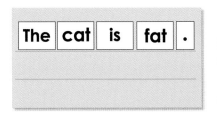

Word Cards: cat, rat, bat, fat, The, is, •

Read the sentence

- Place the cards in the pocket chart to form the sentence. Point to each word as you read out the sentence.
- Read the sentence again with the children as you point.

Find the rhyming words

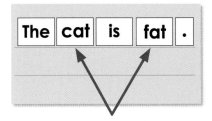

- Can anyone tell what words rhyme in the sentence? Call on a child.
- Yes, ___ and ___ rhyme. Let's all say those rhyming words again.
- Can anyone show us the cards with these rhyming words on them?
- Yes, you found the rhyming words. Now let's read our sentence again and see what these other words say.
- Read the sentence together.

Indentify <u>the</u> and <u>is</u>

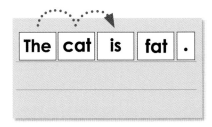

- Point to **The** and ask, What does this say? Call on a child.
- Have everyone repeat, **"The."**
- Let's find out what this other word says.
- Read the sentence together as you point to each word. Point to **is**. Have a child name the word. (If needed, guide the child to reread the sentence, stopping on **is**.)
- Have the class repeat, **"is."** Who heard Sleepy Sammy snoozing?

Change <u>cat</u> to <u>bat</u>, then to <u>rat</u>

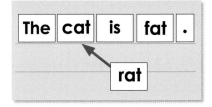

- Change the word **cat** to **bat**. Call on a volunteer to read the new sentence.
- Then everyone read the sentence together.
- Point to each word in a random order and call on a different child to name each word.
- Replace **bat** with **rat** in the sentence. Follow the same steps as above.

Sentence Practice (worksheet)

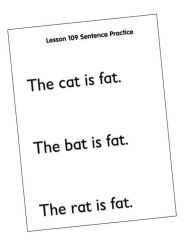

Read the sentence *to* and *with* the children

- Show one copy of 'Lesson 109 Sentence Practice' reproducible page. Read the three sentences to the class.
- Pass out papers to each child. Have children finger-point and read each sentence with you.

Children illustrate as individuals read to you

- The children then draw and color an illustration of one or more sentences.
- Circulate among the class, asking individuals to point to the words as they read the sentences to you.

- If a child has difficulty with pointing or reading, model finger-pointing reading each sentence and then have the child reread it.
- If a child can read and point accurately, point to individual words for the child to identify (**is, cat, The,** etc.). (If this is difficult, guide the child to reread the sentence up to the word you have pointed to.)

Small group/independent activities

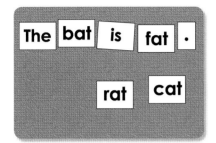

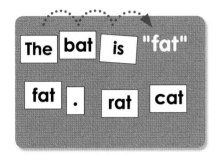

- **Sentence Reading and Building** You may want to place the *Word Cards* on a mat to make it easy to move them around the table within reach of each child. (The mat could be made from construction paper, a carpet square, or a placemat.)

    Word Cards: **The, is, cat, bat, rat, fat, ·**
- Use the *Word Cards* to first practice reading the sentence with children as they take turns pointing to the cards.
- Let children switch nouns to **bat** and **rat** and reread.
- Mix up the words and let each child in turn place a *Word Card* to rebuild the sentence. Reread the whole sentence each time a word is placed.
- **Pocket chart/table spelling** Call out words for the children to build, using the **at** *Rime Card.* Have the children use word-stretching to help segment the words.

    PCCs: **b, c, f, h, m, r, s**

    Rime Card: **at**

    Word Cards: **bat, cat, fat, hat, mat, rat, sat**
- **Concentration Game** As in the previous lesson, lay the pictures and words on the table, printed side down. Have the children take turns. A player turns over one picture and one word. If they match, the player keeps the pair. If the word and picture do not match, the player returns the cards to their original place, and the next player takes a turn.
- **For more challenge** Have children choose a picture first and have them rubber-band stretch the word and give each sound in sequence (or spell the word). Then the child tries to find the matching word.

New Word Family: -ap

Review

- **Word Stretching Warm Up** These words remind us of something we should do everyday. Say the first word, children repeat. One child says each sound, all repeat. (Mystery answer: **Eat breakfast**, or **eat good food**.)

  Words: juice (j-ui-ce), milk (m-i-l-k), fruit (f-r-ui-t) toast (t-oa-s-t), egg (e-gg)

- **PCCs: ă, c, m, n, p, t; Rime Cards: at, ap.** Play 'Guess Who?' with all *PCCs* and *Rime Cards* or use 'Handwriting Review' with whole class or small groups (page 242).

Rhyming Chant for -ap

- Practice saying the chant together several times.
- Ask children which words rhyme.
- Underline the rhyming **ap** words.
- Ask the children which 2 Letterlanders make their sounds in all 4 of these rhyming words.
- You may like to quickly picture-code Annie Apple and Peter Puppy in each rhyming word.
- Ask the children to think of more words that rhyme with **cap, tap, map,** and **nap** (lap, gap, rap, sap, snap, trap, flap, etc).

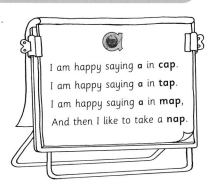

I am happy saying a in **cap**.
I am happy saying a in **tap**.
I am happy saying a in **map**,
And then I like to take a **nap**.

Sentence Building

Read the sentence

- Display the sentence. Point to each word as you read the sentence.
- Point to the words and read the sentence with everyone.
- Call on a child to point to words as the class reads. Let other children do the same. Some may read the sentence on their own, and then point for the class to read.

Identify words in random order

- Point to words in random order and call on children to identify the words.

Substitute rat and bat

- Substitute **rat** and **bat** for **cat** in turn. For each substitution follow the above steps, reading the sentence and pointing to words randomly for identification.

Change the sentence to a question and read

- Change the sentence to read it as a question. Point to the words as you read.
- Read the sentence together. Talk about capital letters and the question mark.
- Let children read and point on their own and for the class.

Materials

- *PCCs:* see Review
- *Rime Card:* **at**, **ap**, *TG CD 2*
- *Unit 1 Word Cards:* **cap, nap, map, tap, sat, fat, mat, rat, cat, bat**, *TG CD 2*
- *Tricky Word Cards:* **is, Is, the, The,** • *TG CD 2*
- *Rhyming Pictures:* **cat, bat, hat, rat, nap, cap, map, tap,** *TG CD 2*

Preparation

- Write chant on chart paper

Small group/independent

- *Rhyming Pictures:* **cat, bat, rat, hat,** *TG CD 2*

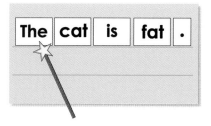

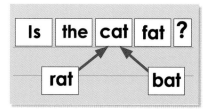

Identify words in random order
● Point to words in random order and call on students to identify the words. (Guide them in rereading up to the word if needed.)

Substitute <u>rat</u> and <u>bat</u> in the question
● Substitute **bat** and **rat** in the sentence and follow the steps above with each new sentence.

Rhyming Picture sort

Rhyming Pictures: **cat, bat, hat, rat, nap, cap, map, tap**

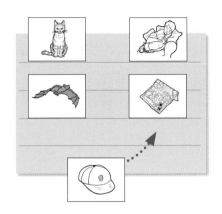

Name the pictures
● Display one picture for each rhyming word family.
● Point and name the pictures. Repeat with the children.

Model the matching of rhyming pictures
● Now, here's another picture. It is a **map**. Let's see if **map** rhymes with one of these words. Hold the new picture under each card in the top row and name the two pictures. **Cat, map**, no, these don't rhyme. **Nap, map**, yes, I hear a rhyme. Say these with me… "**nap, map**."
● Now, we are going to find some more rhymes, but don't say the answer unless I ask you. Show the next picture and name it.

Children match rhyming pictures
● Hold the picture under each top-row picture. Everyone names the two pictures together.
● Who can come up and put **bat** under the picture it rhymes with?

Check the rhyme with the class
● Now, let's see if we agree with that? Let's say these. Point to the pictures in the column as children name them.
● If you hear a rhyme, raise your hand.
● Good, yes, **bat** and **cat** rhyme. Let's try another picture.
● Continue with the same steps with each picture.

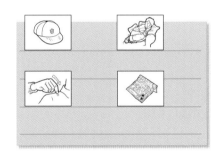

Read the column and question to elicit the word 'rhyme'
● Each time a card is placed and checked, everyone rereads all the rhyming words in that column.
● Ask questions to get the children used to using the word **rhyme**: Why do these words go together? "**They rhyme**." Nap and cap are words that… "**rhyme**."

Live Spelling

Rhyming Pictures: **cap, nap, map, tap** (on the pocket chart)

PCCS: **c, m, n, p, t**

Rime Card: **ap**

Word Cards: **nap, map, cap, tap**

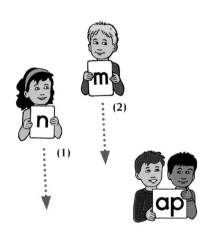

Name the pictures and begin Live Spelling
● Name the rhyming pictures as you point.
● Distribute *PCCs* and **ap** *Rime Card* (held by two children).
● Rubber band-stretch to segment the first word.
● Children Live Spell the word for the first picture.

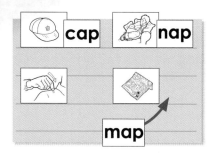

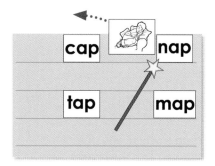

Check the Live Spelling and show the Word Card

- Review arm-blending for onset/rime and check the word. (Touch shoulder for the onset, slide hand down forearm for the rime.)

- Show children the *Word Card* and place it next to the picture.

- Reread all the words

- Live Spell the remaining words by changing the beginning sound and keeping the *Rime Card*.

Practice reading words with and without pictures

- After all the *Word Cards* are placed, point in random order for reading by the class and then by individuals.

- Remove pictures and practice reading the words some more.

a p

Word Card

I'm happy saying 'a' in **cap**

I'm happy saying 'a' in **map**

I'm happy saying 'a' in **tap**

And then I like to take a **nap.**

And then | I like to | take a **nap.**

Small group/independent activities

- **Picture-coding** Provide copies of the large, plain **ap** and display **a** and **p** PCCs. Children picture-code and illustrate with pictures of rhyming words.

- **Rhyming Sort** Sort *Rhyming Pictures* into rhyming columns, then match *Word Cards*. The group always rereads the column each time a child places a picture. Practice reading with and/or without pictures.

  For more challenge: Sort only words and practice reading in order and out of order.

- **Concentration Game** Play the game with words and pictures as described in Lesson 108 on page 67.

  For more challenge play with just **ap** and **at** *Word Cards*. Any two words that rhyme are a match.

- **Pocket chart/table spelling** See details of this group spelling activity (Vol 1, page 239).

  PCCs: l, m, n, p, ch, th plus **Rime Cards: ap, at**

  Words to spell: nap, lap, chap, chat, that, mat, pat

- **Review Rhyming chants** For children who need more practice with the chants, write each line on a sentence strip. Let each child read their sentence of the chant in turn. Then exchange sentences and read again.

- **Independent or pairs activity** Cut up sentence strips and let children reconstruct the chant using the chart tablet as a model.

Working with –ap and –at

Review

● PCCs **ă, d, c, f, n, r, s, s=z, ŭ, y, th, <u>th</u>** Rime Cards: **at, ap** Use 'Quick Dash'.

Word-picture matching

Materials
- *PCCs*: see Review
- *Rime Cards*: **at, ap**, *TG CD 2*
- Unit 1 *Word Cards*: **cat, hat, bat, rat, nap, cap, map, tap**, *TG CD 2*
- *Tricky Word Cards:* **The, is, on, the**, *TG CD 2*
- *Rhyming Pictures* **cat, hat, bat, rat, nap, cap, map, tap**, *TG CD 2*

✔ **Preparation**
- Print copies of 'Lesson 111 Sentence Practice,' *TG CD 2*

✔ **Small group/independent**
- *Letterland Word Builders*, or individual letter sets

Word Cards: **cat, hat, bat, rat, nap, cap, map, tap**

Rhyming Pictures: for the same words

Name pictures, match words/pictures, reread column

● Have the children name *Rhyming Pictures* as you point. Hand out *Word Cards*, one per child.

● Point to a picture and ask the children to look to see if their word matches. The child with **hat** comes and places the *Word Card* to the right of the picture. Each time a word is placed, have the class read the word and any others in the same column.

Read words without pictures in columns, then randomly

● After all words are placed, remove the pictures leaving two columns of rhyming words on the pocket chart.

● Point and read columns of words together.

● Point randomly to words in either column for the class to read.

● Call on a volunteer and point to several words for another child to read. Repeat with a number of children.

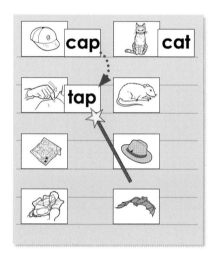

Sentence Building

Word Cards: **cat, hat, rat, map, cap**

Tricky Word Cards: **The, is, on, the, ·**

Picture Cards: **cat, hat, rat, map, cap**

Read the sentence, place pictures, reread

● Point to each word as you read the sentence.

● Arrange picture cards so that they illustrate the sentence (i.e., The **cat** picture is placed just above the **map** picture showing **The cat is on the map**. Ask the children to think of a real cat walking around on a map.

● Everyone read the sentence while you point. Repeat a little faster each time.

Read the words in random order

● Point to the words in a random order. Have children read them as a group.

● Do the same with a few individual children.

Change the sentence. Child changes pictures

● Change one or two of the nouns in the sentence and ask a volunteer to read it, followed by everyone reading it.

● Another volunteer changes the pictures to match the sentence.

Reread to check. 'Thumbs Up' if sentence and picture match
- Point to each word as everyone rereads the sentence. Children give thumbs up sign if the sentence and pictures match.

More sentence/picture changes
- Make several sentences, following the same steps.

Mix up words and use as flash cards
- Pick up *Word Cards* and mix them up. Show words one a time in random order. Have individuals/group read the words.

Sentence Practice (worksheet)

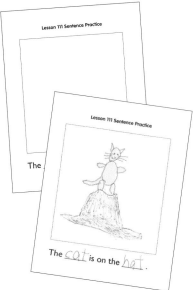

Materials: Copy of 'Lesson 111 Sentence Practice' for each child

Word Cards: cat, rat, hat, bat, map, cap

Model reading the sentence and filling in the blanks
- Project 'Lesson 111 Sentence Practice' or write the sentence with blanks on the board. Read to students saying "blank" for blank spaces. All reread together.
- Tell children that they will choose words for the blanks from the words on the pocket chart. Ask for a suggestion for the first blank, and then the second blank. Fill in words and read with class.
- Change the words and reread with class. Move your model out of sight.

Children fill in the blanks and illustrate the sentence
- Pass out a copy of 'Lesson 111 Sentence Practice' to all the children.
- Children write in words and illustrate the sentence they have created.

Children read to you and then partners
- Circulate and listen as individuals finger-point and read their sentences. Point to words at random for students to identify.
- Children share their sentences in pairs, then move to a new partner and share again.

Small group/independent activities

- **Rhyming Picture Sort** For children needing more practice hearing rhymes, sort rhyming pictures, carefully segmenting the onset and rhymes orally, **c-ap**, as children sort. Always repeat the column each time a further card is placed.
- **Reading with Individual letter sets** (Vol 1, p 241) Have children read the words they make with onset and rime arm-blending.

  Letters needed: a, b, c, f, h, m, r, p, t, t

  Words to build and read: fat, that, bat, mat, map, cap, rap
- **Sentence Building with Pictures** On a table or pocket chart, display sentence words and pictures used with whole class lesson. Arrange pictures to show, for example, 'The hat is on the bat.' Have children take turns placing each word in the sentence, rereading the sentence before the next word is placed.

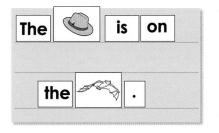

- **Word/Picture Matching, Sorting, Concentration Game** Match pictures and words, then turn over, mix up and play *Concentration Game* (see page 67).

  For more challenge Sort words only (no pictures) into rhyming columns, then play *Concentration Game*, matching rhyming words.

New Word Family: –an

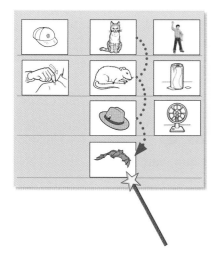

Materials
- *PCCs*: see Review
- *Rime Cards*: **at, ap, an**, *TG CD 2*
- Unit 1 *Word Cards*: **man, pan, fan, can**, *TG CD 2*
- *Rhyming Pictures*: all 12 for **-at, -ap, -an**, *TG CD 2*

Preparation
- Write chant on chart paper
- Copy 'Lesson 112 Onset-Rime Spelling, *TG CD 2*

Small group/independent
- Copy **an** picture-coding page, *TG CD 2*

Review

- **Word Stretching Warm Up** You can do these things in one place, but you cannot in another. Say the first word, children repeat. One child says each sound, all repeat. (Mystery answer: **You can on the playground, but not inside the school.**)

    Words: **jump (j-u-m-p), run (r-u-n), skip (s-k-i-p), race (r-a-ce), yell (y-e-ll)**

- **PCCs ă, c, f, h, m, n, p, r, s, t, v Rime Cards: at, ap, an**. Play 'Guess Who' with *PCCs* and *Rime Cards*, or use 'Handwriting Review' with the whole class or small groups (page 242).

Rhyming chant for –an

- Practice saying the chant together several times.
- Ask children which words rhyme.
- Underline the rhyming **an** words.
- Ask the children which two Letterlanders make their sounds in all 4 of these rhyming words.
- You may like to quickly picture-code Annie Apple and Noisy Nick at the end of each rhyming word.
- Ask the children to think of more words that rhyme with **can** (**ran, tan, plan, van**).

> I am happy saying **a** in **can**.
> I am happy saying **a** in **fan**.
> I am happy saying **a** in **man**,
> and happy saying **a** in **pan** and **than**!

Rhyming Picture sort

Rhyming Pictures for: **-ap, –at, -an**

- Display the top row of pictures.
- Name the pictures and children repeat.
- Let individuals place additional pictures that rhyme under the first word in each column. **Remember to:**
  - Ask class to raise their hands if words rhyme.
  - Have the group name all the pictures in a column after each picture is placed.
  - Ask occasionally, Why do these go together? Answer: **"They rhyme."** This gets children used to using the term.

Live Spelling

Rhyming Pictures: **man, pan, fan, can** Word Cards: **man, pan, fan, can**

PCCs: **c, f, m, n, p** plus Rime Card: **an**

- Name the rhyming pictures as you point. Children repeat.
- Distribute *PCCs* and **an** *Rime Card* (held by two children).
- Rubber-band stretch to segment the first word.
- Children Live Spell the word for the first picture.

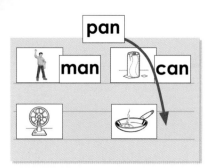

Check the Live Spelling and show the Word Card

- Review arm-blending for onset/rime and check the word. (Tap shoulder for the onset, slide hand down forearm for the rime.)
- Show children the *Word Card* for the word and place it next to the picture.
- Each time a word is placed, everyone rereads all the words.

Onset-Rime Spelling (worksheet)

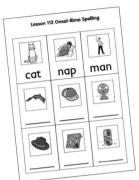

- Project the page or hold up a copy of 'Lesson 112 Onset-Rime Spelling'. Ask the children to write in the rhyming words in each column on their paper.
- Children will then write the rhyming word for each picture. On the bottom line they think of another rhyming word to write that is not pictured on the page.

Vocabulary Cards and rhyming

Vocabulary Cards: van, lamp

- Show students the fronts and backs of the *Vocabulary Cards*.
- Explain how they can read lots of words by using the first sound and making a rhyme.
- Everyone reads the big word in the middle and the rhyming words in the corners.
- Leave cards out for children to read with a partner.

Small group/independent activities

- **Picture-coding** Provide copies of the large, plain **an** and display **ă**, and **n** *PCC*s. Children picture code and illustrate with pictures of rhyming words.
- **Rhyming Sort** Sort picture cards for **at, ap**, and **an** families into rhyming columns, then match *Word Cards*. Practice reading with, and then without the pictures.

    For more challenge Sort only words and practice reading in order and out of order.

- **Pocket chart/table reading** Make words using the **at, an**, and **ap** *Rime Cards*. Have the children use Onset and Rime type arm-blending.

    PCCs: h, m, r, s, t, v plus **Rime Card: at, an, ap**

    Word Cards: sat, hat, mat, map, rap, tap, tan, van, ran

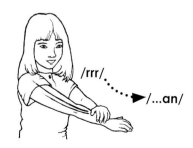

/rrr/........▶/...an/

Working with –an and –ap

Materials

- *PCCs*: see Review
- *Rime Cards*: **at, ap, an**, *TG CD 2*
- Unit 1 *Word Cards*: **cat, rat, bat, hat, man, can, pan, fan, nap, cap, map, tap**, *TG CD 2*
- *Tricky Word Cards*: **Is, on, the** (2), **The, Yes, No,** ⌷ **?** *TG CD 2*
- *Rhyming Pictures*: **man, can, pan, fan, nap, cap, map, tap, cat, rat, bat, hat**, *TG CD 2*

Small group/independent

- *Letterland Word Builders,* or individual letter sets

Review

- **Word Stretching Warm Up** All of these live in the same kind of place. Say the first word, children repeat. One child segments saying each sound, all repeat. (Mystery answer: **The ocean or sea**.)(You might ask children to name other sea creatures.)
- **Words: eel (ee-l), whale (wh-a-le), crab (c-r-a-b), seal (s-ea-l), fish (f-i-sh)**
- **PCCs ă, c, f, h, i, l, m, n, p, t, sh, th** **Rime Cards: at, ap, an**. Use the 'Quick Dash'.

Word/picture matching

Word Cards: man, can, pan, fan, nap, cap, map, tap

Rhyming Pictures: Same as word cards

Name the pictures, match the words/pictures, reread column

- Have the children name *Rhyming Pictures* as you point. Hand out *Word Cards*, one per child.
- Point to a picture and ask the children to look to see if their word matches. The child with **man** comes and places the *Word Card* to the right of the picture.
- Each time a word is placed, have the class read the word and any others in the same column.

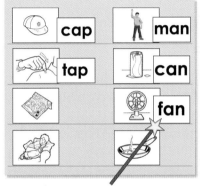

Read words without pictures in columns, then randomly

- After all words are placed, remove the pictures leaving two columns of rhyming words on the pocket chart.
- Point and read columns of words together.
- Then point randomly to words in either column for the class to read.
- Call on a volunteer to point to several words for another child to read. Repeat with a number of children.

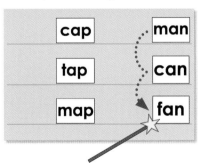

Reading with individual letter sets

Words: hat, that, fat, fan, man, can, cap, nap, lap

Letters: a, c, f, h, l, m, n, p, t, t

Use this activity with your whole class, or save it for small group time.

- Give the sounds or name the letters in the word. (Don't give away the word.) Children repeat and then build the word with letters or tiles.
- Have children point to the first letter (or digraph) and say the sound.
- Then children slide their fingers under the rime (**at, an,** or **ap**), saying the sound of the two letters together.
- Next they slide their finger under the whole word to blend it.
- Use the word in a brief phrase or sentence.

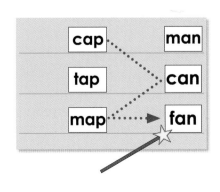

- If the next word varies by just one letter, tell children to take that letter away, e.g. for **tap-nap**, take out **/t/** and put **/n/** in the same spot (or use letter names).

Sentence Building

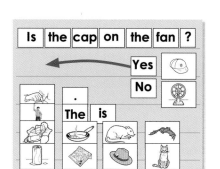

Rhyming Picture Cards: cat, rat, hat, map, cap, fan

Word Cards: cat, rat, hat, map, cap, fan

Tricky Word Cards: Is, on the, the (2 cards of **the**), **Yes, No**

- Display *Word Cards* on the pocket chart as shown, leaving space to drop in the nouns. Place the picture of a **cap** in the pocket chart just above the picture of a **fan**.
- Point to the pictures of the **cap** and the **fan**. Tell the class to pretend someone has left a **cap** on the **fan**.
- Name the pictures: **cap, fan**.
- Point to the words and read the sentence: Is the **cap** on the **fan**?
- Read the sentence together.
- Point to and read the words **yes** and **no**.
- Let's read our question again and then pick the answer, yes or no. Reread the sentence with the class. Select **yes** and move it into place just below the sentence. Then reread question and answer together.
- Leave the pictures in place and change the words in the sentence to read, '**Is the rat on the fan?**' Read the sentence with the class and have them choose the answer **No**.
- Let students experiment, taking turns changing words and pictures. Have them take turns pointing to the words and leading the class in reading and answering the question.
- Take all the *Word Cards* from the pocket chart and use them as flash cards, having the students read the words, fast, then faster, then fastest!

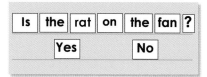

Small group/independent activities

- **Pocket Chart/table spelling** Call out words for the children to build, using the **at**, **ap**, and **an** *Rime Cards*. Have the children use word-stretching to segment the words.

    PCCs: c, l, m, th **Rime Cards: an, ap, at**

    Word Cards: that, cat, can, than, man, map, lap

- **Sort/Concentration Game** Sort words or pictures into rhyming columns. Then mix words or pictures up to play the *Concentration Game* (see Lesson 108, page 67), matching rhyming pairs.

    Rhyming Picture Cards: cat, bat, hat, rat, cap, nap, tap, map, fan, man, can, pan

    OR, **Word Cards: rat, hat, bat, fat, van, man, fan, pan, tap, nap**

- **Sentence Building** Spread the words out within reach of the children or place them on a mat. Call out a sentence, all repeat it, and then let children take turns placing the words in sequence. Each time a card is played, everyone rereads the sentence as one child points. Make two or three sentences if time allows.

    Word Cards: bat, hat, pan, fan, map, cap,

    Tricky Word Cards: The, the, is, Is, on

More on Word Families with ă

Materials

- *PCCs*: see Review
- *Rime Cards*: **at, an ap**, *TG CD 2*
- Unit 1 *Word Cards*: **cat, bat, hat, sat, rat, that, man, can, ran, fan, van, nap, lap, map, tap**, *TG CD 2*
- *Tricky Word Cards*: **The, is, on, the,** ● *TG CD 2*
- *Rhyming Pictures*: **cat, bat, hat, rat, nap, cap, map, tap**, *TG CD 2*

Preparation

- Copy 'Lesson 114 Sentence Practice' worksheet, *TG CD 2*

Small group/independent

- *Letterland Word Buliders*, or individual letter sets
- Rhyming chants. Option: write each line on a sentence strip

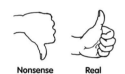

Nonsense   Real

Review

- **PCCs: c, f, g, l, m, n, r, s, v, z, sh, th** Rime Cards: **at, an, ap**. Play 'Guess Who?' with *PCCs* and *Rime Cards* or use 'Handwriting Review' with whole class or small groups (page 242).

Pocket chart: Real and Nonsense words

PCCs: c, f, g, l, m, n, r, s, v, z, sh, <u>th</u>

Rime Cards: at, an, ap

Words To Read: sat, that, gat*, van, zan*, than, shan*, cap, lap, thap* (starred words are nonsense words)

Everyone arm-blend the words. Give thumbs up or down

- Make the first word **sat** and remind class how to arm-blend with rimes.
- Children give thumbs up for real words; thumbs down for nonsense words. For words like '**that**' and '**than**' say a simple sentence using the word to clarify.

One child arm-blends, others follow

- For some words, choose one child to arm-blend the word and then have the whole group repeat the arm-blending. (This allows you to observe each child's skill at this task.) Be sure to include those whose mastery is in doubt. Provide a model by arm-blending with the child if the child is having difficulty.

Sorting words

Word Cards: bat, hat, sat, rat, that, man, can, ran, fan, van, nap, lap, map, tap

Read the top row of cards

- Place the *Word Cards* for **bat, man**, and **nap** across the top of the pocket chart.
- Ask children to read the words to themselves first, so they will be ready to read them together.
- Point to each word and read with the children.

Model matching rhyming words

- Hold up a word such as **cap**. Say, I am going to put this word under the word it rhymes with.
- Hold the card for **cap** under the *Word Card* **bat**. Say the two words **bat, cap**. Then say, Those don't rhyme. Let me try here: **man, cap**. No, those don't rhyme. Let's see, **nap, cap**. Yes, those rhyme. Let's all read them: **nap, cap**.
- Repeat with one or two more words to demonstrate the sorting.

Individual children sort words. All read the column

- Call on children to do the same with the rest of the words. Help with corrections.
- Point while everyone reads down the column each time a word is added.
- Continue until all words are placed.

Tractors, Trains, Planes, and Helicopters

● Tell the children you will all practice the words by playing *Tractors, Trains, Planes, and Helicopters.*

Tractors: Read slowly sounding out each word in the column

Trains: Read down the column at a slow but steady pace

Planes: Read a little faster down the column

Helicopters: After reading all the columns with the steps above, point to words in a random order hopping from one column to another like an agile helicopter.

● Let a few children read some words using their choice of Tractor, Train, Plane, or Helicopter.

Sentence Practice: Irregular word spelling

Word Card: cat, hat

Tricky Word Cards: The, is, on, the, | • |

Worksheet: Copy 'Lesson 114 Sentence Practice' worksheet for each child.

Read the sentence

● Make the sentence: **The hat is on the cat.**

● Point to the words and read the sentence with the class.

Air-trace <u>the</u> aloud, in a whisper, with silent mouth movements

● Point to the word **the** and ask, What is this word?

● Let's spell **the**. Point to each letter on the card as you say the letter names with the class, **"t-h-e"**

● Ask, What does that spell? **"the"**

● Write a huge **the** on the chalkboard with a line underneath.

● Lead the class in air-tracing as they spell the word aloud, then air-trace the underline and say the word **"the."**

● Repeat air-tracing with spelling-aloud two more times: the first time in a whisper, the second time with no sound, but moving mouths silently.

Erase and trace with 'magic chalk'

● Erase the board. Now let's imagine you have magic chalk in your fingers that can reach up to the board. Let's trace **the** again three times, naming the letters: 1) aloud, 2) whispering, and 3) silently mouthing the letter names.

Compare <u>The</u> and <u>the</u>

● Ask children to find the word a second time in the sentence. Talk about why one **the** has a capital **T** and the second a lowercase **t**.

Sentence Practice (worksheet)

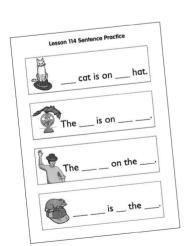

● Pass out copies of the worksheet, 'Lesson 114 Sentence Practice'.

● Project the worksheet or write the first sentence on the board with blanks.

● Work with the class on reading and completing the first two sentences.

Observe and assist on last two sentences

● Have them try the last two sentences on their own. Circulate to help those that need it.

All write their own sentences and illustrate them
- Challenge students to make a picture on the back of the paper and write a sentence to go with it. They may follow the model of the worksheet sentence using any nouns they like or simply create an original sentence and illustration.

Small group/independent activities

- **Spelling with Individual letter sets** After you say each word, have children repeat and then segment each word into onset and rhyme (**th-at, n-ap, v-an**).

  Letters: a, c, h, n, p, r, t, t

  Words: that, rat, rap, chap, tap, tan, ran, than

- **Reading Sentence Practice 3** Reread completed worksheets with choral reading. Let pairs read to each other. Children read their original sentences to the group.

- **Sort Words/Concentration Game** Sort rhyming words in columns on the table or a mat. All read the column each time a word is placed. Practice reading the words with *Tractors, Trains, Planes, and Helicopters* as on page 80. Shuffle cards and play the *Concentration Game*, matching any words that rhyme.

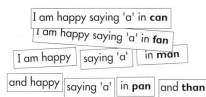

I am happy saying 'a' in **can**
I am happy saying 'a' in **fan**
I am happy | saying 'a' | in **man**
and happy | saying 'a' | in **pan** | and **than**

- **Review Rhyming chants** For children who need more practice with the **-an** chant or earlier ones, write each line on a sentence strip. Let each child read their sentence of the chant in turn. Then exchange sentences and read again.

- **Independent or pairs activity** Cut up sentence strips and let children reconstruct the chant using the chart tablet as a model.

Unit 1: Lesson 115

Putting it all together

✓ **Materials**
- *PCCs*: see Review
- *Rime Cards*: **at, an ap**, *TG CD 2*
- Unit 1 *Word Cards*: **cat, hat**, *TG CD 2*
- *Tricky Word Cards*: **is, on, The, the,** ⋅ *TG CD 2*
- *Rhyming Pictures*: **cat, bat, hat, rat, nap, cap, map, tap**, *TG CD 2*

✓ **Preparation**
- Copy 'Lesson 115 Sentence Practice' and prepare for projection or copy to board, *TG CD 2*
- Copy and assemble Decodable booklet 'Is the Hat on the Cat?' *TG CD 2*

✓ **Small group/independent**
- Copy 'Lesson 115 Sentence Practice' (*TG CD 2*). Pepare for projection, or copy the boxes to your board

Review

- **Word Stretching Warm Up** What can we do with all of these things? Say the first word, children repeat. One child segments, saying each sound, all repeat. (Mystery answer: **Travel, go places**.)

- **Words: bike (b-i-ke); car (c-ar); boat (b-oa-t); plane (p-l-a-ne); bus (b-u-s)**

- **PCCs: c, f, n, p, v, t, th** Rime Cards: **at, ap, an**. Use the 'Quick Dash'.

Live Reading: Consonants-go-marching

Rime Cards: at, an, ap

PCCs: c, f, n, p, v, t, th

Distribute cards
- Pass out the *PCCs* and *Rime Cards* (each one held by two children).
- Have the two children holding the **at** card stand facing the class.
- Line up students with the consonant *PCCs* on one side of the room where they can still see the words being made.

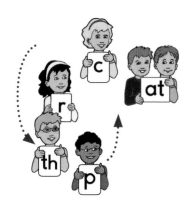

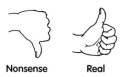

Nonsense   Real

Try each consonant with the rime
- Have the child with **c** come and stand beside **at** and say Clever Cat's sound. The children with **at** then say 'at' together.
- Have the class arm-blend and then say the word: "c–at, cat."

List real and nonsense words
- Write the titles **Real** and **Nonsense** on the board. The children decide where the word **cat** goes, using a thumb signal to tell you, Real or Nonsense.
- If it's a real word but unfamiliar to most children, briefly give the meaning and write it under **New Words**.
- Each child with a consonant comes in turn to stand beside **at**, etc.
- Go through all the consonants with the other *Rime Cards*: **ap, an**.

Practice reading the lists
- Practice reading the lists of Real and Nonsense words a bit faster each time.

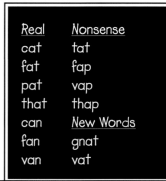

Real	Nonsense
cat	tat
fat	fap
pat	vap
that	thap
can	New Words
fan	gnat
van	vat

Sentence Building

Rhyming Pictures: **cat, hat**

Word Card: **cat, hat**   Tricky Word Cards: **The, the, is, on**

Children build the sentence
- Place the picture of the **hat** just above the picture of the **cat** to illustrate the sentence to be built.
- Place the *Word Cards* in a mixed-up order below the pictures.
- Say, Let's make a sentence about these pictures. I want you to help make the sentence: The hat is on the cat. Let's all say the sentence. **"The hat is on the cat."**
- One child chooses the first word and puts it in place. Discuss the reason for a capital letter.
- After children place each word, point to and reread the sentence with the class.
- Discuss the reason for the period at the end.

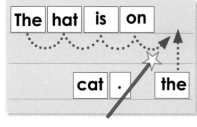

Turn cards over to make an invisible sentence
- Read the sentence together one more time. Then turn each *Word Card* over to its plain white side.
- Tell the students, You can read the invisible words! Say the sentence as you point to each plain card.
- Let the class read the invisible words as you point.
- Tell them you want them to make the invisible sentence reappear on their own papers.

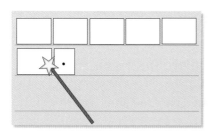

Sentence Practice (worksheet)

'Read the boxes'
- Project the worksheet 'Lesson 115 Sentence Practice' or make the boxes on the board.
- Point to the word boxes and say the sentence, The hat is on the cat.
- Give out worksheets.

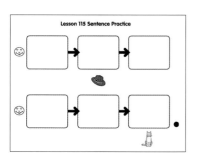

Lesson 115 Sentence Practice

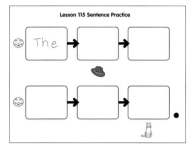

- Students point to the boxes on their worksheets and say the sentence.

Guide the writing of the first word

- What word goes in this first box? "**The**".
- Let's see if we remember how to spell **the**. Let's do our air-writing. "**t-h-e, the.**"
- What kind of letter do we start our sentence with, a capital or lowercase letter?
- Have children spell **the** aloud as you write **The** in your first box.

Children continue on their own. Give help as needed

- Children write **The** in the first box and work on the rest of the sentence.
- Circulate and help as needed.
- Suggest that students who finish early draw a picture of a cat with a hat on, or create their own sentence and illustration on the back.

Decodable Booklet: 'Is the Hat on the Cat?'

Show the title on the board, talk about capital letters

- Show a copy of the booklet: 'Is the Hat on the Cat' to the class. Tell them that this book uses some of the words they have been learning recently.
- Write the title on board, **Is the Hat on the Cat?** Guide reading the title.
- Talk about which Letterlanders are doing their *Capital Letter Tricks* in all the important words. (Unless it is at the beginning of a title, the word '**the**' is less important.)
- Hand out booklets.

Children attempt to read the booklet alone or in pairs

- Let children try reading them to themselves or with a partner. Help as needed.

Read as whole group, then two groups read alternate pages

- Everyone reads the booklet together.
- Divide the class into two groups. Groups alternate reading pages, but all read the final page together.
- Read again, beginning with the second group this time.
- Take up booklets to reread another day or send home for home reading.

Small group/independent activities

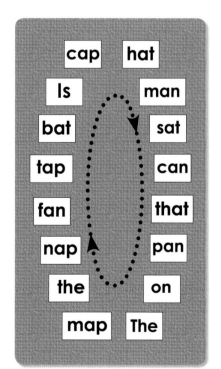

- **Reread Booklet** Divide group in halves. Halves alternate reading pages in 'Is the Hat on the Cat?' booklet. Then do partner reading.
- **Sentence Dictation** Call out this sentence and have children repeat it: The cat is on my lap. Children write the sentence with help. Show them the spelling of **my**, if needed.
- **Word Race** Lay a few *Tricky Word Cards* along with word family words out in a square or oval pattern on a mat. The group reads the words in sequence as you point. Tell children this is a race track and challenge them to read a bit faster on the second and third turn. If time allows, let individual children have a run around the track of words.

Unit 2 Word Families with ĭ

Rhyming with –ig, –in, –ip

Materials

✔
- *PCCs*: see Review
- *Rime Cards*: **in, ig, ip**, *TG CD 2*
- *Rhyming Pictures*: **pig, wig, dig, in, pin, win, fin, lip, sip ship, chip**, *TG CD 2*
- Unit 2 *Word Cards*: (same as pictures listed above), *TG CD 2*
- *Vocabulary Cards*: **pig, in, six**

✔ **Small group/independent**
- Large **ig** for picture-coding, *TG CD 2*

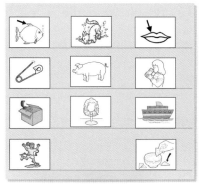

Review

- **Word Stretching Warm Up** What do we do with all of these things? Say the first word, children repeat. One child segments saying each sound, all repeat. (Mystery answer: **Eat a meal**.)

  Words: cup (c-u-p), plate (p-l-a-te), knife (kn-i-fe), spoon (s-p-oo-n), fork (f-or-k)

  PCCs: b, d, f, g, ĭ, l, n, p, s, w, ch, sh Use the 'Quick Dash'.

Rhyming Picture sort

Rhyming Pictures: ig, in, ip words

Sort Rhyming Pictures in columns

- Place one picture for each rhyming word family in a horizontal row on the pocket chart with room below for additional cards.
- Let individuals place additional pictures that rhyme with the first word in each column. **Remember to:**
  - Ask the class to raise hands if they agree that the word rhymes.
  - Have the whole group name all the pictures in a column after each picture is placed.
  - Ask occasionally, Why do these go together? Answer: **"They rhyme."** So children get used to using the term.

Live spelling

Rhyming Pictures: wig, dig, pig, in, pin, win, fin, lip, sip, ship, chip (in rhyming columns on the pocket)

PCCs: d, g, ĭ, l, n, p, w, sh, ch

Rime Cards: ig, in, ip (ready to use)

Word Cards: the same as the pictures above (ready to use)

Name the Rhyming Pictures
- Name the first set of *Rhyming Pictures* as you point.

Live spell the word. Add the Rime Card
- Live spell the word for the first rhyming picture. (For details, see Live Spelling, Vol 1, page 238.)
- Once the first word has been spelled, replace the two final *PCCs* with the special *Rime Card*. Two children hold the *Rime Card* together.

Arm-blend. Then put the Word Card with the picture
- Review arm-blending. (Tap shoulder for onset, slide hand down forearm for the rime.)

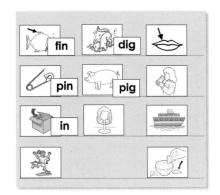

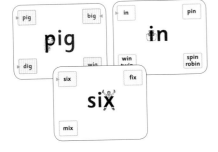

- Place the *Word Card* for the first word beside the picture, **"dig"**.
- Read the *Word Card*, **"dig"**.

Live Spell with PCCs and Rime Card. Add the Word Card and read the column

- Live Spell the remaining words by changing the beginning sound and keeping the *Rime Card*.
- After live-spelling each word, place the *Word Card* beside its picture.
- Everyone reads all the words in the column each time.

Live Spell -in, -ip words and practice reading the words

- Follow the same steps with **in** and **ip** words.
- After all *Word Cards* are placed, point to the cards in random order for individual children to read.

Vocabulary Cards and rhyming

Vocabulary Cards: pig, in, six

- Show students the backs of the three *Vocabulary Cards*.
- Explain and demonstrate how they can read lots of word by using the first sound and making a rhyme.
- Read the corner words together as you point.
- Leave several cards out for children to try reading with a partner when time is available.

Small group/independent activities

- **Independent Picture-coding** Provide copies of the large, plain **ig** and display *PCC*s as a model. Children picture-code and add rhyming words and pictures around the Letterlanders.
- **Vocabulary Cards** One child holds the card and points to the words on the back while the other child reads. Then they switch.
- **Pocket chart/table reading** Make words using the **ig**, **ip**, and **in** *Rime Cards*. Have the children arm-blend the onset and rime.

   PCCs: b, s, w, ch, sh plus

   Rime Cards: ig, ip, in

   Words: wig, big, sip, ship, in, win, chin

- **Sort Rhyming Pictures** Display pictures for **pig, sip,** and **pin** in a horizontal row. Children take turns placing pictures of rhyming words under each of the first row pictures. Each time a card is placed, point to all the cards in the column for everyone to name.
- **Match words to pictures** Leave the *Rhyming Pictures* in columns and have children match *Word Cards* to them.

More about –ig, –in, –ip

Materials
- *PCCs* and *Rime Cards*: see Review
- *Unit 2 Word Cards*: **dig, pig, wig, pin, win, lip, ship, chip,** *TG CD 2*
- *Tricky Word Cards*: **in, I, see, a,** ● *TG CD 2*
- *Rhyming Pictures*: **dig, pig, wig, in, pin, win, lip, ship, chip,** *TG CD 2*

Preparation
- Write chant on chart paper.

Small group/independent
- *Unit 1 Word Cards*: **man, cap, rat,** *TG CD 2*
- A large **in** for picture-coding, *TG CD 2*

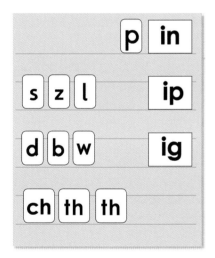

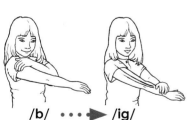

/b/ •••➤ /ig/

Review

- **PCCs b, d, ĭ, p, w, z, ch, sh, th Rime Cards: in, ig, ip**. Play 'Guess Who' with all *PCCs* listed. Use 'Handwriting Review' with whole class or small groups (page 242).

Rhyming Chant for –in

- Practice saying the chant together several times.
- Ask children which words rhyme.
- Underline the rhyming **in** words.
- Ask the children which two Letterlanders make their sounds in all 4 of these rhyming words.
- If practical, quickly picture-code Impy Ink and Noisy Nick at the end of each rhyming word.
- Ask the children to think of more words that rhyme with **pin** (**win, kin, grin, spin**).

Hello, I'm Impy Ink.
Listen to my ĭ sound in words like **pin**.
Listen to my ĭ sound in words like **fin**.
Listen to my ĭ sound in words like **chin**.
Look: each time I write a word I use my ink again!

Pocket chart: Word Building

Rime Cards: ig, ip, in

PCCs: b, d, l, p, z, ch, th

Words To Make: big, pig, chig*, lip, dip, thip*, chin, thin, zin*
(*Starred words are nonsense words)

- Quickly review the *Rime Cards* with the class: **ig, ip, in**.

Make the word. Everyone use arm-blending
- Make the first word, **big**.
- Rollercoaster the words (arm-blending).
- The children give a 'thumbs up' for a real word, 'thumbs down' for a nonsense word.

Children take turns to lead the blending
- Continue with the word list, asking individual children to "lead the class" in arm-blending. (The child blends the word first; then the class blends the same word.)

Review rhyming words quickly without blending first
- If time allows, go back and quickly make each **ig** word again to focus on fluency *without* arm-blending. Then you might try changing the beginning letters and reading the **ig** words a third time, a bit faster as a challenge.
- Follow the same steps with each set of rhyming words.

Word/picture matching

Word Cards: dig, pig, wig, in, pin, win, lip, ship, chip

Rhyming Pictures: same as words above

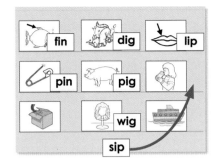

Preparation: Place each group of *Rhyming Pictures* in a column with space to the right of each picture for a *Word Card*.

Name pictures. Distribute Word Cards
- Point to the pictures and have the children name them.
- Hand out *Word Cards*. One at a time, have children place their words beside the matching picture.

Match the words to the pictures. Read the column
- Each time a card is placed, have students read all the words in the same column.

Remove pictures. Read the words
- After all words are placed, remove the picture and practice reading the words together, first by columns, then by pointing to words randomly.
- Let a few children have turns reading words.
- Leave the words and pictures out and suggest that children try matching them up at other times during the day.

Sentence Building

Word Cards: **pig, wig, ship, chip, pin** Tricky Word Cards: **I, see, a**

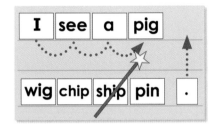

Read the sentence *to* and *with* the children
- Place the cards in the pocket chart to form the first sentence, as pictured. Point to each word as you read out the sentence. Remind the children of the importance of the period.
- Point to the words while you read the sentence together.

Talk about punctuation
- Ask someone to tell what the period on the end of the sentence is for (the stop sign).

Children take turns pointing and leading the reading
- Call on a student to point to words as the class reads. Let other students do the same. Some could read the sentence on their own first, and then point while class reads.

Identify words. Try other nouns on the end
- Point to words in random order. Call on students to identify them.
- Experiment with the new meanings by substituting other final words.

Small group/independent activities

- **Picture-coding** Provide copies of the large, plain **in** and display *PCCs* as a model. Children picture-code and add rhyming words and pictures around the Letterlanders.
- **Chant review** Let pairs of children reread the **in** chant and the **a** family chants from Unit 1.
- **Pocket chart/table spelling** Call out words for the children to build, using the **in**, **ig**, and **ip** *Rime Cards*. Have the children use word stretching to segment the words.

    PCCs: **f, r, n, w** plus **Rime Card: in, ig, ip**

    Words: **fin, win, wig, rig, rip, nip**

- **Word Card Reading** Display the words in rhyming columns. Practice reading the words first in columns as you point. Then point to words randomly for reading.
- **Sentence Building** Spread the *Word Cards* out within reach of all the children or place them on a mat to move around. Call out a sentence, all repeat it. Then let children take turns placing the words in sequence. Each time a card is played, everyone rereads the sentence as one child points. Make two or three sentences if time allows.

> Word Cards: **I, see, a, pig, wig, ship, chip, pin**
>
> From Unit 1: **man, cap, rat**

Unit 2: Lesson 118

Sentence Building

✔ Materials
- *PCCs* and *Rime Cards*: see Review
- Unit 2 *Word Cards*: **lip, ship** (2), **dip, chip, dig, wig, pig** (2), **big, pin, win, fin, chin**, *TG CD 2*
- *From Unit 1*: **cat, rat, bat, cap, fan**, *TG CD 2*
- *Tricky Word Cards*: **a, Can, can, I, No, see, Yes, you** ⬝ , ? *TG CD 2*
- *Rhyming Pictures*: **pig, ship, wig, cat, cap, rat, fan, bat, chip, pin**, *TG CD 2*

✔ Preparation
- Write chant on chart paper.

✔ Small group/independent
- Large **ip** for picture-coding, *TG CD 2*
- Letter sets for each child

Review

- **PCCs b, f, p, r, t, w, z, ch, th, sh**. Rime Cards: **at, an, ap, ip, ig, in**. Play 'Guess Who?' with all *PCCs* listed or use the 'Handwriting Review' with whole class or small groups (page 242).

Rhyming Chant for –ip

- Practice saying the chant together several times.
- Ask the class which words rhyme.
- Underline the rhyming **ip** words.
- Ask the children which two Letterlanders make their sounds in all 4 of these rhyming words.
- If practical, quickly picture-code Impy Ink and Peter Puppy at the end of each rhyming word.

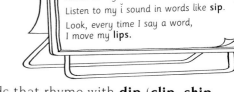

Hello, I'm Impy Ink.
Listen to my ĭ sound in words like **dip**.
Listen to my ĭ sound in words like **rip**.
Listen to my ĭ sound in words like **sip**.
Look, every time I say a word,
I move my **lips**.

- Ask the children to think of more words that rhyme with **dip** (**clip, ship, chip, hip**).

Live Reading: Consonants-go-marching

- **PCCs b, f, p, r, t, w, z, ch, th, sh** Rime Cards: **ig, ip, in**

Make words with Rime Cards by changing the onset
- Pass out the 10 *PCCs* and the 3 *Rime Cards* listed above. Each *Rime Card* should be held by two children.
- Have the two children holding **ig** stand in front of the class. Review the sounds made by these letters.

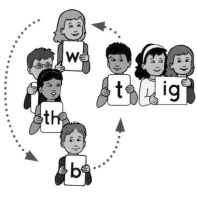

- Those children with the 10 consonant *PCCs* line up on one side of the room where they can see the words as they are made.
- Consonant children go up one at a time and stand by **ig**.

Real	Nonsense	New Words
big	tig	fig
pig	bip	shin
wig	rin	
rip	zin	
chip	thig	
fin		
pin		

All children blend the words and vote with their thumbs

- Children arm-blend, onset-rime style, and give the thumb sign to show their decision whether you should write the word on the board under **Real** or **Nonsense**. If it is a real word but unfamiliar to most children, briefly explain the words and write it under **New Words**.

- Do the same with the other *Rime Cards*: **ip, in**.

Reread word lists, Fast, Faster, Fastest

- Read the 2 lists of real and nonsense words on the board with the class using the *Fast, Faster, Fastest* routine (see Vol 1, page 201).

Sorting words: -ig, -in, and -ip

Word Cards: **lip, ship, dip, chip; dig, wig, pig, big; pin, win, fin, chin**

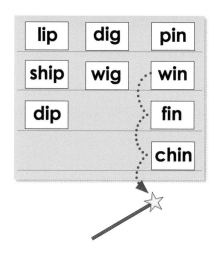

Children sort words under lip, dig and pin

- Place the 3 *Word Cards* for **lip**, **dig** and **pin** across the top of the pocket chart.
- Ask children to read the words to themselves so they can be ready to read them with the class.
- Point to each word and read with the class.
- Model sorting of one word under its rhyming top card (as on previous days).

All read the column of words after each card is sorted

- Always have the class read down the column after a word is placed.
- Call on a child to place the next word in a column. Help with corrections if needed.

Practice word with 'Tractors, Trains, Planes, and Helicopters'

- After all words are placed, practice pointing to and reading the words by playing *Tractors, Trains, Planes, and Helicopters* with the class (see page 80). Let some individuals read a column of words by themselves.

Sentence Building

Word Cards: **Can, can, pig, pig, wig, ship, ship, chip, pin.** From Unit 1: **cat, rat, cap, fan, bat** (also, cards for one period and one question mark).

Tricky Word Cards: **a, I, you, Yes, No, see**

Rhyming Pictures: **pig, ship, wig, cat, cap, rat, fan, bat, chip, pin**

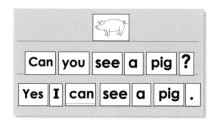

Read the sentences *to* and *with* the class

- Place the *Word Cards* and picture as shown to the left. Point to each word as you read the sentences. Read the sentences together.

Discuss terms: Question, answer, question mark

- Talk about the first sentence as a question (with a question mark) and the second sentence as an answer.

One child points while the class reads

- Let a student point while the class reads. Let a few other children take turns.

Change the pictures and words

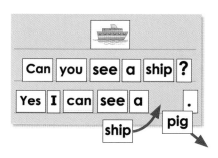

- Replace the **pig** picture with the **ship** picture. Change the word **pig** to **ship** in the first sentence.
- Reread sentences and ask the class what needs to be changed in the second sentence (**pig** to **ship**).

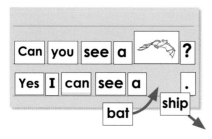

- Reread the changed sentences together.
- Remove the **ship** picture and replace the word **ship** with the **bat** picture as shown. (For most words, e.g. **bat**, you will only have one *Word Card*. In this case, use the picture in place of the word in one of the sentences.)
- Ask children to change the word in the answer to match.
- Let a child point as all read the changed sentences.

Children experiment. All read the results

- Let individual children experiment, changing the pictures and sentences.
- Let another child point to the words and lead the class in reading the sentence altered by a classmate.
- Show the children pictures and questions that lead to an answer with **No** at the beginning as shown.

Small group/independent activities

- **Picture-coding** Children picture-code **ip**, adding rhyming words and pictures around these two Letterlanders.
- **Chant Review** Let pairs of children choose chants to practice reading and to later present to the class.
- **Reading with letter sets**

    Letters to use: **a, c, f, g, h, i, l, n, p, w**

    Words to make and read: **lip, chip, chin, pin, pan, fan, wig**

- **Hide-a-Word** Place *Rhyming Picture Cards* for **pig, fin,** and **sip** in a horizontal row. Have children match *Word Cards* with the pictures they rhyme with. Each time a *Word Card* is played, hide it under the picture so that each player has to use the pictures to decide if the next word rhymes. After all the words are hidden, spread them out in rhyming columns, take away the pictures and practice reading the words.
- **Sentence Conversation** (Use the same *Word Cards* as used with the whole class lesson.) Display the question sentence on the left. Have children read the sentence. The children construct an answer each in turn adding a word, and all reading the partial sentence after each word is added. If time allows, let children construct a new question for you to respond to by making a further sentence to answer them.

Written Word Sort

Materials

- *PCCs* and *Rime Cards*: see Review
- Unit 1 and 2 *Word Cards*: **pig, pig** (2), **wig, ship, ship** (2), **chip, pin, cat, rat, cap, fan, bat**, *TG CD 2*
- *Tricky Word Cards*: **I, Can, can, you, Yes, No, see, a,** **.** **?** *TG CD 2*
- *Rhyming Pictures*: **pig, ship, wig, cat, cap, rat, fan, bat, chip, pin**, *TG CD 2*
- *Letterland Word Builders,* or individual etter sets

Preparation

- Copy 'Written Word Sort' worksheet.' Prepare for projection, or copy on the board, *TG CD 2*
- Copy 'Lesson 119 Sentence Practice,' *TG CD 2*

Small group/independent

- (same materials as above)

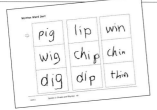

Review

- **PCCs c, d, g, h, ĭ, l, n, o, p, s, s, t, w**. **Rime Cards: at, an, ap, ip, ig, in**. Use the 'Quick Dash'.

Children make words with letter sets

- **Reading and Spelling** Use this activity with the whole class, or save it for small group instruction.

    Letters: c, d, g, h, i, l, n, p, s, s, t, w (for each child)

    Words for reading: lip, dip, dips, chip, chin, thin, win, wig

    Words for spelling: dig, digs, dip, sip, sips, ships

Written Word sort

- **Preparation** Make copies of 'Written Word Sort' for each child. Make a transparency of this sheet or draw similar boxes on your board. (You can place these sheets in clear plastic sheet protectors. Children can write on them with wipe-off markers. Then they can be reused many times.)

Children copy the top row from the board or projection

- Write in the words **pig, lip**,and **win** in the boxes going across.
- Read the words you have written with the class and have them write the same words on their *Written Word Sort* pages.
- Say the word **chin**. Have children repeat the word and point to their chins.

Try chin with each word in the top row to find a rhyme

- Tell them you are going to listen for words that rhyme with **chin** as you point to the words in your boxes.
- **Pig, chin**, no rhyme with these, **Lip, chin**, do they rhyme? **"No." Win, chin**, do they rhyme? **"Yes."** I am going to write **chin** right there under **win** because they rhyme. You write it on your paper, too.

Children write each word under the word that rhymes

- Call out other words and let children find the word that rhymes and write the word in the correct column. You may want them to point to the box on their *Written Word Sort* copy first, and wait until you have had a chance to see that everyone has the correct box, before they write the word.
- Write the word in your box after most of the children have written theirs. Ask them to check their word with yours and make corrections as needed.

All read the column after each word is written

- After each word you write, point to the words in that column and have children read them with you.
- When the page is complete, have each child match up with a partner to read the all the words on their page.

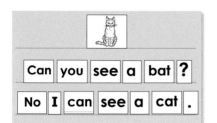

Can | you | see | a | bat | ?
No | I | can | see | a | cat | .

Sentence Building

Word Cards: **pig, pig, wig, ship, ship, chip, pin, cat, rat, cap, fan, bat,**

Tricky Word Cards: **I, Can, can, you, Yes, No, see, a,** •, ?

Rhyming Pictures: **pig, ship, wig, cat, cap, rat, fan, bat, chip, pin**

Children build questions and all read the answers

- Arrange words and pictures on the pocket chart to make the sentences used on the previous day, '**Can you see a ___? Yes,** (or **No**) **I can see a ___.**

- Let the children build various sentences just as you did the day before.

Sentence Practice (worksheet)

- **Preparation** Copy 'Lesson 119 Sentence Practice' worksheet for each child. Project transparency or write the first two sentences on the board with blanks as on the worksheet.

Model filling in the blanks in the first question and answer

- Read your copy of first two sentences with the children and ask them to decide which words go in the blanks.

- Have children write words on their worksheet in the first pair of sentences. Fill in the blanks on your copy for children to check their writing by. Reread the sentences with the class. They may make corrections as needed.

Children complete the page as you circulate to support

- Let children try the rest of the page on their own as you circulate and help those who need it.

Children pair up. One reads questions, the other answers

- After children finish reading, have them take partners. One can read the questions. The other one the answers. Then they switch roles.

- Children who finish early may draw and write on the back of the page.

Small group/independent activities

- **Sort Word Cards** Sort rhyming words in columns on the table or a mat. All read the column each time a word is placed.

- **Concentration Game** Mix up cards and turn them face down. Players try to find two words that rhyme, reading each word as they turn it over (see details of how to play the game on page 67).

- **Sentence Practice** Have half the children read the questions on their completed worksheet. The other half respond by reading the answers. Then switch. Pair children up to reread worksheet with a partner.

New Decodable Booklet

Review

- **Word Stretching Warm Up** What do all these things do? Say the first word, children repeat. One child segments saying each sound, all repeat. (Mystery answer: **make light, shine**.)

    Words: sun, (s-u-n), star (s-t-ar), fire (f-i-re), lamp (l-a-m-p), bulb (b-u-l-b)

- PCCs **ă, c, ĕ, ĭ, m, n, ŏ, s, s=z, ck, ng, th, <u>th</u>** Rime Cards: **at, an, ap, ig, in, ip**. Play 'Guess Who?' with all *PCCs* listed or use the 'Handwriting Review' with whole class or small groups (page 242).

Rhyming Chant for –ig

- Practice saying the chant together several times.
- Ask children which words rhyme.
- Underline the rhyming **ig** words.
- Ask the children which two Letterlanders make their sounds in all 4 of these rhyming words.
- If practical, quickly picture-code Impy Ink and Golden at the end of each rhyming word.

Hello, I'm Impy Ink.
Listen to my ĭ sound in words like **wig**.
Listen to my ĭ sound in words like **dig**.
Listen to my ĭ sound in words like **pig**.
And other things that are very **big**.

Practice Irregular words

Tricky Word Cards: see, you

- Children use wipe-off boards or paper.

Show the Word Card, say the word, then children say it
- Show the word **see** and tell children the word.
- Point to the word **see** and ask, What is this word?

Spell aloud and say the word
- Let's spell "**see**." Point to each letter as you say the letter names with the class, "**s-e-e**."
- Ask, What does that spell? Class answers, "**see**."

Write a huge word on board, children air-trace and spell
- Write a very large **see** on the board with an underline.
- Lead class in air-tracing, saying each letter name as you trace the letters.

Air-trace the underline and say the word; trace again
- Trace the underline and say the word '**see**.'
- Repeat air-tracing and saying the word two more times.

All write the word
- Erase the word and have the children write the word on their board or paper.
- Follow the same steps with **you**.

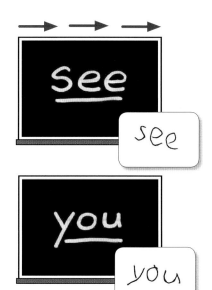

Decodable Booklet: 'Can you See?'

- **Preparation** Make two-sided copies of the Decodable Booklet 'Can You See?' for each child. Fold, cut, and staple as you have with other booklets.

Write the title on the board, discuss and review Capital Letter Tricks

- Write the booklet title 'Can You See?' on the board. Guide the children in reading the title. Talk about how each of the Letterlanders does their *Capital Letter Trick* to show that the word he or she is starting is an important word.

Children attempt to read on their own or with a partner

- Let children try reading to themselves or with a partner. Help as needed.

Lead choral rereading

- Next, everyone read it together. Let half the class read the questions and the other half read the answers. Switch sides and choral read it again.
- Take up the booklets to reread as a part of next day's lesson.

Small group/independent activities

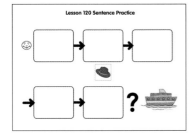

- **Sentence Practice** Have children repeat this sentence twice, "**Can you see a ship?**" Distribute 'Lesson 120 Sentence Practice' worksheet. Have children point to one box for each word as they repeat the sentence. Have children write the sentence, one word in each box. Provide enough support to ensure success.

- **Sight Word Review** Practice reading these *Tricky Word Cards*: **a, the, you, see** (words chosen from the booklet, *Can You See?*) and add them to your Word Wall. Hold up a card, say the word, wait 3 seconds, then have children repeat the word when you point to it. Do the same with each word. Mix the cards up and go through the set of words two more times, pointing to the word for children to name. Pass out the booklet and let children find and read these words.

- **Reread the Booklet** in one or more of these ways: choral read, partner read, half the group reads one page, and the other half the next page, etc.

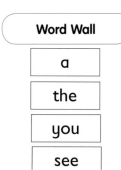

at ap an ig ip in

Review ă and ĭ Families

Materials

- *PCCs* and *Rime Cards*: see Review
- Units 1 and 2 *Word Cards*: **cat, can, than, fan, pan, van; cap, lap, nap, tap; pin, win, thin, chin; big, pig, wig, dig; lip, ship, sip, dip, chip,** *TG CD 2*
- *Tricky Word Cards*: **Can, you, see, a,** **?** *TG CD 2*
- Decodable Booklet: 'Can You See?', *TG CD 2*

Preparation

- Write chant on chart tablet
- Make sentence strips from the booklet

Review

- **Word Stretching Warm Up** What can all of these things do? Say the first word, children repeat. One child segments saying each sound, all repeat. (Mystery answer: **Grow up**.)

   Words seed (s-ee-d), egg (e-gg), child (ch-i-l-d), pup (p-u-p), calf (c-a-lf), cub (c-u-b)

- **PCCs: a, c, f, g, i, l, n, p, s, t, w, ch, sh, th, <u>th</u>** Rime Cards: **at, an, ap, ig, in, ip**. Use the 'Quick Dash'.

Live Reading and Spelling

   PCCs: a, c, f, g, i, l, n, p, s, t, w ch, sh, th, <u>th</u> (plain side of **s**=**z** for **sips**)

   Words for Live Reading: lip, ship, tap, than, thin, wig

   Words for Live Spelling: sip, sips, chips, pan, fat, fit

- For more details see Live Reading and Live Spelling, Vol 1, pages 237 and 238.

Live Reading

- Pass out the 13 *PCCs*. Line up the **l, a,** and **p** children to form **lap**.
- Tell the children to sound out the words to themselves but not to say them until you signal them, perhaps by saying, What's our word?
- Say, Now we need Annie Apple to sit down and Impy Ink to take her place.
- Continue the Live Reading list above.

Live Spelling

- The children listen while you say the word to be spelled, e.g. **sip**. Have them rubber-band stretch the word.
- Ask the class which Letterlander needs to come up first, which one in the middle, and which one last, to Live Spell the word.
- Have the class sound out the word to check their spelling. Then make **sips**.
- Say the next word, e.g. **chips**. The children repeat the word and then stretch it. Ask who needs to sit down, who needs to take their place, and who ends this word.

Find your Word Family

   Word Cards: can, than, fan, pan, van; cap, lap, nap, tap; pin, win, thin, chin; big, pig, wig, dig; lip, ship, sip, dip, chip

Each child gets a Word Card and sounds out the word

- Give each child one *Word Card*. Be sure that you give out at least two or three words for each rhyming family.
- Ask children to sound out their words.

Model looking for your rhyming family

- Hold up a leftover *Word Card* or write one of the *Rhyming Cards* on the board. Read the word and tell the class that you are looking for another word in your family. You will know it is your family if the word rhymes with your word.

- One child, or several, with a rhyming word, come up. Show and read the cards.

Children walk about finding their word family

- Tell the children to walk around the room and find their rhyming word family.
- When a child finds another child with a rhyming word they hold hands, or just walk together, while they try to find other family members.

Each family reads their words aloud in turn. Then the class reads them

- When they have all found their families, have families sit together. Let each family stand up in turn to read their words.
- Then before each family sits back down, they hold up their *Word Cards* for the rest of the class to read.

Reread Decodable Booklet

Children retell the story from memory

- Before distributing the booklets, ask children what they remember about the booklet from the previous day.

Choral read, then two teams reading alternate pages

- Reread the booklet together. Children should point to the words as they read.
- Then divide the class into two groups. Let all read the title, then have one group read the question pages and the other group read the answer pages. Have them read the last two pages together. Switch parts and read again.

Children partner-read three times, changing partners each time

- Pair up children to read the booklet. One partner reads the questions, the other the answers. Both read the title and last two pages. Switch and read again.
- After reading the booklet twice with one partner, each child finds another partner until they have read with at least three partners.
- If children need additional practice to comfortably read the book, save them for small group work. Later, send them home to read with a family member.

Small group/independent work

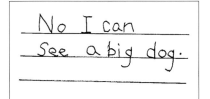

- **Word Race** Lay out a number of *Tricky Word Cards* and family words from Units 1 and 2 in a square or oval pattern on a mat. The group reads words in sequence as you point. Tell children this is a race track and challenge them to read a bit faster on the second and third turn. If time, let individual children have a run around the track of words. (See example, page 83.)
- **Answer Writing** Use *Word Cards* to make a question sentence, e.g. "**Can you see the big cat?**" Have children read the sentence. Have them each give an oral response first and then write it, e.g. "**No, I can see a big dog,**" "**Yes, I see the cat.**"
- **Sentence strips** Display sentence strips each with a question or answer from the booklet, 'Can You See?' Have children read the sentences and match up questions and answers. If you are using all the sentences from the booklet, have them reconstruct the sequence of sentences with or without referring to the book. These strips can then be put in a center or independent work area for subsequent days.

Can you see a big ship?

Yes, I can see a big ship.

Can you see a big fin?

Yes, I can see a big fin.

Yikes!

Unit 3 Word Families with O

Unit 3: Lesson 122

Rhyming with -op, -ot, -ock

✔ **Materials**
- *PCCs* and *Rime Cards*: see Review plus **op, ot, ock**
- Unit 3 *Word Cards*: **mop, top, hop; lock, rock, sock; dot, hot, pot**, *TG CD 2*
- *Rhyming Pictures*: (same as *Word Cards* listed above), *TG CD 2*

✔ **Preparation**
- Write chant on chart paper

✔ **Small group/independent**
- *Vocabulary Cards*: **dog, fox**
- Unit 1 *Word Cards*: **man, cap, rat**, *TG CD 2*
- Large **op** card for picture-coding, *TG CD 2*

Review

● PCCs **d, ĕ, h, ĭ, l, m, n, ŏ, p, r, s, t, ck, sh**, Rime Cards: **at, ap, ig, ip** Use the 'Quick Dash'. When showing the *Rime Cards*, children say the two sounds together. Then you might ask for some words spelled with that rime.

Rhyming Chant for -op

● Practice saying the chant together several times.
● Ask which words rhyme.
● Underline the rhyming **op** words.
● Ask the children which two Letterlanders make their sounds in all four of these rhyming words.
● If practical, quickly picture-code Oscar Orange and Peter Puppy at the end of each rhyming word.
● Ask the children to think of more words that rhyme with **mop** (**pop, chop, shop, plop**).

Hello, I'm Oscar Orange. Can you spot my **o** sound in words like **mop**? Can you spot my **o** sound in words like **top**? Can you spot my **o** sound in words like **hop**? And then... just **stop**.

Rhyming Picture sort

Rhyming Pictures: mop, top, hop, lock, rock, sock, dot, hot, pot

Children sort and name the Rhyming Pictures
● Place three pictures at the top of the pocket chart; **hot, mop, lock**.
● Let individual children place additional pictures that rhyme under the first word in each column. **Remember to:**

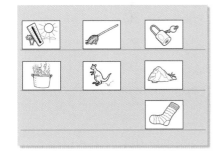

  - Let the child point to each word in the column for the class to say the rhyming words.
  - Ask the class to raise their hands if the words rhyme.
  - When a picture is placed have children say all the rhyming words in that column.
  - Ask occasionally, Why do these go together? Answer: **"They rhyme."**

Live Reading

Rhyming Pictures: mop, top, hop; lock, rock, sock; dot, hot, pot (Leave these pictures in rhyming columns on the pocket chart from above.)

PCCs: **d, h, l, m, o, p, r, s, t, ck**

Rime Cards: **op, ot, ock** (ready to use)

Word Cards: **mop, top, hop, lock, rock, sock, dot, hot, pot**

Live reading m-o-p

- Hand out the *PCCs* listed above.
- Line up children with the *PCCs* to form the word **mop**.
- Have the class sound out the word.

Replace o-p with Rime Card op

- Have the two children with **o** and **p** hold the **op** *Rime Card* instead.
- Have the class sound out "**op**," then "**m-op**" again.

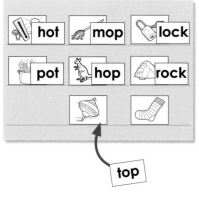

Live reading and Word Cards for -op words

- Show the class the **mop** *Word Card* and have a child place it on the pocket chart next to the **mop** picture.
- Live read **top** and **hop** by changing the first letter.
- Add the **top** and **hop** cards to the pocket chart next to their pictures.
- Each time a word is added to the pocket chart, have the class read all the rhyming words in the column.

Words with -ot and -ock

- Follow the same steps with **ot** and **ock** words.
- Finally, remove all the *Rhyming Pictures* and practice reading the *Word Cards* using the *Tractors, Trains, Planes, and Helicopters* game (see page 80).

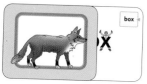

Vocabulary Cards and rhyming

- Show the children the fronts and backs of the *Vocabulary Cards*, **dog** and **fox**.
- Point out that the big word in the middle and the words in the corners all have the same two letters at the end and that they rhyme.
- Practice reading the words on the cards with the children.
- Ask for volunteers to try reading a few of the words.
- Leave the cards out for independent exploration with a few other decodable *Vocabulary Cards* (those with the thin blue frame around the picture). Suggest that pairs of children explore reading the words when your schedule allows.

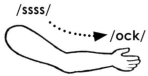

Small group/independent activities

- **Picture-coding** Provide copies of the large, plain **op** and display *PCCs* as a model. Children picture-code and add rhyming words and pictures around the Letterlanders.
- **Vocabulary Cards** One child holds the card and points to the word on the back while the other child reads; then they switch.
- **Pocket chart/table reading** Make words using the **op**, **ot**, and **ock** *Rime Cards*. Have the children arm-blend the onset and rime.

    PCCs: h, l, n, s, sh

    Rime Cards: op, ot, ock

    Word Cards: hop, shop; shot, not, lot; lock, sock

- **Hide-a-Word** Display pictures for **hot, mop,** and **lock** in a horizontal row. Children take turns matching rhyming *Word Cards* and hiding them under the picture. After all *Word Cards* are hidden, point to a picture and see how many rhyming words the children can name. Then take the cards out and have children read them, one rhyming group of words at a time.

Sentence Practice

Materials
- *PCCs* and *Rime Cards*: see Review
- Units 1-3 *Word Cards*: **hop, mop, top; lock, rock, sock; dot, hot, pot; chip, hat, map,** *TG CD 2*
- *Tricky Word Cards*: **This, is, for, you,** • *TG CD 2*
- *Rhyming Pictures*: **hop, mop, top, lock, rock, sock, dot, hot, pot,** *TG CD 2*

Preparation
- Write chant on chart paper
- You may want to use an interesting rock, or other real items, in place of pictures for sentence building
- Optional: Children's names on cards for sentence building in whole class or small group

Small group/independent
- Copies of large **ot** for picture-coding, *TG CD 2*
- Additional *Word Cards* and *Rhyming Pictures, TG CD 2*

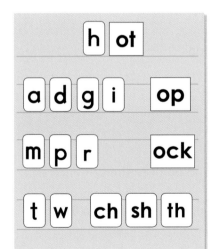

Review

- **Word stretching warm up** What do all these words tell us about? Say the first word below, children repeat. One child segments saying each sound, all repeat. (Mystery answer: **The weather**.)

  Words: **hot (h-o-t), cool (c-oo-l), wind (w-i-n-d), rain (r-ai-n), snow (s-n-ow)**

- PCCs: **ă, g, h, ĭ, l, m, n, p, r, t, w, ch, sh, th** Rime Cards: **op, ot, ock, an, in ap, ig.**
  Play 'Guess Who?' or use the 'Handwriting Review' with whole group or small groups (page 242).

Rhyming Chant for -op

- Practice saying the chant together several times.
- Ask which words rhyme.
- Underline the rhyming **ot** words.
- Ask the children which two Letterlanders make their sounds in all four of these rhyming words.
- If practical, quickly picture-code Oscar Orange and Talking Tess at the end of each rhyming word.
- Ask the children to think of more words that rhyme with **hot** (**pot, shot, got, not**).

Hello, I'm Oscar Orange. Can you spot my **o** sound in words like **hot**? Can you spot my **o** sound in words like **not**? Can you spot my **o** sound in words like **dot**, and other words? There really are a **lot**!

Make words on the pocket chart

PCCs: **d, h, m, r, w, ch, sh, th**

Rime Cards: **ot, op, ock, ig, ap**

Words to make: **hot, dot, chot*, hop, chop, rock, thock*, shock, wig, hig*, map** (*Nonsense words)

Make words with PCCs and Rime Cards
- Review the latest *Rime Cards* with the class: **op, ot, ock**
- Make the first word, **hot**
- Arm-blend the word with the children. (Touch the shoulder and say /**h**/, slide hand down your forearm and say /**ot**/. Then slide your hand from shoulder to wrist and say "**hot**.") Continue with the word list as above.

Thumbs up for real words, thumbs down for nonsense words
- The children give a "thumbs up" for a real word, "thumbs down" for a nonsense word.
- After children give the sign, write the real words in one list on the board and nonsense words in another list.
- Continue with the word list asking individual children to "lead the class" in arm-blending. (The child blends the word first. Then the class blends the same word.)

Read the word lists

● Read the real and nonsense word lists with the children several times, going a little bit faster each time.

Word/picture matching

Word Cards and Rhyming Pictures: hop, mop, top, lock, rock, sock, dot, hot, pot

Preparation: Place each group of *Rhyming Pictures* in a column with space to the right of each picture for a *Word Card*.

Match the words with the pictures

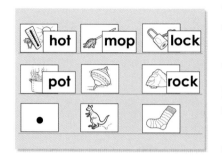

● Point to the pictures and have children name them.

● Hand out the *Word Cards*. Have children, one at a time, place the words beside the pictures.

● Each time a card is placed have everyone read all the words in the same column.

Practice reading the words without the pictures

● After all the words are placed, remove the pictures, and practice reading the words together by columns, then by pointing to the words randomly.

● Let a few children have turns reading some words on their own.

Independent practice

● Leave the words and pictures out for children to match up at other times during the day.

Sentence Building

Word Cards: rock, top, lock, pot, chip, hat, map

Tricky Word Cards: This, is, for, you

Rhyming Pictures: rock, top, lock, pot, chip, hat, map

Read the sentence

● Point to the words as you read the sentence aloud.

● Point and read it together.

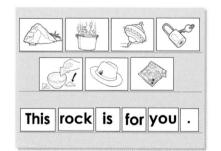

● Show everyone the *Rhyming Picture* of a rock (or an actual rock) and explain that they will take turns holding the rock picture and pointing to the sentence and reading the words.

Children lead the sentence reading

● Give the rock picture to a child and have that child point to the sentence as the class reads.

● Tell the first child to give the rock to a classmate and say, **"This rock is for you."**

● Repeat with several children. The classmate then leads the rereading of the sentence and passes the rock on to another.

Change the words

● Change the word in the sentence from **rock** to **top**.

● The next child leads the reading of the sentence and must pick out the picture of the **top** to give to another child.

● Substitute other words and let different children lead the reading and deliver the pictures.

Variation: Replace the word **you** with the children's names, and deliver the picture of the **rock** or **top** to them.

Practice the words
- Point in a random order to words in the sentence and have individuals or the whole class read them.
- Pick up the words from the sentence, show them in a random order, and have children read them.

Small group/independent activities

- **Picture-coding** Provide copies of the large, plain **ot** and display *PCCs* as a model. Children picture-code and add rhyming words and pictures around the Letterlanders.

- **Chant review** Let pairs of children reread the **ot** chant and other previously introduced chants.

- **Pocket chart/table spelling** Call out words for the children to build, using the *PCCs* and **ot**, **op**, and **ock** *Rime Cards*. Have the children use word stretching to segment the words.

  PCCs: h, l, p, n, s, sh

  Rime Cards: op, ot, ock

  Words: not, lots; pop, shop, hop; lock, locks

- **Word Card reading** Display the words in rhyming columns. Practice reading the words in columns at first as you point. Then point to the words randomly for reading. You may want to use the *Tractors, Trains, Planes, and Helicopters* activity (see page 80).

- **Sentence Building** Use name cards for each child in the group. Make a sentence such as "This hat is for Marcus." All read the sentence and then Marcus picks up the picture of the hat. Then Marcus changes the word "hat" for another pictured word and replaces his name with another child's. All read the new sentence and the named child follows the same steps, and so on until all have had a turn.

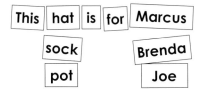

  Word Cards: pot, top, rock, sock, fan, pan, chip, pin, plus name cards for each child

  Tricky Word Cards: This, is, for, ▪

  Picture Cards: pot, top, rock, sock, fan, pan, chip, pin

Word Building

Materials
- *PCCs* and *Rime Cards*: see Review
- Units 1-3 *Word Cards*: **cat, map, wig mop, top, hop; lock, rock, sock; dot, hot, pot**, *TG CD 2*
- *Tricky Word Cards*: **This, is, for, you,** • *TG CD 2*
- *Rhyming Pictures*: **top**, *TG CD 2*
- *Letterland Word Buiders*, or individual letter sets

✔ Preparation
- Write chant on chart paper

✔ Small group/independent
- Copies of large, plain **ock** for picture-coding, *TG CD 2*
- Cards with chilren's names

Review

- PCCs **ă, b, d, ĭ, l, ŏ, t, ch, ck, sh, ch**. Rime Cards: **op, ot, ock, at, ip** Use the 'Quick Dash'.

Rhyming Chant for -ock

- Practice saying the chant together several times.
- Ask which words rhyme.
- Underline the **ock** words.
- Ask the children which two Letterlanders make their sounds in all four of these rhyming words.
- If practical, quickly picture-code Oscar Orange and Peter Puppy at the end of each rhyming word.
- Ask the children to say any of the words they can remember from the chant that rhyme with **rock**.

Hello, I'm Oscar Orange. Can you spot my **o** sound in words like **rock**? Can you spot my **o** sound in words like **sock**? Can you spot my **o** sound in words like **lock**, and say my words all around the **clock**?

Children make words to read and to spell

Words to read: **dot, lot, hop, shop, ship, lip, lick, lock**

Words to spell: **back, bat, hat, hot, pot, pop, chop**

Letters: **a, b, c, d, h, i, k, l, o, p, p, s, t**

Guide the children in building words to read
- This activity may be saved for small group time.
- Say the letter sounds in the word with a pause in between (e.g. /d/ /ŏ/ /t/). Children pull down the letters to form a word to read. *Let's put our fingers under each letter as we say the sounds, /d/ /o/ /t/. Now, let's slide them under the letters as we blend the sounds together, dot. Impy Ink has a dot at the top.*
- Guide the children in changing one or two letters and reading the new word they make.
- Continue with the word list above.

Say words for the children to spell
- Say the new word.
- Children repeat.
- Stretch the word with them.
- Children change one letter to make the new word.

/d/ /o/ /t/
/d/ /ŏt/

a b h i l p p
r s sh ch
d o t

Sorting words: op, ot and ock

Word Cards: **mop, top, hop, lock, rock, sock, dot, hot, pot**

Read the three words at the top
- Place the three *Word Cards* for **pot, rock,** and **hop** across the top of the pocket chart.

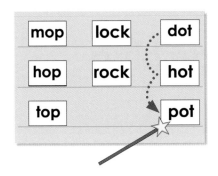

- Ask children to read the words to themselves, so they can be ready to read them with the class.
- Point to each word and read with the class.

Model sorting, then let children sort rhyming words
- Model sorting of one word under its rhyming top card (as in previous days).
- Always have everyone read down the column after each word is added.
- Call on a child to place the next word in a column. Help individuals with corrections if needed.

Practice the words
- After all the words are placed, practice pointing to and reading the words by playing the *Tractors, Trains, Planes, and Helicopters* game (see page 80).
- Let some individuals try a sequence of words by themselves.

Sentence Practice (worksheet)

Word Card: top

Tricky Word Cards: This, is, for, you

Rhyming Picture: top

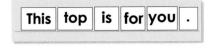

Practice sentence reading
- Form the sentence as shown on the pocket chart.
- Point to the sentence as the children read it twice.
- Point to words in the sentence at random for children to read.

Work through 'Lesson 124 Sentence Practice' worksheet with the class
- Guide children in finger-point-reading the worksheet and filling in the blanks.
- Each child may choose their own words to complete the third box.

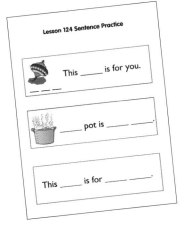

Small group/independent activities

- **Picture-coding** Provide copies of the large, plain **ock** and display *PCCs* as a model. Children picture-code and add rhyming words and pictures around the Letterlanders.
- **Chant review** Let pairs of children reread the earlier chants.
- **Word practice and Concentration Game** Display the **o** family *Word Cards* in rhyming columns. Practice reading the words using the *Tractors, Trains, Planes, and Helicopters* game (see page 80). Then play the *Concentration Game* (see page 67).
- **Sentence Building** Spread the *Word Cards* out within reach of all the children, or place them on a mat they can move around. Call out a sentence. All repeat it. Then let children take turns placing the words in sequence. Each time a card is played, everyone rereads the sentence as one child points. Make two or three sentences if time allows.

  Word Cards: top, sock, map, cap, wig, • plus name cards for each child

  Tricky Word Cards: This, is, for, you

"This sock is for you."

Consonants-Go-Marching

✔ **Materials**
- *PCCs* and *Rime Cards*: see Review
- Units 1-3 *Word Cards*: **rock, top, lock, not, pot, chip, hat, map,** *TG CD 2*
- *Tricky Word Cards*: **this** (2), **Is, is, for, me, you, no, . , ?** *TG CD 2*
- Chart tablet with previous chants

✔ **Preparation**
- Copies of 'Lesson 125 Written Word Sort,' *TG CD 2*
- Optional: Make name cards for sentence building

✔ **Small group/independent**
- *Letterland Word Builders,* or indivudual letter sets
- Units 1-3 *Word Cards*: **mop, top, hop; lock, rock, sock; dot, hot, pot,** *TG CD 2*

<u>Real</u>	<u>Nonsense</u>	<u>New Words</u>
hop	dop	lop
pop	gop	tot
chop	gock	
dot	tock	
got		
dock		
shock		

Review

- **Word stretching warm up** What do all these words tell us about? Say the words below, children repeat. One child segments saying each sound, all repeat. (Mystery answer: **Family, relatives,** or **kin**.)

  Words: son (s-o-n), aunt (au-n-t), mom (m-o-m), dad (d-a-d), sis (s-i-s)

  PCCs: b d, g, h, l, p, t, sh, ch Rime Cards: op, ot, ock, ig, in, at. Play 'Guess Who?' or use 'Handwriting Review' with the whole class or in small groups (page 242).

Live Reading: Consonants-Go-Marching

Rime Cards: op, ot, ock

PCCs: d, g, h, l, p, t, sh, ch

Try each consonant with the Rime Card

- Pass out the eight *PCCs* and three *Rime Cards* listed above. Two children hold a *Rime Card* together.
- Review the sounds of the first *Rime Card*.
- The children with the eight consonant *PCCs* line up on one side of the room, and try each consonant with the rime, as in previous lessons.

Arm-blending and thumb signs

- Children arm-blend and give the thumb sign to show their decision whether you should write the word under **Real** or **Nonsense**. If it is a word most children are not familiar with, briefly explain and write it under **New Words**.
- Read the lists of words with the class using the 'Fast, Faster, Fastest' routine (see Vol 1, page 201).

Written Word Sort

Preparation: You will need copies of the 'Lesson 125 Written Word Sort' *(TG CD 2)* for each child. Make a transparency of this sheet or draw similar boxes on your board. For detailed instructions see Lesson 119, page 91.

Word List: hop, pot, rock, sock, top, chop, not, lock, got

Write hop, pot, rock on the board. Children copy the words.

- Write the three words in three top boxes and have children copy them.

Call out words, children write in columns

- Call out the other six words and have children select the rhyming column and write them in it.
- Read the column of words with children each time they write down a new word.
- Have children read their completed pages to wa partner.

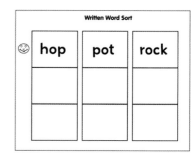

Written Word Sort		
☺ **hop**	**pot**	**rock**

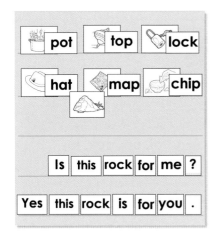

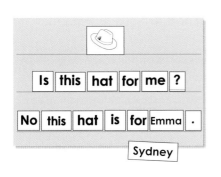

Sentence Building

Word Cards: **rock, rock, top, lock, pot, chip, hat, map** (Optional: cards with the children's names.)

Tricky Word Cards: **this, this, Is, is, for, for Yes, me, you, No, •, ?**

Rhyming Pictures: **rock, top, lock, pot, chip, hat, map**

Teacher reads, class reads, then two children read. Build the sentences shown on the left

● Read sentences *to* the class. Then *all* read them together.

● One child points to the *Word Cards* while reading the question sentence.

● The second child reads the answer sentence and gives the *Rhyming Picture* (or an actual rock) to the other child.

● Change the nouns and let several pairs of children do the above steps.

Optional activity with children's names

● First child reads the question.

● Second child reads the answer: **"No, this rock is for Sydney."** (Teacher has placed this third child's name in the blank space.)

● First child sits. Second child reads the question.

● Sydney reads the answer, which now has a fourth child's name in the blank space (e.g. Emma), etc.

Rhyming Chants for -ot, -op, -ock

● Conclude the lesson by reviewing the rhyming chants from Lessons 120, 121, and 122.

Small group/independent activities

● **Chant review** Let pairs of children choose chants to practice reading and to later present to the class.

● **Reading with letter sets**

Letters: **ă, c, h, ĭ, k, l, n, ŏ, p, s, t**

Words to make and read: **lock, shock, shop, chop, not, hot, hit, hat, chat**

● **Hide-a-Word** Place pictures for **hop**, **lock**, and **hot** in a horizontal row. Have children match *Word Cards* with the picture they rhyme with. Each time a *Word Card* is played, hide it under the picture so that each player has to use the pictures to decide if the next word rhymes. After all the words are hidden, spread them out in rhyming columns, take up the pictures and practice reading the words.

Rhyming Pictures: **hop; lock, hot**

Word Cards: **mop, top, hop; lock, rock, sock; dot, hot, pot**

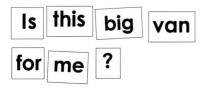

● **Sentence conversation** Use the same *Word Cards* as used with the whole class lesson plus the word **big**. Display the question sentence, pictured left. Have children read the sentence. The children construct an answer, each in turn adding a word and all reading the partial sentence after each word is added. If time allows, let children construct a new question for you to respond to.

Spelling New Words

Materials
- *PCCs* and *Rime Cards*: see Review
- *Tricky Word Cards*: **see, you, Yes, is, for, this, me, you,** ⟨ • ⟩, ⟨ ? ⟩ *TG CD 2*
- *Word Card:* **cap**, *TG CD 2*
- Paper, chalk, or white boards

✔ Preparation
- Print 'Lesson 126 Sentence Practice' from *TG CD 2*, and prepare for projection, or copy on the board

✔ Small group/independent
- Units 1-3 *Word Cards:* **sock, lock, rock; sip, lip, chip, dip; can, pan, man, fan**, *TG CD 2*

Review

- **PCCs ă, b, g, h, ĭ, ŏ, s, t, ch, ck, th, th** Rime Cards: **ot, op, ock, ip, an, ap**. Use the 'Quick Dash'.

Writing the words

Words to spell: **got, map, hop, sock, than, chip**

Call out words for children to spell
- Tell children you will call out words for them to write.
- Suggest that they may want to stretch the words as they write so they don't miss any sounds.
- Have children keep their papers or boards for the next activity, to write the irregular words below.
- Use their writing to decide who needs more work on rhyming words with short **a, i,** and **o**.

Practice Tricky Words

Preparation: Children can use boards, or papers from the above activity.

Tricky Word Cards: you, for

Explain Tricky Words
- Ask if the children sometimes surprise their parents by behaving differently, depending on who they are with. Well, so do the Letterlanders! When they do behave differently, there is usually a reason. But while we don't know the reason, the words where they behave differently can be difficult to spell. These words are called "Tricky Words." Sometimes only part of the word is tricky, but sometimes all of it is. To spell these Tricky Words, the best way is to learn their letter names by heart, all in a row.

Tell about the Tricky Word <u>you</u>
- The word **you** is irregular. We can hear Yellow Yo-yo Man making his usual sound, all right, but the next letters aren't Oscar Orange and Uppy Umbrella. They are Mr. O (surprising us by saying nothing at all in this word) and Mr. U (saying his name). Show the *Word Card* **you** and have everyone listen to their own voices as they say the word: "**yyyyyou.**"

Children say and spell <u>you</u>
- Show the *Word Card* **you** and have the children say the word.
- Have a few children use the word in an oral sentence.
- We're going to spell the word **you** by learning the letter names by heart. Point to each letter as you say the letter names, **y-o-u**.
- So, what does **y-o-u** spell? Class answers, "**you.**"

Write <u>you</u> on the board and air-trace
- Underline a very large version of **you** on the chalkboard.

you
Word Card

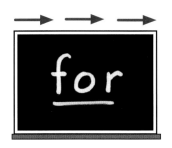

- You could also picture-code Yellow Yo-yo Man, and stick men for Mr. O and Mr. U in a contrasting color, with Mr. O's hand over his mouth.
- Lead the class in air-writing with everyone saying each letter name as you trace the letters in the air. (**"y-o-u"**)
- Trace the underline and say the word **"you"**.
- Repeat air-writing, say the word twice more, then children write it.

Learning the Tricky Word 'for'

- Follow the same steps with the word **for**. Use the explanation below to explain the tricky parts of this word.
- We can hear Firefighter Fred making his usual **fff** sound, but Oscar Orange has been captured by the Robot! So neither of them is behaving as usual. (You could picture-code them with the Robot's sack around Oscar.) We'll be learning the full story later, but right now to spell this Tricky Word the best way is for us to learn the letter names by heart: **"f-o-r."**

Sentence Building

Word Card: **cap**   Tricky Word Cards: **Yes, is, Is, for, this, me, you, · , ?**

Children build the sentences

- Say the sentence and have the class repeat it twice: **"Is this cap for me?"**
- Have a child come up and place the first word. Continue with each child adding one word to the sentence.
- Talk with children about the capital letter at the beginning of the sentence and the question mark at the end.

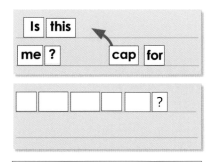

Turn words to blank and "read" the invisible sentence

- Turn each word of the first sentence to the blank side. (Leave the question mark visible.)
- Tell children that they can now read the "invisible sentence." Point to the blank cards as you say the sentence together.
- Tell the class that they will now make the invisible sentence reappear on their papers. (Lesson 126 Sentence Practice worksheet).

Sentence Practice (worksheet)

Children point to boxes and say the sentence

- Point to your boxes on the board or transparency as the children point to their boxes on the 'Lesson 126 Sentence Practice' worksheet and say the sentence: **"Is this cap for me?"**
- Have children say the first word in the sentence.

Children write the sentence

- Have children write the first word and continue to write the sentence, one word per box, on the worksheet.
- Observe as children write and help individuals as needed.
- After children write the first sentence, return to the pocket chart and follow the steps above for the second sentence, **"Yes, this cap is for you."** Then return to the worksheet to make another sentence visible.

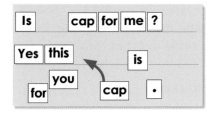

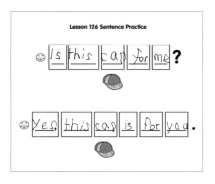

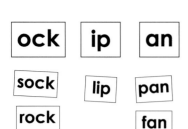

ock   ip   an

sock   lip   pan

rock   fan

chip   man

Word Wall

Continue to add
words as needed.

Small group/independent activities

- **Sort Word Cards** Use words with the rimes **ock, ip**, and **an**. Sort rhyming words in columns on the table or a mat. All read the column each time a word is placed in it.

- **Concentration Game** Mix up cards and turn them face down. Players try to find two words that rhyme, reading each word as they turn it over (see page 59).

- **Sentence practice** Have half the children read the questions on their completed worksheet. The other half responds by reading the answers. Then switch. Pair children up to reread the worksheet with a partner.

- **Spelling practice** For children who had difficulty spelling with the whole group, practice Tricky Words and decodable words. For Tricky Words, show the *Word Card* and have children trace the letters on the table with their fingers as they say the letter names, underline the traced word and repeat it. Then write the word. For decodable words, practice stretching the words to connect each sound to the correct letter. Then write the word.

Unit 3: Lesson 127

New Decodable Booklet

✔ **Materials**
- *PCCs* and *Rime Cards*: see Review
- Units 1-3 *Word Cards*: **bat, that, rat; can, than, van; win, thin, chin; big, pig, wig; lip, ship, chip; hop, top, mop; lock, rock, sock; dot, hot, pot,** *TG CD 2*

✔ **Preparation**
- Copies of 'Is This for Me?' Decodable booklet, *TG CD 2*

✔ **Small group/independent**
- Write the sentence from the booklet 'Is it for Me?' on sentence strips
- *PCCs:* **b, c, n, p**

Review

- **Word stretching warm up** What do all these words tell us about? Say the word, children repeat. One child segments saying each sound, all repeat. (Mystery answer: **Directions, ways to move**.)

    Words: **up** (u-p), **down** (d-ow-n), **left** (l-e-f-t), **right** (r-igh-t), **back** (b-a-ck)

- **PCCs: ă, b, g, h, ĭ, ŏ, s, t, ch, ck, th, th Rime Cards: ock, ot, op, at, in, ig**. Play 'Guess Who?' or use the 'Handwriting Review' with whole class or small groups (page 242).

Find your Word Family

- **24 Word Cards: bat, that, rat, can, than, van, win, thin, chin; big, pig, wig; lip, ship, chip; hop, top, mop; lock, rock, sock; dot, hot, pot** (Add or subtract cards or families to match the number of children you have.)

Children read words, find families, present words to class
- Give each child a *Word Card*.
- Have each child read the word aloud.
- Have children find other children with words that rhyme (Word Families).
- Children sit with their family, and present their words to the class by reading them.
- After each family presents, the class reads the family's three words in unison.
    Variation: Have groups make up a sentence or two using their three words.

A Letterland Take-Home Reader Lesson 127

Decodable Booklet: 'Is This for Me?'

Read the title on the board, distribute booklets

- Write the title on board, 'Is This for Me?' Guide the children in reading the title. Talk about how Impy Ink and Munching Mike do their *Capital Letter Trick* to show that the words they start are important words in the book title.
- Hand out prepared booklets.

Read on their own, with a partner, whole class

- Let children try reading the booklet to themselves or with a partner.
- Next, everyone read it again together.
- Have half the class read the questions and the other half read the answers. Then switch roles and reread.
- Have children read questions and answers with a partner in the same way.

Small group/independent activities

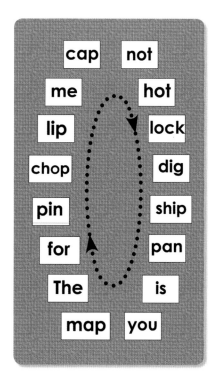

- **Word Race** Lay out a number of *Tricky Word Cards* and word family words from Units 1, 2, and 3 in a square or oval pattern on a mat. Tell children this is a race track. The group reads words in sequence as you point. Time them reading all the words and then challenge them to read a bit faster on the second and third trial. If time, let individual children have a run around the track, or part of it.

> Is this bear
> for me?
> Yes.
> Help !!!

- **Writing** Use *Word Cards* to make the partial sentence:
  Is this _____ for _____? Have children read the sentence. Have them each respond orally, making up their words for the blanks. Have them write their own questions and possibly their own answers.
- **Sentence strips** Display the *PCCs* shown below and sentence strips with questions and answers from the booklet. 'Is This for Me?' Have children read the sentences and match up the Letterlanders, questions, and answers. These strips can then be put in a center or independent work area for subsequent lessons.

Is This For Me?

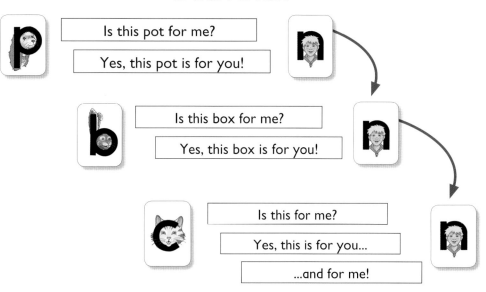

Unit 4 Word Families with U

Rhyming with –un –ug -ut

Materials
- *PCCs* and *Rime Cards*: see Review
- Unit 4 *Word Cards*: **bun, sun, run; nut, cut, shut; bug, rug, hug**, *TG CD 2*
- *Rhyming Pictures*: the same as the *Word Cards* listed above, *TG CD 2*

Preparation
- Write chant on chart tablet

Small group/independent
- Large **un** to picture-code

Review

- **PCCs b, c, h, g, n, r, s, t, ŭ, sh Rime Cards: un, ut, ug, ock, op**. Use 'Quick Dash'.

Rhyming Chant for -un

- Practice saying the chant together several times.
- Ask which words rhyme.
- Underline the rhyming **un** words.
- Ask the children which two Letterlanders make their sounds in all four of these rhyming words.
- If practical, quickly picture-code Uppy Umbrella and Noisy Nick at the end of each rhyming word.
- Ask the children to recall the words from the chant that rhyme with **sun**.

Hello, I'm Uppy Umbrella.
It's **fun** saying i in words like **sun**.
It's **fun** saying i in words like **run**.
It's **fun** saying i in words like **bun**,
and after that,
I'm all done.

Rhyming Picture Sort

Rhyming Pictures: bun, sun, run, nut, cut, shut, bug, rug, hug

Place three cards on the pocket chart
- Place one picture for each *Rhyming Picture* set in a horizontal row on the pocket chart with room below for additional cards.

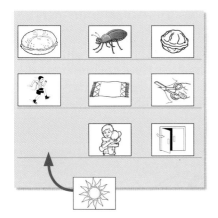

Children sort and name the Rhyming Pictures
- Let individuals place additional pictures that rhyme under the first word in each column. **Remember to:**
  - Let the child that places the word point to each word in the column for the class to read.
  - Ask the class to raise their hands if the words rhyme.
  - Ask occasionally, Why do these go together? Answer: **"They rhyme."**

Live Reading

Rhyming Pictures: bun, sun, run; nut, cut, shut; bug, rug, hug (leave in rhyming columns on the pocket chart)
PCCs: b, c, h, g, n, r, s, t, ŭ, sh
Rime Cards: ut, un, ug (ready to use)
Word Cards: bun, sun, run, nut, cut, shut, bug, rug, hug

ut	un
ug	

Live reading s-u-n
- Hand out the 10 *Picture Code Cards* listed above.
- Line up the children with the *PCC*s to form the word **sun**.
- Have the class sound out the word.

Replace u-n with Rime Card "un"
- Have the **s** child take a step away from the **u** and **n**.
- Have the class sound out **un**.
- Replace the **u** and **n** *PCC*s with the **un** *Rime Card* held by the same two children.
- Move the child with the **s** back in place and have the class sound out **sun** on their arms, saying the onset and then the rime: **"sss-un"**.

Live Reading and Word Cards for -un words
- Show class the **sun** *Word Card* and have a child place it on the pocket chart next to the *Rhyming Picture* for **sun**.
- Live read **bun** and **run** by changing the first letter.
- Add the **bun** and **run** cards to the pocket chart next to their pictures.
- Each time a word is added to the pocket chart, have the class read all the rhyming words in the column.
- Follow the same steps above with **ug** and **ut** words.

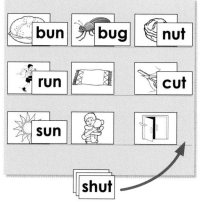

Practice reading Word Cards without pictures
- Finally, remove all the pictures and practice reading the *Word Cards* using the *Tractors, Trains, Planes, and Helicopters* game (see page 80).

Small group/independent activities

- **Picture-coding** Provide copies of the large, plain **un** and display *PCC*s as a model. Children picture-code and add rhyming words and pictures around the Letterlanders.
- **Pocket chart/table reading** Make words using the **un**, **ug**, and **ut** *Rime Cards*. Have the children arm-blend the onset and rime.

    PCCs: **b, h, n, r, s, sh** Rime Cards: **un, ug, ut**

    Words to make: **sun, run, rug, bug, hug; hut, shut, nut**

- **Hide-a-Word** Display pictures for **sun, bug,** and **nut** in a horizontal row. Children take turns matching *Word Cards* with the pictures they rhyme with and hiding them under the picture. After all the *Word Cards* are hidden, point to a picture and see how many rhyming words the children can name. Remove the rhyming pictures and have children read one rhyming group of words at a time.

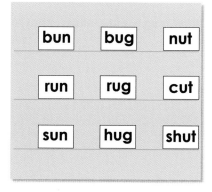

Sentence Building

Materials
- PCCs and *Rime Cards*: see Review
- *Units 3-4 Word Cards*: **sun, run, bun; bug, hug, rug; cut, nut, shut; runs, hops, big, rock,** TG CD 2
- *Tricky Word Cards*: **He, She, and, to, the,** ▪ , TG CD 2
- *Rhyming Pictures*: **sun, run, bun; bug, hug, rug; cut, nut, shut,** TG CD 2
- Cards with the children's names for sentence building

✔ **Preparation**
- Write chant on chart tablet

✔ **Small group/independent**
- Large **ug** to picture-code

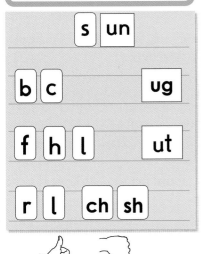

Review
- **PCCs b, c, d, f, h, j, l, r, s, s=z, v, ch, sh, Mr. E** Rime Cards: **un, ug, ut, it, ip, op**. Play 'Guess Who?' or use the 'Handwriting Review' with the whole class or in small groups (page 242).

Rhyming Chant for -ut
- Practice saying the chant together several times.
- Ask which words rhyme.
- Underline the rhyming **ut** words.
- Ask the children which two Letterlanders make their sounds in all four of these rhyming words.
- If practical, quickly picture-code Uppy Umbrella and Talking Tess at the end of each rhyming word.
- Ask the children to recall words from the chant that rhyme with **cut**.

Hello, I'm Uppy Umbrella.
It's **fun** saying u in words like **cut**.
It's **fun** saying u in words like **nut**.
It's **fun** saying u in words like **hut**,
and finally
in words like **fun**.

Make words on the pocket chart
PCCs: **b, c, f, h, l, r, s, s=z, ch, sh**
Rime Cards: **un, ug, ut, it, ip, op**
Words to make: **sun, fun, chun*; rug, rugs, bugs, cug*; cuts, shuts, shut, lut*; lit, lip, hop** (*nonsense words)

Make words with PCCs and Rime Cards
- Make the first word **sun**, with the Sammy Snake *PCC* and the **un** *Rime Card*.
- Arm-blend the word with the children. (Touch your shoulder and say /**s**/, slide your hand down your forearm saying /**un**/. Repeat faster, shoulder to wrist, while saying **sun**.)

Thumb signs, lists on the board
- The children decide if a word is a real word or a nonsense word and give the thumb sign.
- Write the words in **Real** and **Nonsense** columns on the board.
- Read the two lists of real and nonsense words on the board with the class using the Fast, Faster, Fastest routine (Vol 1, page 201).

Word/picture matching
Word Cards and Rhyming Pictures: **sun, run, bun; bug, hug, rug; cut, nut, shut**

Match the words with the pictures
- Place groups of *Rhyming Pictures* in columns with space for adding *Word Cards*.

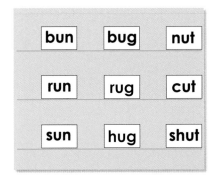

- Point to the pictures and have the children name them.
- Hand out *Word Cards*. Have the children, one at a time, place the words beside the pictures.
- When a card is placed, the children read all the words in the column.

Practice reading the words without the pictures

- After all the words are placed, remove the pictures and practice reading the words together, first by columns, then by pointing to the words randomly.
- Let a few children have turns reading a few words on their own.

Independent practice

- Leave the words and pictures out and suggest that the children try matching them up at other times during the day.

Sentence Building

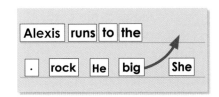

Word Cards: **runs, hops, rock, big, and**

Tricky Word Cards: **He, She, to, the, and**

PCCs: **sh, h, Mr. E**

Build the sentence

- Place the cards in a random order on the pocket chart.
- Say the sentence using one of your children's names: ___**runs to the big rock.**
- Have children take turns placing words in the sentence.
- Each time a word is placed, point to the words in the partial sentence and read it with the children.
- Ask a child, Which word comes next?
- Once the sentence is completed, ask the children to reread it. The child whose name is in the sentence should run in place as if "running to the big rock."

Introduce "she"

- Make the word **she** with *PCCs* (**sh + Mr. E**) showing the picture side.
- Remind students that Mr. E is always eager to appear and say his name in *little* words, and the little word **she** is one of them. Sound out **she** with the children.
- Show the *Word Card* **She**. Replace the child's name in the sentence with **She**.
- Read the sentence with the class and talk about how **she** can be any girl or woman that we were just talking about.
- Try another girl's name in the sentence and then replace it with **She**. Point out the **She** now means the second girl.

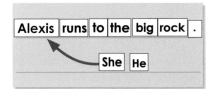

Introduce "he"

- Next put a boy's name in the sentence and read it with the class. The boy whose name is used runs in place.
- Ask, Now, can we put **she** in place of a boy's name?
- Guide the children to come up with the word **he**.
- Is this is another of Mr. E's favorite little words? Yes! Make the word **he** with the **h** and **Mr. E** *PCCs*, and all read it.
- Replace the boy's name with the **He** *Word Card*.

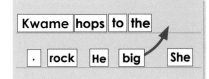

Switch the words around

- Try different children's names and have classmates choose **He** or **She** to replace it.

- Change the word **runs** to **hops** and try more children's names. Now whoever's name goes up in the sentence must hop in place.

Read silently for meaning

- Try quickly switching both a name and the verb. Explain that now the child whose name is in the sentence has to do what it says: either **hop** or **run** in place. The others need to decide if the action is correct.
- Give several children a turn.

Small group/independent activities

- **Picture-coding** Provide copies of the large, plain **ut** and display *PCCs* as a model. Children picture-code and add rhyming words and pictures around the Letterlanders.
- **Chant review** Let pairs of children reread the **ut** chant and other previously introduced chants.
- **Pocket chart/table spelling** Call out words for the children to build with *PCCs* and *Rime Cards*. Have the children use word stretching to segment the words.

  PCCs: b, c, f, j, r, sh
  Rime Cards: ug, un, ut
  Words to spell: rug, jug; fun, bun; cut, shut

- **Word Card reading** Display the Unit 4 words in rhyming columns. Practice reading the words in columns first as you point. Then point to the words randomly for reading.

Unit 4: Lesson 130

Word Building

Materials
- *PCCs* and *Rime Cards*: see Review
- Unit 4 *Word Cards*: **sun, run, bun; bug, hug, rug; cut, nut, shut**, *TG CD 2*
- *Letterland Word Builders*, or individual letter sets

Preparation
- Write the chant on the chart
- Print copies of 'Lesson 130 Sentence Practice' and prepare for projection, *TG CD 2*

Small group/independent
- Character name cards: **Bouncy Ben** and **Golden Girl**
- Units 1, 3 and 4 *Word Cards*: **van, sat, cat, lap, rock, hops, runs**, *TG CD 2*
- *Tricky Word Cards*: **on, to, the, her, The**, *TG CD 2*
- Large **ug** for picture-coding

Review

- **Word stretching warm up** All these are parts of something you all have. Say the word, children repeat. One child segments saying each sound, all repeat. (Mystery answer: **Your mouth**.)

  Words: **lip (l-i-p), tongue (t-o-ngue), teeth (t-ee-th), roof (r-oo-f), cheek (ch-ee-k)**

- **PCCs ă, b, c, f, g, h, ĭ, n, r, t, u, sh** Rime Cards: **ug, un, ut, ock, an, ig**. Use the 'Quick Dash'.

Rhyming Chant for -ug

- Practice saying the chant together several times.
- Ask which words rhyme.
- Underline the rhyming **ug** words.
- Ask the children which two Letterlanders make their sounds in all four of these rhyming words.

Hello, I'm Uppy Umbrella.
It's **fun** saying **u** in words like **bug**.
It's **fun** saying **u** in words like **rug**.
It's **fun** saying **u** in words like **hug**,
and after that
I am feeling all **snug**.

- If practical, quickly picture-code Uppy Umbrella and Golden Girl at the end of each rhyming word.
- Ask the children to recall words from the chant that rhyme with **bug**.

Children build words with letter sets

Words to make for reading: nut, shut, hut, hit, hug, rug, run, fun, fan

Words to make for spelling: hut, but, bat, bun, run, rug, bug, big

Letters: ă, b, c, f, g, h, ĭ, n, r, t, ŭ, sh

Make words to read. Use this activity with the whole class or small groups.

- Make the word on the pocket chart while you direct children to make the word on their mats.
- First, let's put our fingers under each letter as we say the sounds, /n/ /ŭ/ /t/. Now, let's slide our fingers under the letters as we blend the sounds together, **nnnŭŭŭt**, **nut**. A nut fell from the tree.
- Guide the children to change one or more letters and read the new word in the same way.
- Continue with the word list above.

Make words to spell

/n/ /u/ /t/
nŭŭt, nut

- Say the new word: e.g. **hut**. Children repeat: **hut**
- Have them rubber-band-stretch the word.
- Children place letter(s) to make the word.
- Make the word on the pocket chart for children to check.
- Say, Eyes shut and spell. Children cover the new word with their hands, close their eyes, spell out the sounds, and say the word.
- Continue with the next word.

Sorting Rhyming Words

Word Cards: bun, sun, run; nut, cut, shut; bug, rug, hug

Read the three words at the top. Place word cards for bun, nut, and bug across the top of the pocket chart.

- Ask children to read the words placed across the top of the pocket chart to themselves. Point to each word and read with the class.

Model sorting by rhyme, then let children sort

- Model sorting one word under the top card it rhymes with.
- Class reads down the column after each *Word Card* is placed.
- Call on a child to place the next word in a column.

Practice the words for fluency

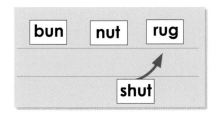

- After all the words are placed, play the *Tractors, Trains, Planes, and Helicopters* game (see page 80).
- Let some individuals try a few words by themselves.

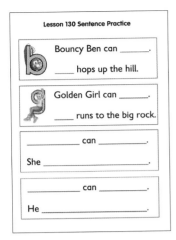

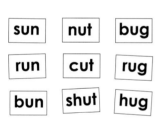

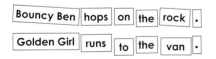

Sentence Practice (worksheet)

Guide the children in reading 'Lesson 130 Sentence Practice' worksheet and filling in the blanks

- Finger-point to your copy as children point to their page, and read the first sentence together.

- Children fill in blanks with your guidance. **"Bouncy Ben can hop. He hops up the hill."**

- Continue with the second sentence in the same way.

- Point to the third sentence and suggest orally how they might fill in the blanks. You may use parts of the previous sentences or make up a new sentence, such as **"Ms. Jenkins can hop. She hops on the rug."**

- Point out that the first blank in the third sentence will be a girl's name, to go with "she" in the second sentence.

- Have several children suggest sentences that they might write.

- Let them fill in their third sentence while you walk around to help.

- Work with children to fill in the fourth sentence.

Small group/independent activities

- **Picture-coding** Provide copies of the large, plain letters **ug** and display *PCCs* as a model. Children picture-code and add rhyming words and pictures around the Letterlanders.

- **Chant review** Let pairs of children reread the previously introduced chants.

- **Word practice and Concentration Game** Display the **u** family *Word Cards* in rhyming columns. Practice reading the words using the *Tractors, Trains, Planes, and Helicopters* game (see page 80). Then play the *Concentration Game* (see page 67).

- **Sentence Building** Spread the *Word Cards* out within reach of all the children. Call out a sentence; children repeat it twice. Then let children take turns placing the words in sequence. Each time a card is played, everyone rereads the sentence as one child points. Make two or three sentences if time allows.

    Letterlander Name cards: Bouncy Ben, Golden Girl

    Word Cards: hops, runs, rock, van, sat, cat, lap

    Tricky Word Cards: on, to, the, her, The, •

    Suggested sentences:

    Bouncy Ben hops on the rock.   **Golden Girl runs to the van.**

    Bouncy Ben sat on the rock.   **The cat sat on her lap.**

New Decodable Booklet

Materials
- *PCCs* and *Rime Cards*: see Review
- *Tricky Word Cards*: **he, she, to**, TG CD 2

Preparation
- Copy the 'Written Word Sort' worksheet, *TG CD 2*
- Copy 'Fun in the Sun' Decodable booklet *TG CD 2*

Small group/independent
- Units 1-3 *Word Cards* for sorting: **hop, top, mop; map, cap, nap, tap; pin, win, fin, chin**, *TG CD 2*
- Units 1-4 *Word Cards* for sentences: **run, hop, rock, sun, sit, lap**, *TG CD 2*
- *Tricky Word Cards*: **Can, can, not, you, Yes, No, I, the, on, a**, *TG CD 2*

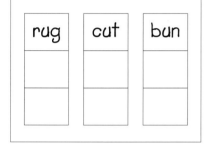

Review

● **PCCs b, c, d, h, j, n, r, s Rime Cards: ug, un, ut, ot, ap, in**. Play 'Guess Who?' or use the 'Handwriting Review' with the whole class or in small groups.

Written Word Sort

Word list: **rug, cut, bun, fun, tug, shut, dug, run, hut**

Project a copy of the Written Word Sort worksheet or draw boxes on the board. Call out the words, children write them.
● Write the three words in the top three boxes and have children copy them.
● Call out the other words. Children select the rhyming column and write them.
● After each word the children write, read that column of words together.
● Have the children read their completed page to a partner.

Practice writing: he, she, and to

Tricky Word Cards: **she, he, to**

● Children can use chalk boards, white boards, or pencil and paper.

Children say and spell "he" and "she"
● Show the **he** and **she** *Word Cards*. Children say the words.
● Have a few children use each word in an oral sentence.
● Ask, Who loves to appear in little words? Yes, Mr. E. We can hear him when we say **hēēē** and **shēēē** can't we? So we can spell these words by sounding them out.
● Write **he** large on the board. Add a stickman through the **e**. Air-trace **he** while saying the sounds /**h**/ /**ē**/.
● Children say and write down **he**, then do the same with **she**.

Spell the Tricky Word "to"
● Write a large **to** on the board. Use the word in a sentence. This is a Tricky Word because there is a surprise sound at the end. So I'm going to put a wavy line under the tricky bit to warn us that this letter is not behaving as usual. The best way to remember how to spell some Tricky Words is by saying their letter names. Let's use letter names to spell **to**: **t-o**.
● Point to each letter as you say the Letter Names with the class, **t-o**.
● Ask, What does that spell? The class answers, **"to."**
● All air-trace together while saying the Letter Names.
● Erase the word and the children write **to**.
● Now have them write all three words, **he**, **she**, and **to**.

Live Reading: Consonants-Go-Marching

PCCs: **b, c, d, h, j, n, r, s** Rime Cards: **ug, un, ut**

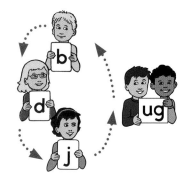

Try each consonant with the Rime Card

- Pass out the eight *PCCs* and three *Rime Cards* listed above. Two children hold a *Rime Card* together.
- Review the sounds of the first *Rime Card*: **ut**.
- The students with the eight consonant *PCCs* line up on one side of the room, and try each consonant with the rime, as in earlier lessons.

Arm-blending and thumb signs

- Children arm-blend the onset and rime and give the thumb sign to show you their decision whether you should write the word under the **Real** or **Nonsense** headings on the board. You can briefly explain words that may not be familiar to the children such as **jut** and **rut**. You will want to leave out any of the nonsense words that can be confused with real words such as dun (done).
- Repeat with the **ug** and the **un** *Rime Cards*.
- Read the lists of real and nonsense words together using the Fast, Faster, Fastest routine (see Vol 1, page 201).

Real	Nonsense	New Words
bug	cug	jut
dug	nug	rut
hug	sug	
jug	jun	
bun		
run		
sun		

Decodable Booklet: 'Fun in the Sun'

Read the title on the board and distribute the booklets

- Write the title on the board, and guide the children in reading it. Ask how we can tell which words are the most important ones in the title.
- Hand out the booklets. Can you see why it is one of Bouncy Ben's favorite books?

Children read: On their own, with a partner, with whole class

- Let children try reading the booklet to themselves, or with a partner. Help as needed.
- Next, everyone read it again together.
- Give children turns reading a page.
- Take up the booklets to reread as a part of the next lesson.

Fun in the Sun

A Letterland Take-Home Booklet Lesson 132

Small group/independent activities

- **Sort Word Cards** Use words with the rimes **ot**, **ap**, and **in**. Sort rhyming words in columns on the table or a mat. All read the column each time a word is placed.
- **Concentration Game** Mix up the words just sorted and play the *Concentration Game* (see details in Lesson 108, page 67).
- **Sentence conversation** Build a question with *Word Cards*. Then the children build an answer. Continue building questions with *Word Cards* and let children answer with *Word Cards*. Build another question and have children write the answer. Leave all *Word Cards* in view, or for more challenge, remove them.

Word Cards: **Can, can, not, run, hop, on, rock, sun, sit, lap,**
Tricky Word Cards: **you, Yes, No, I, the, a, ⟨•⟩, ⟨?⟩**

Questions	Answers
Can you run?	**Yes, I can run.**
Can you hop on a rock?	**Yes, I can hop on a rock.**
Can you hop on the sun?	**No, I can not hop on the sun.**
Can you sit on a lap?	**Yes, I can sit on a lap.**

Find Your Word Family

Materials
- *PCCs* and *Rime Cards*: see Review
- Units 1-4 *Word Cards*: **cap, nap, map; thin, chin, pin; chip, lip, ship; hop, top, chop; lock, rock, sock; nut, cut, shut; bun, sun, fun; bug, rug, hug**, *TG CD 2*
- *Tricky Word Cards*: **he, she, to**, *TG CD 2*
- *Vocabulary Cards*: **up, sun, nut**
- 'Fun in the Sun' Decodable booklet, *TG CD 2*

Preparation
- Lined paper for the class to write sentences for dictation

Small group/independent
- Additional *Tricky Word Cards* from previous Units, for 'Word Race' and a mat to put them on
- Write sentences from the booklet on sentence strips
- *Tricky Word Cards*: **I, can, on**

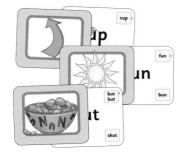

Review

- **Word stretching warm up** What might make you want to do these things? Say the first word, children repeat. One child segments saying each sound, all repeat. (Mystery answer: **Music**.)

  Words: **clap (c-l-a-p), snap (s-n-a-p), sway (s-w-ay), sing (s-i-ng), dance (d-a-n-ce)**

- PCCs: **ă, ā, ĕ, ē, ĭ, ī, o, ō, ŭ, u** Rime Cards: **ap, in, ip, op, ock, ut, un, ug**. Use the 'Quick Dash' and/or 'Handwriting Review' with whole class or in a small group.

Vocabulary Cards and rhyming

- Show the fronts and backs of the *Vocabulary Cards* **sun, nut,** and **up**.
- Point out that the big word in the middle and the words in the corners all have the same two letters at the end and that they rhyme.
- Practice reading the words on the cards with the children.
- Ask for volunteers to try reading a few of the words.
- Leave the cards out for independent exploration with a few other decodable *Vocabulary Cards* (those with the thin blue frame around the picture). Suggest that pairs of children explore reading the words when your schedule allows.

Find your Word Family

24 Word Cards: **cap, nap, map, thin, chin, pin, chip, lip, ship, hop, top, chop, lock, rock, sock, nut, cut, shut, bun, sun, fun, bug, rug, hug** (Add or subtract cards or families to match the number of children you have.)

Children read words, find families, present words to class
- Give each child a *Word Card*.
- Have each child read the word aloud.
- Have children find others with words that rhyme (word families).
- Children sit with their family, and present their words to the class by reading them.
- After each family presents, the class reads the family's three words in unison.

  Variation: Have groups make up a sentence or two using their three words.

Dictation

Dictate sentences
- Children will need paper with lines for writing the sentence.
- Say the first sentence, **She can run to the big rock.**
- Have the class repeat the sentence twice.

> She can run to the big rock.
> He can see a bug on the rug.

- Circulate as the children write the sentence, helping them to spell correctly as required. If they need the sentence repeated, say the whole sentence again and have the children repeat it. Do not break the sentence into shorter phrases unless it is necessary for some children.
- After most have finished writing, set out the sentence with the *Word Cards*, or write it on the board for the children to check and correct any mistakes.
- When children are ready, continue with the second sentence: **He can see a bug on the rug.**

Read Decodable Booklet: 'Fun in the Sun'

Fun in the Sun

A Letterland Take-Home Booklet Lesson 132

Read the booklet with whole class
- Before passing out the booklet, ask children to tell what they remember about it from the previous lesson.
- Reread the booklet together. Children should point to the words as they read.

Half of the class reads one page, the other half the next
- Then divide the class into two groups. Let all read the title, then have the two groups read from alternating pages. All read the last two pages together. Switch parts and read the booklet again.

Partner read
- Pair up children to read the booklet. One partner reads the first page, the other the next, etc. Both read the title and last page. Switch and read it again.
- After reading the booklet twice with one partner, children find another partner until they have read with at least three partners.
- Send the booklets home for reading to parents.

Small group/independent activities

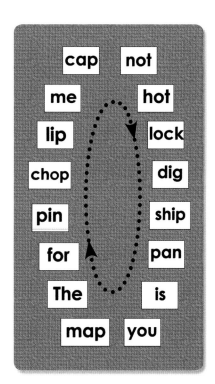

cap   not

me   hot

lip   lock

chop   dig

pin   ship

for   pan

The   is

map   you

- **Word Race** Lay out a number of *Tricky Words* and family *Word Cards* from Units 1–4 in a square or oval pattern on a mat. Tell children this is a race track. The group reads the words in sequence as you point. Time them as a group reading all the words and then challenge them to read a bit faster on the second and third trial. If time allows, let individual children have a run around the track or part of it.
- **Writing** Use *Word Cards* to make the partial sentence: **I can_____ on _____.** Have children read the sentence. Have them each respond orally, making up their own words for the blanks. Then have them write their own sentences.
- **Sentence strips** You may want to draw or enlarge pictures of the mother and her bunny. Write sentences from the booklet on sentence strips. Have children read the sentences and match up the pictures with each character and put them in sequence. Then have half the group read the sentences about the mother, alternating with the other half reading about the bunny. These strips can then be put in a center or independent work area to be worked with on other lessons.

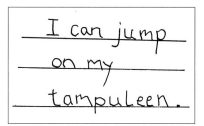

I can jump on my tampuleen.

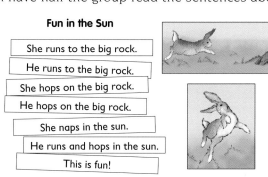

Fun in the Sun

She runs to the big rock.

He runs to the big rock.

She hops on the big rock.

He hops on the big rock.

She naps in the sun.

He runs and hops in the sun.

This is fun!

Unit 5 Word Families with ĕ

Rhyming with -et,-ell,-eck

Review

- **PCCs: b, d, ĕ, j, n, t, v, w, ch, ck, ll, sh** Rime Cards: **ug, ap, ot, in, ock** Use the 'Quick Dash'.

Rhyming Chant for -et

- Practice saying the chant together several times.
- Ask which words rhyme.
- Underline the rhyming **et** words.
- Ask which two Letterlanders make their sounds in all four of these rhyming words.
- If practical, quickly picture-code Eddy Elephant and Talking Tess at the end of each rhyming word.
- Ask the children to give other words that rhyme with **net** (**yet, let, get, pet, bet, set, met**).

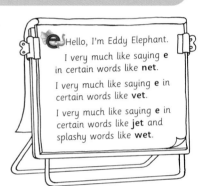

Hello, I'm Eddy Elephant.
I very much like saying **e** *in certain words like* **net**.
I very much like saying **e** *in certain words like* **vet**.
I very much like saying **e** *in certain words like* **jet** *and splashy words like* **wet**.

Rhyming Picture Sort

Rhyming Pictures: **neck, deck, check; well, bell, shell; net, vet, jet**

Place three cards on the pocket chart
- Place one picture for each *Rhyming Picture* set in a horizontal row on the pocket chart with room below for additional cards.

Children sort and name the Rhyming Pictures
- Let individuals place additional pictures that rhyme under the first word in each column. **Remember to:**
  - Let the child who places the word point to each word in the column for the class to say the rhyming words.
  - Ask the class to raise their hands if the words rhyme.
  - Ask occasionally, Why do these go together? Answer: **"They rhyme."**

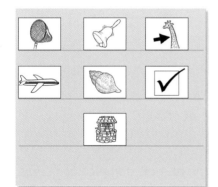

Live Reading

Leave the pictures in rhyming columns from the previous activity.

PCCs: **b, d, ĕ, j, n, t, v, w, ch, ck, ll, sh**
Rime Cards: **et, ell, eck** (ready to use)
Word Cards: **net, vet, jet; neck, deck, check; well, bell, shell**

et	eck

ell

Live reading n-e-t

- Hand out the 12 *PCCs* listed above. Two children could share each of the digraphs **ch, ck, ll**, and **sh**.
- Line children up with the *PCCs* to make **net**.
- Have the class sound out the word.

Replace e-t with Rime Card "et"

- Have the **n** child take a step away from the **e** and **t**.
- Have the class sound out **et**.
- Replace the **e** and **t** *PCCs* with the **et** *Rime Card* held by the same two children.
- Move the child with the **n** back in place and have the class sound out **net** on their arms, saying the onset and then the rime: **"nnn-et."**

Live reading and Word Cards for -et words

- Show the class the **net** *Word Card* and have a child place it on the pocket chart next to the **net** *Picture Card*.
- Live read **vet** and **jet** by changing the first letter.
- Children add the **vet** and **jet** cards to the pocket chart next to their pictures.
- Each time a word is added to the pocket chart, have the class read all the rhyming words in the column.
- Follow the same steps above with **eck** and **ell** words

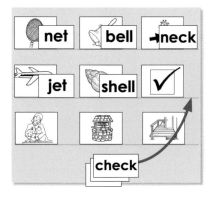

Practice reading the Word Cards with the pictures, then without

- Practice reading the *Word Cards* with the pictures in place.
- Finally, remove all the *Rhyming Pictures* and practice reading the *Word Cards* for fluency, using the *Tractors, Trains, Planes, and Helicopters* game (see page 80).

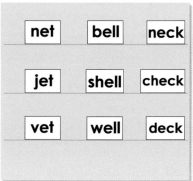

Small group/independent activities

- **Picture-coding** Provide copies of the large, plain **et** *(TG CD 2)* and display *PCCs* as a model. Children picture-code and add rhyming words and pictures around the Letterlanders.

- **Pocket chart/table reading** Make words using the **et, eck**, and **ell** *Rime Cards*. Have the children arm-blend the onset and rime.

   PCCs: **b, l, g, n, p, t, w, ch, ll**

   Rime Cards: **et, ell, eck**

   Words to make: **net, let, get, pet; peck, check; bell, well, tell**

Sentence Building

Materials

- *PCCs* and *Rime Cards*: see Review list
- Units 3 and 5: *Word Cards*: **rock; net, vet, jet; bell, well, shell; neck, check; deck,** *TG CD 2*
- *Tricky Word Cards*: **at, in, is, Now, now, on** (2), **She, she, He, he, the** (2), **was,** ◻ (2), *TG CD 2*
- *Rhyming Pictures*: **rock, net, vet, jet; bell, well, shell; neck, deck, check,** *TG CD 2*
- Character name cards: **Clever Cat, Eddy Elephant,** *TG CD 2*

Preparation
- Write the chant on the chart

Small group/independent
- Copies of large plain **ell** to picture-code, *TG CD 2*

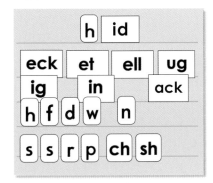

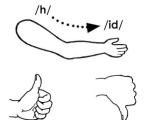

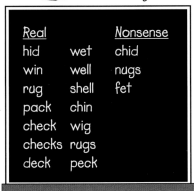

Real		Nonsense
hid	wet	chid
win	well	nugs
rug	shell	fet
pack	chin	
check	wig	
checks	rugs	
deck	peck	

Review

- **PCCs b, c, d, ĕ, f, g, h, l, n, p, r, s, s=z, w, y, ch, sh**
- **Rime Cards: ack, id, ig, in, ug, et, ell, eck.** Play 'Guess Who?' or use the 'Handwriting Review' with the whole class or in small groups.

Rhyming Chant for -ell

- Practice saying the chant together several times.
- Ask which words rhyme.
- Underline the rhyming **ell** words.
- Ask which three Letterlanders make their sounds in all four of these rhyming words.
- If practical, quickly picture-code Eddy Elephant, Lucy Lamp Light, and Linda Lamp Light at the end of each rhyming word.
- Ask the children to recall words from the chant that rhyme with **fell**.

Hello, I'm Eddy Elephant. I very much like saying **e** in certain words like **bell**. I very much like saying **e** in certain words like **well**. I very much like saying **e** in certain words like **shell** and I enjoy these words. Can you **tell**?

Make words on the pocket chart

PCCs: d, f, h, n, p, r, s, s=z, w, ch, sh

Rime Cards: ack, eck, et, ell, id, ig, in, ug

Words to make: hid, chid*, chin, win, wig, rug, rugs, nugs*, pack, peck, check, checks, deck, wet, fet*, well, shell (*nonsense words)

Make words with PCCs and Rime Cards
- Make the first word **hid**, with the **h** PCC and the **id** *Rime Card*.
- Arm-blend the word with the children. (Touch your shoulder and say /**h**/, slide your hand down your forearm saying /**id**/. Repeat faster, shoulder to wrist, while saying "**hid**.")

Thumb signs, lists on the board
- The children decide if a word is a real word or a nonsense word and give the thumb signal: up for real, down for nonsense.
- Write the words in **Real** and **Nonsense** columns on the board.
- Read the two lists of real and nonsense words on the board with the class using the Fast, Faster, Fastest routine (see Vol 1, page 201).

Word/picture matching

Word Cards and Rhyming Pictures: net, vet, jet; bell, well, shell; neck, deck, check

Match the words with the pictures
- Place groups of *Rhyming Pictures* in columns with space for adding *Word Cards*.

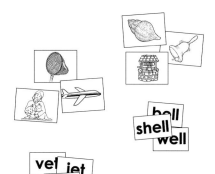

- Point to the pictures and have children name them.
- Hand out *Word Cards*. Have the children, one at a time, place the words beside the pictures.
- When a card is placed, the children read all the words in the column.

Practice reading the words without the pictures
- After all words are placed, remove the pictures and practice reading the words together, first by columns, then by pointing to the words randomly.
- Let a few children have turns reading other words on their own.

Independent practice
- Leave the words and pictures out and suggest that children try matching them up at other times during the day.

Sentence Building

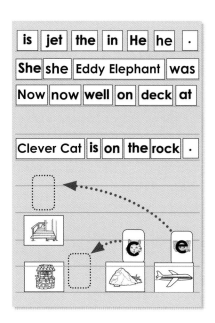

Word Cards: **deck, jet, rock, well**

Tricky Word Cards: **at, in, is, Now, now, on** (2), **She, she, the** (2), **He, he, was, •** (2)

Character Name Cards: **Eddy Elephant, Clever Cat**

PCCs: **c, ĕ**

Rhyming Pictures: **deck, rock, well, jet**

Build the sentence
- Place the *Word Cards* in random order on the pocket chart. Do not build the sentence yet.
- Place Clever Cat's *PCC* above the rock picture as shown.
- Point to Clever Cat and say, Where is Clever Cat?
- Elicit from the children, **"Clever Cat is on the rock."**
- Build the sentence with a different child picking out and placing each word.

Move Clever Cat and change the sentence
- Move Clever Cat over beside the *Picture Card* of the well.
- Ask, Is Clever Cat on the rock? **"No."**
- Show the word **was** and guide them to discover that **was** is a *Tricky Word* because the **a** does not sound like it should. Make a wavy line under the **a**.
- Replace the word **is** in the sentence with **was**.
- Read the sentence with the class, **"Clever Cat was on the rock."**

Add a new sentence about Clever Cat using "she" and "now"
- Ask, Where is Clever Cat now? **"At the well."**
- Show the word **Now** which has Noisy Nick's sound but an unusual sound for **ow**. Make a wavy line under the **ow**.
- Make a new sentence underneath the previous sentence, **"Now, she is at the well."**
- Read the old and the new sentences with the class. Let several children take turns pointing to the words and lead the class in rereading the sentences.

Experiment moving the name cards and the Picture Cards
- Move the Clever Cat *PCC* above the **deck** picture and change the sentences to read **"Clever Cat was at the well. Now, she is on the deck."**

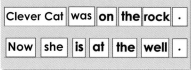

- Experiment with the children, moving Clever Cat and then Eddy Elephant to different positions.
- With the children helping to place the cards, make sentences such as:

    Clever Cat was on the deck. Now she is in the jet.

    Eddy Elephant was in the jet. Now he is on (or at) the rock.

    Eddy Elephant was on the rock. He is at the well now.

Review the Word Cards

- Finish the lesson by picking up a number of the *Word Cards* including **was** and **now**. Hold each one up for the class to read. Go through the cards a few times, a little faster each time.

Small group/independent activities

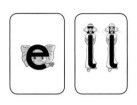

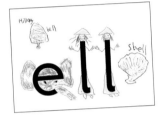

- **Picture-coding** Provide copies of the large, plain **ell** (*TG CD 2*) and display the *PCCs* **e** and **ll** as a model. Children picture-code and add rhyming words and pictures around the Letterlanders.
- **Chant review** Let pairs of children reread the **ell** chant and other previously introduced chants.
- **Pocket chart/table spelling** (Vol 1, page 239) Call out words for the children to build with *PCCs* and *Rime Cards*. Have the children segment the words and then take turns placing the cards to build the word.

    PCCs: b, d, f, l, n, y, ch, sh

    Rime Cards: et, ell, eck

    Word to spell: shell, bell, fell, yell; yet, let, net; neck, check, deck

- **Word Card reading** Display the Unit 5 words in rhyming columns. Practice reading the words first in columns as you point. Then point to words randomly for reading.

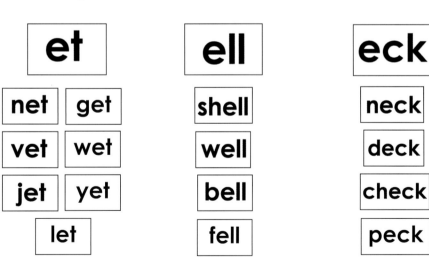

et		**ell**	**eck**
net	get	shell	neck
vet	wet	well	deck
jet	yet	bell	check
	let	fell	peck

Sorting Words

Materials
- *PCCs* and *Rime Cards*: see Review list
- Units 2,3 and 5 *Word Cards*: **neck, deck, check; well, bell, tell; get, wet, jet; rock, ship,** *TG CD 2*
- *Tricky Word Cards*: **was, on, the** (2), **Now, she, he, is, at,** *TG CD 2*
- *Rhyming Pictures*: **well, jet, rock, ship,** *TG CD 2*
- Character name card: Clever Cat, *TG CD 2*
- Copies of 'Lesson 135 Sentence Practice,' *TG CD 2*

Preparation
- Write the chant on the chart

Small group/independent
- Copy the large, plain **eck** page for picture-coding, *TG CD 2*
- *Letterland Word Builders*, or individual letter sets

Review

- **Word stretching warm up** Think about where you could find all these. Say the word, children repeat. One child segments saying each sound, all repeat. (Mystery answer: **The ocean**.)

   Words: shell (sh-e-ll), fish (f-i-sh), ship (sh-i-p), waves (w-a-ve-s), whale (wh-a-le)

- PCCs ă, ĕ, ĭ, ŏ, ŭ, ch, ng, sh, th Rime Cards: **et, ell, eck, ap, in, ock, ug** Use the 'Quick Dash'.

Rhyming Chant for -eck

- Practice saying the chant together several times.
- Ask which words rhyme.
- Underline the rhyming **eck** words.
- Ask which two Letterlanders make their sounds in all four of these rhyming words.
- If practical, quickly picture-code Eddy Elephant, Clever Cat, and Kicking King at the end of each rhyming word.
- Ask the children to recall words from the chant that rhyme with **neck**.

Hello, I'm Eddy Elephant. I very much like saying **e** in words like **neck**. I very much like saying **e** in words like **deck**. I very much like saying **e** in words like **peck** and when I am done, I give myself a **check**.

Sorting Rhyming Words

neck	jet	bell
check	get	well
deck	wet	tell

   Word Cards: **neck, deck, check; well, bell, tell; get, wet, jet**

Read the three words at the top
- Ask children to read the words placed across the top of the pocket chart to themselves. Then point to each word and read with the class.

Model sorting by rhyme, then let children sort
- Model sorting one word under the top card it rhymes with (as in previous lessons).
- Class reads down the column after each *Word Card* is placed.
- Call on a child to place the next word.
- After all the words are placed, play the *Tractors, Trains, Planes, and Helicopters* game (see page 80).
- Let some individuals try a few words by themselves.

Sentence Practice (worksheet)

Build the sentences from the previous lesson
   Rhyming Pictures: **well, jet, rock, ship**
   Word Cards: **rock, at, well**

Lesson 135 Sentence Practice

Talking Tess was at the _____.
Now ____ is on the _____.

Munching Mike ____ in the jet.
____, he is ____.

I was _____.
Now I am _____.

_____ was ____ the _____.
_____ is ____.

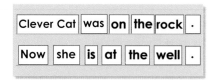

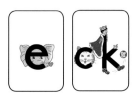

Tricky Word Cards: was, the (2), **on, Now, she, he, is**

Character Name Card: Clever Cat

Sentences: Clever Cat was on the rock. Now, she is at the well.

- Say the first sentence and have children help build it with *Word Cards*. Then do the same with the second sentence.

- Leave the words in the pocket chart for reference as the children do Lesson 135 Sentence Practice. Tell them that they might use the *Rhyming Pictures* for ideas for words as well as the *Word Cards*.

- Guide students as they fill in the worksheet. They may make their own choices for many of the blanks, but the first sentence in each box should use **is** and the second sentence should use **was**.

- In the final box they may use a friend's name in the first sentence and then choose "**he**" or "**she**" in the second sentence to match the name.

- Children who finish early may want to write more or draw on the back of the paper.

Small group/independent activities

- **Picture-coding** Provide copies of the large, plain letters **eck** and display **e** and **ck** *PCCs* as a model. Children picture-code and add rhyming words and pictures around the Letterlanders.

- **Chant review** Let pairs of children reread the previously introduced chants.

- **Reading with individual letter sets** Call out the sounds or the letters and have children build the word. Then have children sound out the word.

   Letters used: b, c, e, h, i, l, l, k, p, s, t, w

   Words: chick, check, peck; pet, wet; well, bell, shell; will, hill

- **Word practice and Concentration Game** Display the **e** family *Word Cards* in rhyming columns. Practice reading the words using the *Tractors, Trains, Planes, and Helicopters* game (see page 80). Then play the *Concentration Game* (see page 67).

Consonants-Go-Marching

Materials
- *PCCs* and *Rime Cards*: see Review list
- White boards and markers, or pencil and paper

Preparation
- Write chant on chart tablet
- Prepare copies of 'Written Word Sort' page from the *TG CD 2*, and project a copy

Small group/independent
- Units 2, 3 and 5 *Word Cards*: **net, jet, vet, get, let; peck, neck, deck, check; rock, sock, lock; ship**, *TG CD 2*
- *Tricky Word Cards*: **the** (2), **Was, was, in, at, No, Yes, Now, he, she,** **.** , **?** *TG CD 2*
- Character name cards: **Noisy Nick, Golden Girl** (or others), *TG CD 2*

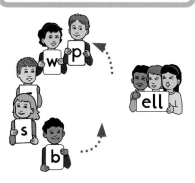

Real		Nonsense
bet	sell	beck
bell	wet	nell
net	well	pell
neck	yet	seck
pet	yell	weck
peck		yeck
set		

Review

- **Word stretching warm up** Think about how these words go together. Say the word, children repeat. One child segments saying each sound, all repeat. (Mystery answer: **the calendar, time**.)

    Words: **week (w-ee-k), May (M-ay), day (d-ay), June (J-u-ne)**

- **PCCs b, n, p, s, w, y Rime Cards: et, ell, eck** Use 'Guess Who?' or the 'Handwriting Review' with the whole class or in small groups.

Rhyming Chant for -et

- Practice saying the chant together several times.
- Ask which words rhyme.
- Underline the rhyming **et** words.
- Ask the children which two Letterlanders make their sounds in all four of these rhyming words.
- If practical, quickly picture-code Eddy Elephant and Talking Tess at the end of each rhyming word.
- Ask the children to recall **et** words from the chant and other rhyming words (**let, net, set, bet, met, get, yet**).

Hello, I'm Eddy Elephant.
I very much like saying **e** in words like **pet**.
I very much like saying **e** in words like **jet**.
I very much like saying **e** in words like **vet**.
I also like to spray myself and get all **wet**.

Live Reading: Consonants-Go-Marching

   PCCs: b, n, p, s, w, y Rime Cards: et, ell, eck

Try each consonant with the Rime Card
- Pass out the six *PCCs* and three *Rime Cards* listed above. Two children hold each *Rime Card* together.
- Review the sounds of the first *Rime Card* **et**.
- The children with the six consonant *PCCs* line up on one side of the room, and try each consonant with the rime, as in the earlier lessons.

Arm-blending and thumb signs
- Children rollercoaster or finger-sound the onset and rime and give the thumb sign to show you whether to write the word under the **Real** or the **Nonsense** heading on the board.
- Repeat with the **ell** and the **eck** *Rime Cards*.
- Read the lists of real and nonsense words together using the Fast, Faster, Fastest routine.

Practice writing Tricky Words

Talk about the tricky part of "was"
- Write **was** on the board in very large letters and underline the whole word.

- Have a few children use **was** in oral sentences.
- Let's rubber-band stretch **was**. **Wwwwŭzzz** (or **wwwwŏzzz**, depending on region). This is a Tricky Word! Elicit from the children that the **a** in **was** "doesn't sound right," and that Sammy Snake is making his snoozing sound /**zzz**/. Put a wavy line under the **a** and picture-code Sleepy Sammy (with small ascending **z**'s above his letter).

Practice writing "was"
- Point to each letter as you say the letter names with the class, **"w-a-s."**
- What does that spell? **"was."**
- Lead the class in air-tracing, saying each letter name as you trace the letters in the air (**"w-a-s"**). Trace the underline and all say, **"was."**
- Repeat the above step twice more.

Children write "was" on paper
- Erase the word and have the children write **was** on their papers, saying the Letter Names and underlining the word as they write.

Introduce the Tricky Word "now"
- Follow the same steps as for **was**. Let the children discover that the **o** and **w** are the tricky parts of **now**. Explain they will learn later why they hear that **ow** sound. Meanwhile, practice spelling it using letter names.

Written Word Sort

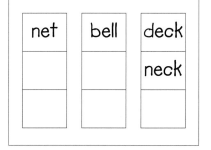

Written Word Sort

Word List: net, bell, deck, neck, vet, well, jet, check, tell

- Write the first three words in your top three boxes and have the children copy them in their boxes.
- Have children point to their words and read them.
- Call out the other words and have the children select the rhyming column and write them.
- Read the column of words with the children each time they write a new word.
- Children practice reading their completed page with a partner.

Small group/independent

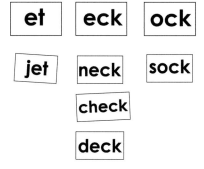

- **Sort Word Cards** Use words with the rimes **et, eck**, and **ock**. Sort rhyming words into columns on the table or a mat. All read the column each time a word is placed.
- **Concentration Game** Mix up the words just sorted and then play the *Concentration Game* (see page 67).
- **Sentence conversation:** Build a question with *Word Cards*. Then the children build an answer. Build more questions and let children answer with *Word Cards* or by writing their answers. Perhaps the children could build questions that you or the other children could answer. Leave all the *Word Cards* in view when the children write (or remove them for more challenge).

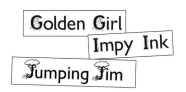

   Word Cards: rock, in, jet, at, ship, well

   Tricky Word Cards: on, Is, the, the, Was, was, Yes, No, Now, he, in, at, she, · ?

   Character Name Cards: Jumping Jim, Golden Girl (or other Letterlanders)

Sample Questions	Sample Answers
Is Jumping Jim on the rock?	No, he is at the well.
Was Golden Girl in the jet?	Yes, she was in the jet.
Is Impy Ink on the ship?	No, he was on the ship.
	Now he is on the rock.

Unit 5: Lesson 137

New Decodable Booklet

Materials
- *PCCs* and *Rime Cards*: see Review
- *Vocabulary Cards*: **leg, red**
- Units 1-5 *Word Cards*: **cap, lap, tap; chin, thin, in; dot, hot, pot; nut, cut, shut; bun, sun, run; net, jet, yet; bell, shell, fell; neck, check, peck**, *TG CD 2*
- Paper and pencils for dictation
- Copies of 'Did You See Eddy Elephant?' Decodable booklet, *TG CD 2*

Small group/independent
- Additional *Tricky Word Cards* from previous Units for Word Race, and a mat to put them on
- Write sentences from the booklet onto sentence strips

Review

- **PCCs ă, ĕ, ĭ, j, ŏ, q, t, ŭ, w, x, y, z Rime Cards: ap, in, ot, ut, un, ell, et, eck** Use the 'Quick Dash'.

Vocabulary Cards and rhyming

- Show children the fronts and backs of the *Vocabulary Cards* **red** and **leg**.
- Point out that the big word in the middle and the words in the corners all have the same two letters at the end and that they rhyme.
- Practice reading the words on the cards with the children.
- Ask for volunteers to try reading a few of the words.
- Leave the cards out for independent exploration with a few other decodable *Vocabulary Cards* (those with the thin blue frame around the picture). Suggest that pairs of children explore reading the words on their own when your schedule allows.

Find your Word Family

24 Word Cards: cap, lap, tap; chin, thin, in; dot, hot, pot; nut, cut, shut; bun, sun, run; net, jet, yet; bell, shell, fell; neck, check, peck (Add or subtract cards or families to match the number of children you have.)

Children read words, find families, present words to class
- Give each child a *Word Card*.
- Have each child read the word aloud.
- Have children find others with words that rhyme (word families).
- Children sit with their word family, and present their words to the class by reading them.
- After each family presents, the class reads the family's three words in unison.
    Variation: Have groups make up a sentence or two using their three words.

Dictation

Dictate sentences
- Children will need paper with lines for writing the sentence.
- Say the first sentence, **She is at the well.**

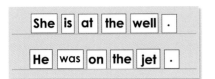

- Have the class repeat the sentence twice.
- Circulate as children write the sentence, helping them spell correctly as required. If they need the sentence repeated, say the whole sentence again and have the children repeat it. Do not break the sentence into shorter phrases unless it is necessary for some children.
- After most have finished writing, set out the sentence with the *Word Cards*, or write it on the board for children to check and correct any mistakes.
- When children are ready, continue with the second sentence, **He was on the jet.**

Read the Decodable Booklet: 'Did you See Eddy Elephant?'

A Letterland Take-Home Reader Lesson 137

Read the title on the board, distribute books

- Write the title on the board, 'Did You See Eddy Elephant?' Guide the children in reading the title.
- Hand out the booklets.

Children read on their own, with a partner, with the whole class

- Let children try reading the booklet alone or with a partner. Help them as needed.
- Next, everyone read the booklet again together.
- Let half the class read Mr. E's questions and the other half read the answers to his questions.
- Let four different children read one part each: **Mr. E, Red Robot, Talking Tess,** and **Quarrelsome Queen.**

Small group/independent activities

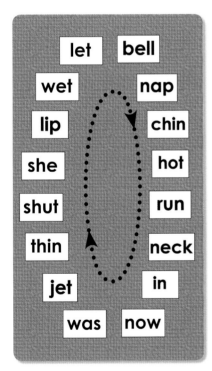

- **Word Race** Lay out a number of *Tricky Words* and *Word Family Words* from Units 1–5 in a square or oval pattern on a mat. Tell children this is a race track. The group reads words in sequence as you point to them. Time them as a group reading all the words and then challenge them to read a bit faster on the second and third lap. If time allows, let individual children have a run around part or all of the track.
- **Writing** Use *Word Cards* to make the partial sentence: "I was _____." Have children read the sentence. Have them each orally respond, making up their own words for the blank. Have them write their own sentences.
- **Sentence strips** Write sentences from the booklet, 'Did You See Eddy Elephant?' on sentence strips. Have children read the sentences and match up the pictures with each character as shown below, and put the sentences in sequence. Then assign characters to read the sentences.

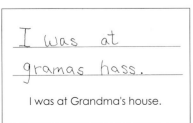

I was at Grandma's house.

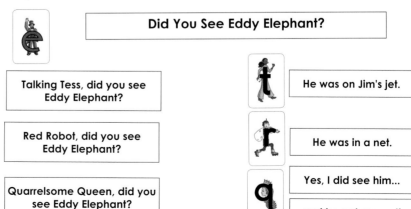

Did You See Eddy Elephant?

Talking Tess, did you see Eddy Elephant?

Red Robot, did you see Eddy Elephant?

Quarrelsome Queen, did you see Eddy Elephant?

He was on Jim's jet.

He was in a net.

Yes, I did see him...

and he got me wet!

Section 3 Assessments

You can assess your children's mastery of the outcomes for Section 3: Onset and Rimes with the following:

Reading Assessments (given individually):

1. Word Reading Accuracy Children read a list of 12 decodable words.

2. Reading Tricky Words Children read a list of 16 high-frequency words that have been presented and practiced in this section.

3. Word Reading Fluency Children read as many decodable words as possible within 60 seconds.

Spelling Assessments (given to small groups or the whole class)

4. Spelling Decodable Words Children write words to match 8 pictures.

5. Spelling Tricky Words Children write 16 words to dictation.

6. Sentence Dictation Children write a sentence to dictation.

Assessment Pages

Teacher's Guide: Student reads from pages 134-135.

Teacher's Guide CD 2: Section 3 Assessment (copymasters including Score Sheet and Spelling Decodable Words)

Assessment Instructions

(1) Word Reading Accuracy (individual administration) The child reads the 12 words on page 134. Encourage the child to 'sound them out.' If the child says the word in a segmented fashion (e.g. **/h/ /a/ /t/**), you may say, Put it together, or, Blend it. Only count the word as correct if the child is able to say it finally without segmentation (e.g. **"hat"**). After about five seconds on a word, have the child move on to the next word. On the Score Sheet (*TG CD 2*) put a line through any words missed, or write the substitution above the word. The goal is at least 10 of 12 words correct.

(2) Reading Tricky Words (individual administration) Tell children that these are Tricky Words that they have worked on and that the words may have letters that do not 'sound right.' The child reads the 16 words on page 134. After about five seconds on a word, have the child move on to the next word. Record errors on the Score Sheet. The goal is at least 12 of 16 words correct.

(3) Word Reading Fluency (individual administration) Instruct the child to read across page 135 and continue reading the words in each row until you say Stop. Time the child for 60 seconds. Put a line through missed words on the Score Sheet and a line under the last word. Count words read correctly. The goal is 10 words correct in one minute.

(4) Spelling Decodable Words (group administration) Give each child a copy of the page (*TG CD 2*) and project or enlarge a copy to demonstrate. Name the first picture and have children repeat it. Ask the children to rubber-band stretch the word on their own and spell it in the box. When everyone is ready, do the same with each picture. On each child's Score Sheet, copy misspellings or put a line through words missed. The goal is at least 6 of 8 words correct.

(5) Spelling Tricky Words (group administration) Provide children with pencil and paper. Dictate the 16 words listed on the Score Sheet by saying the word, a sentence, then repeating the word. Have children repeat the word after you. Then they write the word. You may want to divide this assessment into two sessions of about 8 words each. On the Score Sheet copy misspellings or put a line through words missed. The goal is at least 12 words correct of 16.

(6) Sentence Dictation (group administration) Provide children with pencil and paper. Say the sentence below with rhythm and expression. Have the children repeat the sentence two times and then write it. You may repeat the whole sentence additional times at the request of the children. The child receives one point for each word spelled correctly, one point for correct use of capital and lowercase letters, and one point for a period on the end. There are 8 possible points. On each child's Score Sheet copy misspellings or put a line through words or punctuation missed. Circle letters with capitalization errors. The goal is 6 of 8 points.

   Sentence: **The cat is on the deck.**

You may want to enter all your children's scores on the Section 3 Class Assessment Record.

Children scoring less than the goal numbers on any part of the assessment need additional practice with the items or skills missed. You may want to complete a Section 3-7 Individual Assessment Record (*TG CD 2*), as shown below, for these students and retest them at intervals until the goals are reached.

Individual Record for Section 3–7 Assessments

Child's Name _____ Teacher _____ School _____ School Year _____

Fill in this page for children with scores below the goals on Section 3–7 Assessments. Enter in red any scores that are below the goal for that assessment. Retest unmet goals every 10–20 days until met.

Section ⇒	3 Onsets and Rimes					4 Consonant Blends					5 Vowel Men/Magic e					6 Vowel Men Out Walking					7 The Vowel Stealers				
Assessment	Goal/Number of Items	Initial Test Date:	Retest Date:	Retest Date:	Retest Date:	Goal/Number of Items	Initial Test Date:	Retest Date:	Retest Date:	Retest Date:	Goal/Number of Items	Initial Test Date:	Retest Date:	Retest Date:	Retest Date:	Goal/Number of Items	Initial Test Date:	Retest Date:	Retest Date:	Retest Date:	Goal/Number of Items	Initial Test Date:	Retest Date:	Retest Date:	Retest Date:
Word Reading Accuracy	10/12					10/12					10/12					10/12					10/12				
Reading Tricky Words	12/16					12/16																			
Word Reading Fluency	10 wcpm					10 wcpm																			
Spelling Decodable Words	6/8					6/8					6/8					6/8					6/8				
Spelling Tricky Words	12/16					12/16															12/16				
Sentence Dictation	6/8					6/8																			

wcpm: words correct per minute

Section 3 Assessment Student Page

1. Word Reading Accuracy

hat	chip	lock	run
mop	pan	shell	thin
bug	dot	wig	neck

No. Correct _____/12 (Goal 10)

2: Reading Tricky Words

is	on	me	see
this	to	in	I
the	no	you	for
she	now	he	was

No. Correct _____/16 (Goal 12)

Section 3 Assessment Student Page

3: Word Reading Fluency

top	pig	can	rock	4
lip	nap	in	not	8
that	neck	sun	get	12
lock	cut	hot	than	16
shut	dot	run	hops	20
bug	van	dip	hug	24
wet	dig	tap	check	28
sat	hop	ship	well	32
nut	rug	sock	rat	36
chin	net	peck	thin	40

60 seconds _____ words correct (Goal: 10)

Section 4
Consonant Blends

Lessons 138-148

Consonant Blends

The eleven lessons in this Consonant Blends section help you teach children to read and spell words with initial consonant blends. There are three types of initial blends. They are taught in three units as shown:

Unit 6: Lessons 138-141 Blends with **S** (**sc, sk, sl, sm, sn, sp, st**, and **sw**)

Unit 7: Lessons 142-144 Blends with **L** (**bl, cl, fl, gl**, and **pl**)

Unit 8: Lessons 145-148 Blends with **R** (**br, cr, dr, fr, gr, pr**, and **tr**)

Children are taught blends with the two *Picture Code Cards* for the two letters, (e.g. Sammy Snake and Talking Tess cards for **st**) and are taught to blend the two sounds without stopping in between as they sound out a word (e.g. **step**). This has an advantage over some programs that teach these blends as 20 new sounds for children to learn. With Letterland, the emphasis is on children re-using the sounds they already know and simply blending them together.

Learning Outcomes and Assessments

Outcomes	Assessments (See pages 157-160) Use some or all of the options below
• Read words with initial blends accurately.	1. Word Reading Accuracy
• Recognize high-frequency words accurately,	2. Reading Tricky Words
• Read CCVC words at a rate of at least 10 words correct per minute (wcpm).	3. Word Reading Fluency
• Spell CCVC words correctly.	4. Spelling Decodable Words
• Spell 18 high-frequency words correctly.	5. Spelling Tricky Words
• Write simple sentences with a capital letter for the first word and a period at the end.	6. Sentence Dictation

Tricky Words

• Children are taught to read and spell four additional Tricky Words in this Section:

we   **like**   **my**   **do**

Previous Tricky Words

• In Section 3, children were taught to read and spell the following 18 tricky words:

is	**on**	**me**	**see**	**this**	**to**	**in**	**I**	**yes**
the	**no**	**you**	**for**	**she**	**now**	**he**	**was**	**and**

Learning About Blends

This section continues using many of the fun interactive features in Section 3. It also includes a number of new ways to learn and practice blends:

- For each of the 20 blends listed above there is a song on the *Blends and Digraphs* CD that tells a story about the characters, and features words with the initial blend. These songs make great shared readings, (print copies from the *TG CD 2*) and a number of them can be dramatized, following suggestions in the lessons. In addition, some of the songs can be put on sentence strips for practice in sequencing.

Firefighter Fred and **Lucy Lamp Light**

When flickering flames flare up in a fire and the wind fans the flames higher and higher, Lucy shouts, "Don't let it spread. The man we need is Firefighter Fred!"

Fred flings on his coat and flies down the street, straight to the fire with wings on his feet. He turns on his hose and quickly aims, floods the fire and flattens the flames.

The Blends and Digraph Song lyrics are available on the *TG CD 2*.

- You and your children will enjoy the oral, interactive stories for introducing each set of blends. For example, with the **r**-blends, you will tell a version of the Three Billy Goats with Red Robot playing the troll who's stealing all the first sounds of **r**-blends, so that the Billy Goats can't even say their last name **_ruff**. When they try to go over the **_ridge** to get to the **_reen _rass** the sound of their footsteps is **_rip, _rap, _rip, _rap**. Children help fill in the sounds when cued with the relevant *Picture Code Cards*.

- You will also teach about blends using your *Picture Code Cards* on the pocket chart, for example, when you show them how Sammy Snake likes to **ssss**neak up on words and change them into other words. You will build the word **lip** with the children hissing, **"sssssss,"** as you **sssss**lide Sammy into place to make **slip**.

- In Live Reading and Spelling you will use special variations of these familiar activities to emphasize the blends. With **l** blends, for example, the child with Lucy Lamp Light's *PCC* shines a flashlight on the other Letterlanders needed to form the word.

- You will also continue many of the activities from Section 3, including Word Sorting and Sentence Building, using the new words containing consonant blends. And you will continue to help children add to their store of high-frequency Tricky Words.

Unit 6

Introducing Blends with S

✔ Materials
- *PCCs:* Review list plus **ck, ll, ng**

✔ Small group/independent
- Make words for picture-coding, one per page, from the *Decodable Word Bank* below
- *Consonant Blend Cards:* **sc, sl, sn, sm, sp, st, sw**, *TG CD 2*

Decodable Word Bank

scat	spell	still
skin	spill	stop
slam	spin	stuck
sled	spot	stuff
smack	stack	swim
smell	step	swing
snack	stick	
snap	stiff	

"ssslip"

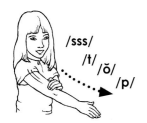

/sss/
/t/ /ŏ/
/p/

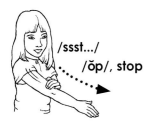

/ssst.../
/ŏp/, stop

Review

● **PCCs ă, c, d, ě, ĭ, k, l, n, ŏ, p, s, t, ŭ, w** Use the 'Quick Dash'.

Introducing blends with S

● Let's play a word game while I tell you a story. In some of the words, I will leave out the first sound. It will always be Sammy Snake's sound. You add his sound to the beginning of the word to work out what the word is. Let's try a few words before we start the story. Listen, Sammy is a long _**nake**. Children say, "**sssnake**." Our bodies are covered with _**kin**... "**ssskin**." (In the story below, you may need to complete the sentence before having children say the word with the missing initial **s**.)

● One day, Golden Granny offered to take Golden Girl and Noisy Nick to the park to play. That put a _**mile** on their faces. They were so happy that they _**kipped** all the way to the park. At the park, they decided to get on the _**wings**. Golden Girl said "I feel like my feet can touch the _**ky**." Next they decided to go down the _**lide**. After taking many turns _**liding**, they went to sit down with Golden Granny and have a _**nack**. Then Golden Granny said, "Are you ready to go home?" "No," said Golden Girl and Noisy Nick, "we want to _**tay** all day." "Okay," said Golden Granny, "What do you want to do next?" Noisy Nick said, "Let's put on our _**kates** and go _**kating**." At the end of the afternoon, they all went home so tired that they had to lie down and take a _**nooze**.

On the pocket chart
● Tell the children, Sammy Snake likes to play word games. One of his favorites is to **sss**lip up to the **sss**tart of words and change their meaning.

● Make the word **lip** with plain *PCCs* in the middle of your pocket chart and have children sound it out. Place the picture side of Sammy Snake's *PCC* to the far left of the word. Have children make Sammy's sound /**sssss**/ as you slide him toward the start of **lip**. Then have them say **ssslip** without stopping between /**sss**/ and **lip**. Try it a few times, if needed, until they can do it. Did Sammy Snake change the meaning? Yes! We had **lip** and now we have the word **slip**. Say the word **slip** and use it in a brief phrase or sentence. Do the same with the other words below.

　　PCCs: ă, ĭ, l, n, ŏ, p, s, t, w, ck, ng
　　Words: s-lip, s-nap, s-pot, s-tack, s-wing

Chalkboard reading
　　Words: stop, swim, scat, skip

● Write **stop** on the chalkboard. Show children how to sound out this word using the Rollercoaster Trick. Have them touch each of four points along their left arms with their right arm, saying the four sounds in the word. Show them how to blend the first two sounds "**sssst**" and then the last two "**ŏŏŏp**." Then blend all together while the right hand rollercoasters down the left arm "**sssstŏŏŏp, stop**." Do the same with the other words.

Small group/independent activities

- **Picture-coding** (**Ind**) Provide children with the large words you have prepared for them to picture-code the whole word.

- **Pocket chart/table reading** (**SG**) Make the words for children to rollercoaster as in the whole group lesson above. Let individuals be the "Leader" by blending a word first and then let the group blend the same word. This allows you to see what each child can do and to help as needed.

  PCCs: ă, ĕ, d, ĭ, k, l, n, p, s, t, ŭ, ck, ll

  Words: spin, skip, spell, snack, stuck, sled

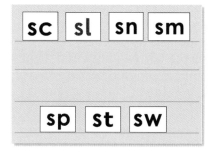

- **Match spoken words to Blend Cards** (**SG**) Display the *Consonant Blend Cards* (*TG CD* 2). Say the first word for the children to repeat. Guide them in rubber-band stretching the word to listen for the first two sounds. Have someone point to the *Blend Card* that begins the word.

  S-Blend Cards: sc, sl, sn, sm, sp, st, sw

  Words: smoke, slow, snake, sweep, spider, scary, stove

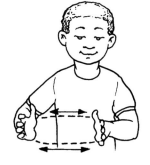

Unit 6: Lesson 139

Read Words with S-blends

Preparation and materials

- *PCCs:* Review list plus **ff, ll**
- *Consonant Blend Cards:* **sc, sl, sn, sm, sp, st, sw** *TG CD* 2
- Unit 6 *Word Cards:* **scat, skin, skip, slip, sled, smell, smog, snack, snap, spill, spin, spot, stuff, stuck, swim, swell, swing**
- *Blends/Digraphs Songs* CD, #23, also available on *TG CD* 2 Project lyrics, or copy on a chart
- A cracker or children's snap blocks for the song "snack"

Small group/independent

- Make words for picture-coding from the *Decodable Word Bank*
- *Letterland Word Builders*, or other letter sets
- Additional *Word Cards:* **We, like, to, and, ⸴ , ▪** *TG CD* 2

Review

- **PCCs ă, c, ĕ, ĭ, k, l, m, n, ŏ, p, s, t, ŭ, w** Use the 'Guess Who?' activity.

Word Reading and sorting

- **Live Reading** Line up the children with *PCCs* to form the words without Sammy Snake. For each word have Sammy slither up to the start of the word hissing his /**sssss**/ sound. Then have children blend the word with their arm rollercoasters, combining the first two sounds, then the last two, and finally blending the whole word, as on page 140.

  PCCs: ă, c, ĕ, ĭ, k, l, m, n, ŏ, p, s, t, ŭ, w, ff, ll

  Words: slam, stuff, spot, scat, skin, smell, swell

- **Word Sort** Place the *Blend Cards* on your pocket chart as shown above. Show the first *Word Card* and have children blend it. Have the class decide which *Blend Card* it should be placed under. Place the card and read the word again. Show the next word and have one child read it. Have the child place it on the pocket chart and then let that child point to all the words placed so far as the class rereads them. Do the same with each card. After accumulating quite a few cards you may have children read just the words that go with the *Blend Cards* in the top row, or just those at the bottom.

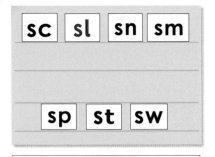

Sammy Snake and Noisy Nick Song

- **Listen** to the *Sammy Snake and Noisy Nick Song*. Then read it with the children a few times, pointing to words on the chart you have prepared. Have some children picture-code or highlight the **sn** at the start of words. Discuss words such as **snatch** and **snarled** that some children may not be familiar with.

- **Plan and play** Talk together about how two children could act out this "story." Reread the first two sentences with them and talk about what the children portraying the two characters would do. Have two children try acting out just the first two sentences. Then do the same with the last three lines. You could use a cracker as the snack, or some children's blocks that snap together and unsnap. Then have the class read the first two sentences followed by two children acting out that part. Next everyone reads the last two lines and then the two children act out this part. Let different pairs of children become the characters with the class continuing to reread several times. Have a different child point to the words for the class each time.

Small group/independent activities

- **Reading with letter sets** Call out the sounds for the first word. Children build the word with their own letters and sound it out. Tell them which sounds to change for the next word. For some words, call on individuals to read the new word, and then the group. For other words, ask for a group response first.

  Letters: a, c, f, f, k, n, p, s, t, u

  Words: snap, snack, stack, stuck, stuff

- **Sort Word Cards** This time lay out the five short vowel *BPCCs* as shown. Have children take turns sorting the Unit 6 *Word Cards* under the vowels. Each time, the child who places the word also points to all the words under that vowel for all to read.

- **Sentence Building** Say the sentence below and have the children repeat it twice. Then have them take turns selecting the words and placing them in order in the sentence. Each time after a child places a word, the child points to each word in the sentence thus far for all to read.

  Sentence: We like to skip, spin and swing.

Spell Words with S-blends

Preparation and materials

- *PCCs:* Review list plus **k, l, m, p, t**
- *Consonant Blend Cards:* **sc, sl, sk, sn, sm, sp, st, sw**, *TG CD 2*
- *Unit 6 Word Cards:* **slip, scat, skip, skin, sled, smell, smog, snap, snack, spill, spot, stuck, stuff, swim, swing, mud**, *TG CD 2*
- *Tricky Word Cards:* **do, not, I, like, to, We, get, in the, my, . ,** *TG CD 2*

Small group/independent

- *Letterland Word Builders*, or other individual letter sets
- Copies of 'Lesson 140 Sentence Practice,' *TG CD 2*

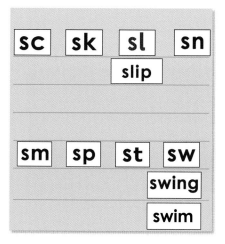

Review

- PCCs **ă, ĕ, g, ĭ, n, ŏ, s, ŭ, w, ck, ll, ng** Use the 'Guess Who?' activity.

Spelling and sorting

- **Live Spelling** Distribute the *PCCs.* Call out the words as usual for children to repeat, stretch, and choose the Letterlanders to build the words. After one or two words let a different child be Sammy Snake.

    PCCs: **ă, ĕ, g, ĭ, k, l, m, n, ŏ, p, s, t, ŭ, w, ck, ll, ng**

    Words: **smog, still, spot, snug, slip, stack, skull, swing**

- **Word Sorting by Sound** Place the *Blend Cards* on your pocket chart as shown. Call out the first word, but do not show it to the children (see list in the green box). Have them rubber-band stretch the word, listening especially for the first two sounds. Decide with the class where the first word belongs. Then call out the other *Word Cards* without showing them and have individual children stretch the word, and place it under the *Blend Card.* Each time a card is placed, have the child point to the words placed so far for all to reread. After a number of words, you could just have the child choose three to five words to point to for the class to read.

Sentence Building

- **Tricky Word Practice** On the board write **we** and **like**. Use the word **we** in a sentence. Then talk about the sounds in **we** with the children, pointing out that Mr. E is saying his name at the end of this word, just like in **he** and **she**. Picture-code Mr. E as a quick stick figure. Have them air-write **we** while saying the letter names, and repeat it three times. Then erase the word and have them write it on their paper, or white board three times, each time saying the letter names and repeating the word.

- Practice **'like.'** Use the word in a sentence. Talk about Mr. I saying his name and the silent **e**. Picture-code Mr. I and rewrite the **e** as a dotted line to show it is silent. Have children practice air-writing and writing the word on paper as with **we** above. Add **like** to your Word Wall.

- Build the first sentence below and have children read it. Change *Word Cards* to make the second sentence. Have children read it. Then build sentences with the other phrases below, and let the class decide if they want the first part of the sentence to be **"like"** or **"do not like."**

    We like to swim.
    We do not like to spill stuff.
    We like to skip.
    I like to skip my snack.
    We like to smell smog.
    We like to sled.
    I like to get stuck in the mud.
    I like to smell my snack.

Word Wall

> like

Small group/independent activities

- **Spelling with letter sets** Call out the words for children to repeat and then sound out using the rubber-band stretch. Children build the words and then spell them aloud (with eyes open or shut).

  Letters: ă, c, d, ĕ, g, ĭ, k, l, k, m, n, ŏ, p, s, t, ŭ, w

  Words: slug, swell, snip, snack, smell, stop, skid

- **Concentration Game** Place all the *Word Cards* with **s**-blends face down. Children take turns turning over and reading two cards. If they begin with the same **s**-blend, the child picks them up. If not, the child turns them back over.

- **Lesson 140 Sentence Practice** Display the *Word Cards* with **s**-blend words and guide children in choosing the words to complete the sentences. They do not have to be limited to the words on the cards, but encourage them to use as least one **s**-blend word in each sentence.

> **Lesson 140 Sentence Practice**
>
> I like to _____
>
> _____
>
> I do not like to _____
>
> _____
>
> S Sammy Snake likes to
>
> _____

Unit 6: Lesson 141

Review S-blends

Preparation and materials
- *Rime Cards*: See Review list
- *Blends/Digraphs Songs* CD, #20, lyrics available on *TG CD* 2
- Project or copy lyrics on a chart
- *Consonant Blend Cards*: **sc, sl, sn, sm, sp, st, sw**, *TG CD* 2
- Copies of 'Lesson 141 Written Word Sort,' *TG CD* 2
- *Word Wall Words*: **my, do**
- Unit 6 *Word Cards*: **slip, scat, skip, skin, sled, smell, smog, snap, snack, spill, spot, stuck, stuff, swim, swing, mud**, *TG CD* 2
- *Tricky Word Cards*: **I like, to, We, get, not, do, in the, my,** ▪ *TG CD* 2

Small group/independent
- Additional *Word Cards*: **was, now, stiff, swell**
- Write the lyrics to the *Sammy Snake and Peter Puppy Song* on sentence strips, one line per strip

Review

- **Rime Cards at, ap, in, ip, ot, op, ell** Use the 'Quick Dash'.

Sammy Snake and Peter Puppy Song

- **Sammy Snake and Peter Puppy** Listen to the *Sammy Snake and Peter Puppy Song*. Then read it with the children a few times, pointing to words on the chart you have prepared. Have some children picture-code or highlight the **sp** at the start of words. Discuss words such as **suspended, spanned,** and **unsuspecting**, that some children may not be familiar with.

- **Plan and play** Discuss a plan for dramatizing the song one stanza at a time. Ask the children to read or sing a stanza, and then act out the scene. **Suggestion:** Act out, The spider can "spin a special spiral web", by drawing a spiral on the board.

Live Reading with blends and rimes

- **Sammy Snake words** Distribute the *Blend Cards* and the *Rime Cards*, one per child. Display Sammy Snake's *PCC*. We are going to do some live reading with these *Blend Cards* and *Rime Cards* and each word we make will tell us something about Sammy Snake. Call children to come forward to build a word by saying the letter names on their cards. For example, for the first word say, We need **s-p** (letter names) and **o-t**. Have the children face the class with their cards as in live spelling. Have the class sound out the onset /**sssssp**/, and then the rime

/ŏt/, and finally the whole word **spot**. Then share the sentence below that uses the word to tell something about Sammy Snake. After a few words, if you like, you or the children may make up your own sentences rather than use those below.

spot Sammy Snake has a favorite spot to take a snooze at the end of some words.

skin Sammy Snake has scaly yellow and green skin.

slip Sammy Snake is so slender he can slip through small spaces.

smell Sammy Snake likes to smell steamy soup.

snug In winter, Sammy likes a snug, warm bed for sleeping.

stop Sammy Snake will stop at the supermarket for some salad for his supper.

swell Sammy Snake swells up to a capital S when he starts his name or someone else's name.

Decodable and Tricky Words

sl	sw	sk	sn

st	sm	sc	sp

Lesson 141 Written Word Sort

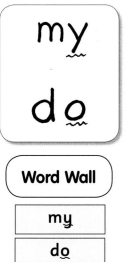

my

do

Word Wall

my

do

- **Written Word Sort** Project a copy of the 'Lesson 141 Written Word Sort' page, or draw similar boxes on the screen and distribute copies. Call out the first word. Children repeat it and then rubber-band stretch the word. Tell children to look at the top row of boxes to find the beginning blend. Each child points to the box under the first two letters in the word. Once children have chosen a box, point to the correct box on your projected page. Have children rubber-band stretch the word again, and write it in the box. After they have written the word, write it on your copy for them to check. After you finish the top row, read the words left to right with the class, and then have them read them to a partner. Continue with the same steps for the bottom row.

  Words for top row: swim, skip, slam, snack

  Words for bottom row: spell, smash, stop, scat

- **Tricky Word Practice** Write **'my'** on the board Use **my** in a sentence and talk about the **y** that sounds like Mr. I. Put a wavy line under **y** and tell children they will soon learn why Yo-yo Man sometimes says Mr I's name for him. Practice air-writing and saying **"em, why"** three times, repeating the word after each spelling. Children do the same while writing the word on paper three times. Add **my** to your Word Wall.

- Practice the word **'do.'** Write **do** on the board and discuss its sounds. Make a wavy line under the **o.** Have children practice air-writing and writing on paper, or white board, three times each as usual. Add **do** to your Word Wall.

Small group/independent activities

- Display the *Word Cards* from the sentence below in a random arrangement. Say the sentence and have children repeat it twice. Then they take turns placing the *Words Cards*. Read the whole sentence again, pointing to the cards. Tell the children they will be writing the sentence in a moment. Turn the cards to their blank side and have children "read the invisible sentence" as they take turns pointing to the blank side of the *Word Cards*. Then have children write the sentence on their papers. When each one finishes, have the child read their sentence to you, and guide corrections. Finally, turn the cards to the word side for children to check their papers.

  Sentence: We do not like to spill stuff.

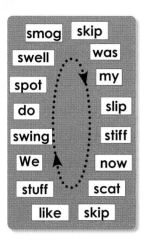

smog · skip · swell · was · spot · my · do · slip · swing · stiff · We · now · stuff · scat · like · skip

- **Word Race** Lay out a number of *Word Cards* with **s**-blends and *Tricky Word Cards* in a square or oval "race track" on a mat. Point to words in sequence around the track as children read them. Repeat a second and third time, going a little faster each time.

  Variations: 1. Time the group on each round trying to reduce the time.
  2. Let individuals point and read alone, or with a partner.

- **Song lyric sequencing** Place the five sentence strips, each one with one line from the *Sammy Snake and Noisy Nick Song* lyrics, on the table or pocket chart in a mixed-up sequence. Read each sentence *to* the children and then *with* the children. Guide children in putting the sentences in the correct order. Read the lyrics together, and then sing the song with the CD.

Sammy Snake and Noisy Nick

Sammy Snake sat down with a snack one day.

Noisy Nick sneaked up to snatch it away.

"Don't snatch," snarled Sammy.

"There's enough for you,"

and kindly snapped the snack in two.

Unit 7

Unit 7: Lesson 142

Introducing Blends with L

✔ Preparation and materials
- *PCCs:* Review list plus **d, p** (Patsy Puppy), **t, ch**

✔ Small group/independent
- Make words for picture-coding, one per page, from the *Decodable Word Bank* below
- *Letterland Word Builders*, or other individual letter sets
- Unit 7 *Word Cards:* **flag, class, blocks, plum, clock, cliff, glass**, *TG CD 2*
- *Tricky Word Cards:* **Do, you, see, a, in, the,** ⬚?⬚
- Make a set of cards with **yes** on one and **no** on the other for each child

Decodable Word Bank

black	cliff	flip
blocks	clock	glad
clap	club	plan
glass	flag	plug
class	flat	plus

Review

- **PCCs ă, b, c, ě, f, g, ĭ, l, ŏ, p** Use the 'Guess Who' game.

Introducing blends with L

- **PCCs** for use with the following story: **b, c, f, g, p**

- Let's play a word game while I tell you a story. In some of the words, I will leave out the first sound. I will hold up the Picture Code Card for the first sound and you say the word correctly. For example, My dog has **_leas** (Hold up the **f** *PCC*.) **"Fleas."** Here's another one, I flew in a **_lane** (Hold up the **p** *PCC*.) **"Plane."** All the words will have Lucy Lamp Light's **l** sound as the second sound in the word because we are learning about how she blends with some of our other Letterland friends, at the beginning of lots of words.

- Lucy Lamp Light wanted to know the time so she looked at the **_lock** (**c**). She was going to work in her garden, and she didn't want to get her hands dirty so she looked for her **_loves** (**g**). She opened a door to look in her **_loset** (**c**). There they were. She went outside. She hoped it would not rain so she looked at the sky to check for **_louds** (**c**). She didn't see any, but she could feel the wind **_low** (**b**). Just then she saw a butterfly **_lying** (**f**) by. It made her feel **_lad** (**g**). She had some things that she wanted to **_lant** (**p**). They were pretty **_lowers** (**f**). Some were red, and some were **_lue** (**b**). She got busy and **_lanted** (**p**) them all. Just as she finished it began to rain. Now that her flowers were in the ground Lucy Lamp Light was happy to have the rain. She listened to the drops go **_lop, _lop** (**p**). She thought the sound was very **_leasant** (**p**).

Live Reading

- Distribute the *PCCs*. Have the five children with **b, c, f, g,** and **p** stand to the left of the class. Let one child hold Lucy Lamp Light's *PCC* and stand at the front of the class. Have the children with other *PCCs* stay in their seats. You will hold the flashlight. You will probably want to dim the room lights a bit.

    PCCs: ă, b, c, d, f, g, l, ŏ, p, p, t, ck

    Words: flat, clock, glad, plop, black

- Explain that the group on the left is the group of Letterlanders that blend with Lucy at the beginning of words. They will line up before Lucy Lamp Light in the word. The children with cards who are sitting down will line up after Lucy. Choose the children to build the words by shining the flashlight on them. After the children are lined up in a word, you might want to use your light to shine on each letter as the children rollercoaster blend. Have them blend the first two sounds and then the rest of the word, and finally put it all together as you sweep the light across the word.

Small group/independent activities

- **Picture-coding (Ind)** Print some of the words in the *Decodable Word Bank* on page 146, one word per page for children to picture-code.

- **Reading with letter sets (SG)** Call out the sounds for the first word. Children build the word with their own letters and sound it out. Tell them which sounds to change for the next word. For some words, call on individuals to read the new word and then the group. For other words, ask for a group response first.

    PCCs: a, b, c, f, g, i, k, l, o, p, s, s, t, u

    Words: flip, plug, plugs, club, glass, block, blocks

- **Sentence Building** Give each child a **yes** card and a **no** card. Make the sentences below with the *Word Cards*. Have a child read the sentence and all respond by holding up **yes** or **no**.

    Do you see a flag in the class?

    Do you see blocks in the class?

    Do you see a plum in the class?

    Do you see a clock in the class?

    Do you see a cliff in the class?

    Do you see a glass in the class?

Read and Spell with L-blends

Preparation and materials

- *PCCs:* Review list plus **d, p** (Patsy Puppy), **ch**
- *Consonant Blend Cards:* **bl, cl, fl, gl, pl,** *TG CD 2*
- Unit 7 *Word Cards:* **black, blocks, clock, cliff, club, flag, flip, glad, glass, plum, plop,** *TG CD 2*
- *Blends/Digraphs Songs* CD, #7
- Project the lyrics on a chart or sentence strips, *TG CD 2*

Small group/independent

- *Letterland Word Builders* or other letter sets
- Copies of 'Lesson 143 Sentence Practice,' *TG CD 2*

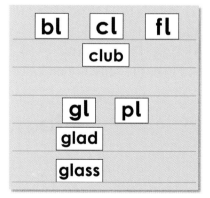

Review

- PCCs **ă, b, c, ĕ, f, g, ĭ, l, ŏ, p,** Use the 'Quick Dash'.

Live Spelling and Word Cards

- **Live Spelling** Distribute the *PCCs*. Have the children with **b, c, f, g,** and **p** stand to the left of the class. Let one child hold Lucy Lamp Light's *PCC*. Lucy stands at the front of the class. The children with other *PCCs* stay in their seat. This time Lucy Lamp Light will hold the flashlight. You will probably want to dim the room lights if possible.

  PCCs: **ă, b, c, d, f, g, ĭ, l, ŏ, p, p, ck**

  Words: **flag, plop, glad, click, black**

- Say the first word. Children repeat and rubber-band stretch the word. Lucy Lamp Light then shines her flashlight on the Letterlander that comes first in the word. Then the children with *PCCs* who are seated hold up their *PCCs* so that Lucy can shine her light on the letters that come after her in the word. After children are lined up, have them blend the first two sounds, then the last two, and finally blend the whole word. Let a different child be Lucy for each word.

- **Word Sort** Place the *L-Blend Cards* on your pocket chart as shown. Show the first *Word Card* (see list in green box) and have children blend it. Have the class decide which *Blend Card* it should be placed under. Place the card and read the word again. Show the next word and have one child read it. Have the child place it on the pocket chart and then let that child point to all the words placed so far as the class rereads them. Do the same with about half of the words.

- Next, read the rest of the words without showing them to the children. Say a word and then guide the children in rubber-band stretching the word. Then tell them to use their eyes to point to the correct blend. (This keeps everyone thinking.) Then call on one child to place the word, and point to other words for the class to read together.

Firefighter Fred and Lucy Lamp Light Song

- **Play the Song** Ask the children to listen to the words, and be ready to tell what happens in the song. Let them listen a few times. Then ask for volunteers to help retell the story. Mention that flashlight begins with the same sounds as many of the words in the song. Hand the **fl**ashlight to a child to begin recounting the story. Ask the other children to listen, and when they get the flashlight, to tell something that no one else has told yet. Pass the flashlight to various children for their comments.

- Read the lyrics on the chart you have made, one sentence at a time, as you point to the words. Then have children echo-read the sentence with you a couple times. Have children highlight or picture-code the **fl** in the words. Play the song again for children to sing along as you point to the words. (You will come back to this song in the next lesson.)

flop

blocks

Small group/independent activities

- **Spelling with letter sets** Call out the words for children to repeat and then sound out with fingers or rubber-band stretch. Children build the words and then spell them aloud (with eyes open or shut).

  Letters: a, b, c, f, f, g, i, k, l, m, o, p, s, s, u

  Words: class, flop, blocks, glass, plums, cliff

- **Sort Word Cards** This time lay out the four short vowel *BPCCs* (or *PCCs*) as shown at the left. Have children take turns sorting a *Word Card* (see list in green box) under the vowels. Each time a child places a word they should point to all the words under that vowel for all to read.

- **Lesson 143 Sentence Practice** Project a copy of the page or write the sentences on the board with blanks to guide the children in completing the worksheet. Children complete each question and then write **yes** or **no** in the blank. Read the sentences together one at a time, and have children fill in the blanks. Then fill in your sentence for them to compare. When finished, each child reads their paper to another child.

Unit 7: Lesson 144

Review L-blends

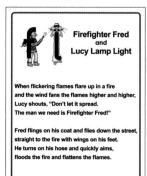

Review

- PCCs **ă, b, c, ĕ, f, g, ĭ, l, ŏ, p, ŭ** Use the 'Guess Who?' game.

Songs and games

- **Firefighter Fred and Lucy Lamp Light Song** (Track 7) As you point to the lyrics on your chart, choral-read them together. Then play and sing the song again.

- **Plan and play** Talk with the children about how to dramatize each stanza. You will want one child to be Lucy Lamp Light, and another to be Firefighter Fred. Some children could be the flames, starting low down, waving their hands above their heads. Other children could be the wind rushing around the flames. Then, as the flames get "higher and higher," the flame children could rise up and wave their arms high up. Other children could be water from the fire hose, pretending to drip water from their fingers and causing the flames to die down. Ask questions to elicit more ideas. How does Lucy react when she first sees the flame? How does she contact Firefighter Fred? What would Fred need to put on besides his coat? Does he put on wings? After the fire is out, what would Lucy and Fred say? What would have happened if Lucy and Fred had not acted so quickly?

- Go over the first stanza together, and then act it out. Do the same with the second stanza. Repeat with different children taking the roles.

- **Lucy Lamp Light Blend Words** Distribute the *Blend Cards* and the *Rime Cards*, one per child. Display Lucy Lamp Light's *PCC*. We are going to do some live reading with these *Blend Cards* and *Rime Cards*, and each word we make will tell us something that Lucy Lamp Light shines her light on. Call children to come forward to build a word by saying the letter names on their cards. For example, for the

first word say, We need **b-l** (letter names) and **o-c-k**. Have the children face the class with their cards. Have the class sound out the onset /**bllll**/, and then the rime /**ŏck**/, and then the whole word **block**. Then share the sentence below that uses the word. Of course, you or the children may make up your own sentences rather than use those below.

block	Lucy shines her lamp light for Bouncy Ben to play with his blue building blocks.
clock	Lucy shines so that Clever Cat can clean her clock with the clown face on it.
flock	Lucy shines so that Firefighter Fred can feed his flocks of farm animals at night.
plug	Lucy shines so that Peter Puppy can plug in his video game to play with his pals.

Written Word Sort

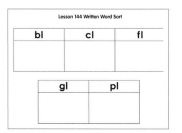

Lesson 144 Written Word Sort

bl	cl	fl

gl	pl

- **Project a copy** of the 'Lesson 144 Written Word Sort' or draw similar boxes on the screen. Call out the first word. Children repeat it and then rubber-band stretch the word. Tell children to look at the boxes to find the Beginning blend. Each child points on their paper to the box under the first two letters in the word. Once children have chosen a box, point to the correct box on your page. Have children rubber-band stretch the word again and write it in the box. After they have written the word, write it on your copy for all to check.

    Words: glass, plan, clip, block, flop

Small group/independent activities

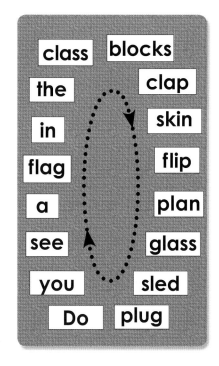

class blocks
the clap
in skin
flag flip
a plan
see glass
you sled
Do plug

- **Word Race** Lay out a number of *Word Cards* with **l**-blends and *Tricky Words* in a square or oval "race track" on a mat. Point to words in sequence around the track as children read them. Repeat a second and third time, going a little faster each time.

    Variations: 1. Time the group on each round trying to reduce the time;
    2. Let individuals take a turn, pointing and reading alone, or with a partner.

- First, say the sentence to the children. They repeat it twice. Then they take turns placing the *Word Cards*. Read the whole sentence again, pointing to the cards. Tell the children they will be writing the sentence in a moment. Turn the cards to their blank side and have children "read the invisible sentence" as they take turns pointing to the blank side of the *Word Cards*.

Do	you	see	a	flag	in	the	class	?

Children write the sentence on their papers. When each one finishes, have the child read their sentence to you, and guide corrections. Finally, turn the cards to the word side for children to check their papers.

							?

- **Song lyric sequencing** Place four sentence strips, each one with one line from the first stanza of the Firefighter Fred and Lucy Lamp Light Song, on the table, or pocket chart in a mixed up sequence. Read each sentence *to* the children and then *with* the children. Guide children in putting the sentences in correct order. Read the lyrics of the first stanza together. Do the same with the second stanza, and then sing the song with the CD.

And the wind fans the flames higher and higher.

The man we need is Firefighter Fred!

When flickering flames flare up in the fire

Lucy shouts, "Don't let it spread!"

Unit 8

Introducing R-blends

✔ Preparation and materials
- *PCCs*: Review list plus **c, p, t**
- *Blends/Digraphs Songs CD*, #14
- Write the lyrics on sentence strips or a chart, or prepare for projection
- Make a reversible red/white mask for Red Robot, or plan another way he can turn from red to white

✔ Small group/independent
- Make words for picture-coding, one per page, from the *Decodable Word Bank* below
- *Letterland Word Builders*, or other individual letter sets
- Write the lyrics from the above song, one line for each sentence strip

Decodable Word Bank

brag	dress	grass
brick	drip	grin
brush	drop	press
crack	fresh	truck
crib	frog	trip
crush	grab	trap

Review

● **PCCs ă, b, d, f, g, ĭ, ŏ, r, ŭ, ck, ng, th** Use the 'Quick Dash' activity.

Introducing R-blends

● **PCCs** Display for use with the following story: **b, c, d, g, l, p, r, t, th**

● Let's play a word game while I tell you a story. In some of the words, I will leave out the first sound. I will hold up the *Picture Code Card* for the first sound and you say the word correctly. For example: The man built his house with **_rick**s (hold up or point to the **b** *PCC*). **"Bricks."** Here's another one. The baby sleeps in a **_rib** (hold up the **c** *PCC*). **"Crib."** All the words will have Red Robot's **/rrr/** sound as the second sound in the word (display the **r** *PCC*) because we are learning about how he often blends his sound with some of our other Letterland friends when they start words.

● This is the story of Three Billy Goats and Red Robot. You may have heard another story about some Billy Goats and a bad guy who lived under the **_ridge** (Hold up **b**: **"bridge"**). He was a **_roll** (Hold up **t**: **"troll"**), but in this story it is Red Robot who lives under the **_ridge** (**b**: **"bridge"**). Red Robot keeps stealing the first letter in words, and that is causing all the Billy Goats lots of **_rouble** (**t**: **"trouble"**). When the Billy Goats talk about what they like to eat it comes out **_reen _rass** (**g**: **"green grass"**). And when the Billy Goats go across the **_ridge** (**b**: **"bridge"**) the sound that they make is all wrong, it sounds like **_rip, _rap, _rip, _rap** (**t**: **"trip, trap, trip, trap"**).

● As a matter of fact the Billy Goats couldn't even say their last name. It came out as Billy Goats **_ruff** (**g**:**"Gruff"**). They couldn't even say how many Billy Goats there were. They kept saying **_ree** (**th**: **"three"**). One day a solution to the Goats' **_roblem** (**p**:**"problem"**) came in a surprising way. It started to rain.

● Red Robot was **_rilled** (**th**: **"thrilled"**). He begin grabbing up first sounds so that the rain went **_rip, _rop, _rip, _rop** (**d**: **"drip, drop, drip, drop"**). But then it started to rain harder and harder, and Red Robot tried to get all of Dippy Duck's **/d/** sounds, but pretty soon his robber sack was all full and he could not get any more sounds in it.

● So from that day on, Red Robot has stopped stealing sounds at the start of words. (Occasionally he manages to capture Walter Walrus and steal away his sound, but that's another story.) But he still *tries* to steal those Dippy Duck sounds, so you have to listen really closely when you say **drip** and **drop** because he makes it hard to hear the **/d/** sound. And he also still tries to steal the **/t/** sound in words like **trip** and **trap**, so listen very carefully so you won't miss the little **/t/** sound in these words.

Live Reading

- **Distribute the PCCs** Let one child hold Red Robot's *PCC* and wait to the left of the class. Have the children with the other *PCC*s stay in their seats.

    PCCs: ă, b, d, f, g, ĭ, ŏ, p, r, t, ŭ, ck

    Words: tuck/truck, bag/brag, fog/frog, dip/drip, tap/trap

- Sometimes Red Robot likes to play a trick. He runs up to words and squeezes in just after the first letter and changes the meaning of the word! We are going to do some live reading to show how he does this.

- Line children with *PCC*s up to form the word **tuck**. Have the class blend the sounds to read the word. Use it in a brief phrase or sentence. Then have Red Robot rush in from the side and change the word to **truck**. Have the children blend this word. Did Red Robot change the meaning of the word? Give a brief phrase or sentence with **truck**. Do the same with the other pairs of words above. You may want to let a different child be Red Robot for each pair of words.

Firefighter Fred and Red Robot Song

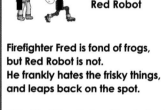

Firefighter Fred
and
Red Robot

Firefighter Fred is fond of frogs,
but Red Robot is not.
He frankly hates the frisky things,
and leaps back on the spot.

"Mind that friendly frog," laughs Fred,
but Red Robot takes fright.
He's so afraid of frogs, you see,
he turns from red to white!

- **Listen** Ask the children to be ready to tell what happens in the song. Play the song (Track 14). If you have a beanbag frog or puppet, children could pass this around as each one tells part of the story. Next point to the words as you read the lyrics from the first stanza *to* the children from your chart or projected image. Then read the lyrics *with* the children a few times. Talk about any unfamiliar words such as **frisky** and **fond**. You might have a few children take turns being the pointer. Also, you might have children highlight or picture-code the **fr** in words. Do the same with the second stanza.

- **Plan and play** Plan with the children how each stanza could be acted out with one child playing Firefighter Fred, another playing Red Robot, and a few playing the part of frisky frogs. How could Red Robot turn from red to white? Perhaps with a reversible paper plate mask. Have them read one stanza, then act it out, etc. You could play it again with different children in the acting roles.

Small group/independent activities

- **Picture-coding (Ind)** Print some of the words in the *Decodable Word Bank* from the previous page, one word per page for children to picture-code.

- **Reading with letter sets (SG)** Call out the sounds for the first word. Children build the word with their own letters and sound it out. Tell them which sounds to change for the next word. For some words, call on individuals to read the new word, and then the group. For other words, ask for a group response first.

    Letters: ă, b, c, d, ĕ, g, ĭ, n, ŏ, p, r, s, s, t

    Words: brag, grab, grass, press, dress, drop, drip, trip, trap, crab, crib, bring

- **Song sequencing** Display the sentence strips you have made of the *Firefighter Fred and Red Robot Song* in random order one stanza at a time. Read each sentence strip *to* the children and then *with* the children. Have the children put the lines in correct sequence. Then reread the whole stanza with them. Do the same with the second stanza. Then read and/or sing the whole song again.

Read and spell with R-blends

Preparation and materials

- *PCCs*: Review list plus **c, f, g, n, p**
- *Consonant Blend Cards*: **br, cr, dr, fr, gr, pr, tr**, *TG CD 2*
- Unit 8 *Word Cards*: **brag, brick, crack, crush, drip, dress, frog, grass, grin, press, truck, trap** *TG CD 2*
- *Blends/Digraphs Songs* CD #13
- Project the lyrics or write on a chart. (The first two lines are repeated three more times, but you may want to just write **'x 3'**)

Small group/independent

- *Letterland Word Builders*, or other individual letter sets
- *Word Cards*: **The, frog, hops, on, the, grass, crab, runs, truck, rolls** *TG CD 2*

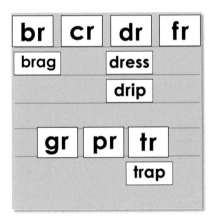

Review

- PCCs **ă, b, d, ĕ, ĭ, ŏ, r, t, ŭ, ng, sh, ss** Use the 'Guess Who?' activity.

Live Spelling and Word Cards

- **Live Spelling** Distribute the *PCCs*. Have the children with **b, c, d, f, g, p,** and **t** stand to the left of the class. Let one child hold the Red Robot *PCC* and stand towards the back of the group. (Let a different child be Red Robot for each word. Other children with *PCCs* stay in their seats.)

  PCCs: **ă, b, c, d, ĕ, f, r, g, ĭ, n, ŏ, p, r, t, ŭ, ng, sh, ss**

  Words: **grin, fresh, trap, crib, dress, bring, press, crush, drop**

- Say the first word. Children repeat and rubber-band stretch the word. Red Robot decides which of the beginning consonants is paired with him. He tags that child, who, with one hand on Red Robot's shoulder, travels with him to the front to begin the word. Then the children decide on the other Letterlanders needed and they take their places in the word. After the children are lined up, have them blend the first two sounds, then the last two and then the whole word.

- **Word Sort** Place the *Blend Cards* on your pocket chart as shown. Show the first *Word Card* (see the list in the Preparation box) and have children blend it. Have the class decide which *Blend Card* it should be placed under. Place the card and read the word again. Show the next word and have one child read it. Have the child place it on the pocket chart and then let that child point to all the words placed so far as the class rereads them. Do the same with about half the words.

- Read the rest of the words without showing them to the children. Say a word and guide the children in rubber-band stretching it. Then tell them to use their eyes to point to the correct blend (this keeps everyone thinking). Next, call on one child to place the word, and to point to other words for the class to read together.

Dippy Duck and Red Robot Song

- **Play the Song** Ask the children to listen to the words, and be ready to tell what happens in the song. Let them listen a few times. Ask the children, **Who likes the rain?** and have them speculate why. Then ask who doesn't like the rain and why. Talk about how real ducks' feathers and their body oils help keep them dry under their feathers like a rain coat. Discuss the word **driving** as it relates to rain. With the children, rubber-band stretch the words **drip** and **drop** to establish that they both start with **d** and **r**. (Children tend to hear a /j/ sound when pronouncing the **dr** blend.)

  - Read the lyrics, one sentence at a time as you point to the words and then have children read the sentence with you a couple times. Have children highlight or picture-code the **dr** in the words. Play the song again for them to sing along as you point to the words.

Small group/independent activities

- **Spelling with letter sets** Call out the words for children to repeat and then rubber-band stretch. Children build the words and then spell them aloud (with eyes open or shut). They should leave the previous word in place each time and decide which letters need to be changed.

  Letters: ă, b, c, d, ĕ, g, ĭ, ŏ, p, r, s, s, t

  Words: **grab, crab, crib, dress, drop, drip, trip, trap**

- **Sort Word Cards** This time lay out the five short vowel *PCC*s as shown at the left. Have children take turns sorting *Word Cards* under the vowels (see the list in the Preparation box). Each time, the child who places the word points to all the words under that vowel, for all to read.

- **Sentence Building** Build the first sentence and have the children read it with you. Change the two *Word Cards* to make the next sentence and let one of the children read it. Then have all the children read it. Do the same with the third sentence. (Tell them the word **rolls**.)

  Words: **The, frog, hops, on, the, grass, crab, runs, truck, rolls**

  Sentences: **The frog hops on the grass.**
  The crab runs on the grass.
  The truck rolls on the grass.

Review R-blends

Preparation and materials
- *R-Blend Cards:* **br, dr, gr, tr**, *TG CD 2*
- *Rime Cards:* **at, in, ip, op**, *TG CD 2*
- *Blends/Digraphs Songs CD #17*
- Project and make copies of 'Lesson 147 Written Word Sort,' *TG CD 2*

Small group/independent
- *Word Cards:* **plan, brick, spin, grass, club, drop, step, crush, Do, like, The, frog on, the, grab, truck, hops, runs, rolls,** • *TG CD 2*
- Writing materials

Review

- **PCCs** ă, ĕ, ĭ, j, ŏ, p, r, t, ŭ, v, x, y, z, ck Use the 'Quick Dash' activity.

Songs and games

- **Talking Tess and Red Robot Song** (Track 17) Read the lyrics to the children. Play the song and have children talk about what they heard in it. Read the lyrics one line at a time *to* the children and then have them echo-read the line with you. Let the children highlight the **tr** blend in words. With the children rubber-band stretch the word **trip** from the story. Help them to hear the /t/ sound and the /rrr/ sound in this word as they will tend to hear a /ch/ sound in this blend. Build this word on the pocket chart and have the children blend it on their arm rollercoasters. Do the same with the words **track** and **trick**.

- **Red Robot Blends** Distribute the *Blend Cards* and the *Rime Cards*, one per child (see Preparation box). Display Red Robot's *PCC*. We are going to do some live reading with these *Blend Cards* and *Rime Cards* and each word we make will tell us something about Red Robot. Call children to come forward to build a word by saying the letter names on their cards. For example, for the first word say, We need **g-r** (letter names) and **a-b**. Have the children face the class with their cards as in Live Spelling. Have the class sound out the onset /**grrr**/ and then the rime /**ăb**/ and then the whole word "**grab**." Then share the sentence below that uses the word.

grab	Red Robot likes to grab things with his **/rrr/** sound.
grin	When Red Robot runs away with things that start with his **/rrr/** sound he has a big **grin** on his face.
grip	Red Robot has a tight **grip** on his robber sack and won't let go.
brat	Red Robot is kind of a **brat**, a selfish, bothersome character.
trip	Do you remember in the song when Talking Tess **trips** Red Robot to keep him from getting away with his loot?
drop	Do you think Red Robot would **drop** his robber sack if he was tripped?

Written Word Sort

- Project a copy of the 'Lesson 147 Written Word Sort' or draw similar boxes on the board. Call out the first word. Children repeat it and then rubber-band stretch the word. Tell children to look at the top row of boxes to find the beginning blend. Each child points on their paper to the box under the first two letters in the word. Once children have chosen a box, point to the correct box on your page. Have children rubber-band stretch the word again and write it in the box. After they have written the word, write it on your copy for all to check. Then do the same with the rest of the words in the top row. Read the words on the top tow together and then have children pair up and read the words to each other. Follow up with the bottom row.

    Top row Words: crib, fresh, drop, brick

    Bottom row Words: grab, truck, press

Lesson 147 Written Word Sort

br	cr	dr	fr

gr	pr	tr

Small group/independent activities

- **Word Race** Lay out a number of *Word Cards* including **r**-blends and review words in a square or oval "race track" on a mat. Point to words in sequence around the track as children read. Repeat a bit faster each time.

    Variations: 1. Time the group on each round trying to reduce the time.
    2. Individuals or pairs take a turn.

- **Sentence Building** Display the *Word Cards* randomly. Build the first sentence below with a blank space (for **hops**). Children read the sentence and choose the word to put in the space. Then let several children point and read. Then change the cards to make the second sentence, etc.

    Sentences: 'The frog ___ on the grass.' (**hops**)

    'The crab ___ on the grass.' (**runs**)

    'The ___ rolls on the grass.' (**rolls**)

- **Sentence Dictation** Rearrange the *Word Cards* into a random order. Say the above sentence to the children. They repeat it twice. Then they take turns placing the *Word Cards*. Read the whole sentence again pointing to the cards. Tell the children they will be writing the sentence in a moment. Turn the cards to their blank side and have children "read the invisible sentence" as they take turns pointing to the blank side of the *Word Cards*. Then have children write the sentence (make it reappear) on their papers. When each one finishes, have each child read their sentence to you and guide corrections. Finally, turn the cards to the word side for children to check their papers.

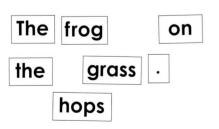

plan brick
Do spin
like grass
The club
frog drop
on step
the crush
grab truck

The frog on
the grass .
hops

Review S, L and R-blends

Review

- PCCs **ă, b, d, ě, ĭ, l, ŏ, p, r, s, ll, ss** Use the 'Quick Dash' activity.

Live Reading and Spelling

- **PCCs for Live Reading and Spelling: ă, b, c, d, ě, f, g, ĭ, l, m, n, ŏ, p, r, s, t, ll, ss**

- **Live Reading** Distribute the *PCCs* to children in their seats. Call them up as needed to form words. Line up the first word. Have children rollercoaster the two sounds before the vowel (onset), then the last two sounds (rime). Then have them rollercoaster the whole word (**/ssst/-/ŏp/, stop**.)

- **Words for Live Reading: spill, slip, snap, trap, press, frog, flag, glad, clap**

- **Live Spelling** Call out words for children to repeat and rubber-band stretch. Children decide which Letterlanders are needed, who needs to sit down, and who needs to replace them. Children then arm blend the word to check their spelling. You may want to have a Blends Race. Write "Blends" on the board, and underneath a quick picture-coding of **l, r,** and **s**. Each time a word is made, children decide which type of blend, and you make a tally mark for that one under the letter. The winner of the race is the one with the most marks at the end.

  Words for Live Spelling: glass, grass, grab, brag, flag, flip, smell, drill, still, step

Preparation and materials

- *PCCs*: Review list plus **c, f, g, m, n, t**
- Project or enlarge the Decodable booklet: 'Clever Cat Gets Stuck' and make copies, *TG CD* 2
- Project Assessment 1, *TG CD* 2

Small group/independent

- Make sentence strips for 'Clever Cat Gets Stuck' Decodable booklet, *TG CD* 2

Clever Cat gets Stuck

A Letterland Take-Home Reader Lesson 148

Clever Cat's car is stuck in the mud.

The wheels just spin.

Clever Cat is glad to see Talking Tess.

Talking Tess has a plan.

Talking Tess brings her tractor.

She drags Clever Cat's car.

Clever Cat has a big grin.

Read the Decodable Booklet: 'Clever Cat Gets Stuck'

- Project or enlarge the booklet or write the title on the board. Provide copies for each child. (There are three words in this booklet that children may need help with (car, wheels, calls). The children might like to underline the tricky parts of these words in their booklets.) Read the title *with* the children and look at the cover. Have them predict how Clever Cat might get stuck. Read pages 2 and 3 with the children. Have them predict how Clever Cat might get her car out of the mud. Read the rest of the pages together.

- Reread several times with different groups of children reading each page.

Small group/independent activities

- **Reread Clever Cat Gets Stuck** with the group. Then children partner read.
- **Sentence Strips** Read sentence strips from pages 2-5 with the children in a random order. Have children arrange them in sequence. Then read the strips from pages 6-8 and do the same. Have children reread the strips.
- **Play a new game called 'Take-Away'** Have children hide their eyes. Remove one sentence strip and then close up the gap where it belongs. Then have children read the sentence that was taken out and try to place it back in the sequence. Have them reread the story to make sure the sentence is in the correct place. Repeat a few times. Leave the sentence strips and a copy of the booklet out for children to use during group or independent time.

Section 4 Assessments

You can assess your children's mastery of the outcomes for this section with the following:

Reading Assessments (given individually):

1. Word Reading Accuracy Children read a list of 12 decodable words.

2. Reading Tricky Words Children read a list of 16 high-frequency words that have been presented and practiced in this section or previously.

3. Word Reading Fluency Children read as many decodable words as possible within 60 seconds.

Spelling Assessments (given to small groups or the whole class)

4. Spelling Decodable Words Children write words to match 8 pictures.

5. Spelling Tricky Words Children write 16 words to dictation.

6. Sentence Dictation Children write a sentence to dictation.

Assessment Pages

Teacher's Guide: Student reads from pages 159-160.

Teacher' Guide CD 2: Section 4 Assessment (copymasters including 'Score Sheet' and 'Spelling Decodable Words')

Assessment Instructions

(1) Word Reading Accuracy (Ind) The child reads the 12 words on page 159. Encourage the child to 'sound them out.' If the child says the word in a segmented fashion (e.g. /s/ /n/ /a/ /p/), you may say, Put it together, or, Blend it. Only count the word as correct if the child is able to say it finally without segmentation (e.g. "**snap**"). After about five seconds on a word, have the child move on to the next word. On the Score Sheet put a line through any words missed, or write the substitution above the word. The goal is at least 10 of 12 words correct.

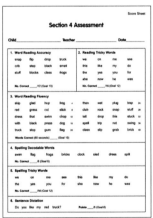

(2) Reading Tricky Words (Ind) Tell children that these are Tricky Words that they have worked on and that the words may have letters that do not 'sound right.' The child reads the 16 words on page 159. After about five seconds on a word, have the child move on to the next word. Record errors on the Score Sheet. The goal is at least 12 of 16 words correct.

(3) Word Reading Fluency (Ind) Instruct the child to read across the page (page 160) and continue reading the words in each row until you say stop. Time the child for 60 seconds. Put a line through missed words on the Score Sheet and a line under the last word. Count words read correctly. The goal is 10 words correct in one minute.

(4) Spelling Decodable Words (SG) Give each child a copy of the page (*TG CD 2*) and project or enlarge a copy to demonstrate. Name the first picture and have children repeat it. Ask the children to rubber-band stretch the word on their own, and spell it in the box. When everyone is ready, do the same with each picture. On the Score Sheet, copy misspellings or put a line through words missed. The goal is at least 6 of 8 words correct.

(5) Spelling Tricky Words (SG) Provide children with pencil and paper. Dictate the 16 words listed on the Score Sheet by saying the word, a sentence, then repeating the word. Have children repeat the word after you. Then they write the word. You may want to divide this assessment into two sessions of about 8 words each. On the Score Sheet copy misspellings or put a line through words missed. The goal is at least 12 words correct of 16.

(6) Sentence Dictation (group administration) Provide the children with pencil and paper. Say the sentence below with rhythm and expression. Have the children repeat the sentence two times and then write it. The child receives one point for each word spelled correctly, one point for correct use of capital and lowercase letters, and one point for a question mark on the end. There are 8 possible points. On the Score Sheet copy misspellings or put a line through words or punctuation missed. Circle letters with capitalization errors. The goal is 6 of 8 points.

Sentence: **Do you like my red truck?**

You may want to enter all your children's scores on the Section 4 Class Assessment Score Sheet (*TG CD 2*).

Children scoring less than the goal numbers on any part of the assessment need additional practice with the items or skills missed. See 'Small Group Intervention,' pages 222-238. You may want to complete a Section 3-7 Individual Assessment Record (*TG CD 2*) for these students, and retest them at intervals until the goals are reached.

Score Sheet

Section 4 Assessment

Child_____ Teacher _____ Date_____

1. Word Reading Accuracy

snap	flip	drop	truck
crib	step	black	smell
stuff	blocks	class	frogs

No. Correct _____/12 (Goal 10)

2. Reading Tricky Words

we	on	me	see
this	like	my	do
the	yes	you	for
she	now	he	was

No. Correct _____/16 (Goal 12)

3. Word Reading Fluency

skip	glad	hop	frog	4	then	wet	plug	trap	24
red	grass	cut	stick	8	club	rock	snap	stuff	28
dress	that	swim	chop	12	tell	drop	this	stuck	32
with	black	press	dog	16	spell	trip	not	swing	36
truck	stop	gum	flag	20	class	slip	grab	brick	40

Words Correct (60 seconds) _____ (Goal 10)

4. Spelling Decodable Words

| swim | flag | frogs | bricks | clock | sled | dress | spill |

No. Correct _____/8 (Goal 6)

5. Spelling Tricky Words

| we | on | me | see | this | like | my | do |
| the | yes | you | for | she | now | he | was |

No. Correct _____/16 (Goal 12)

6. Sentence Dictation

Do you like my red truck?   Points _____/8 (Goal 6)

Section 4: Class Assessment Score Sheet

Section 4 Assessment: Student Page

1. Word Reading Accuracy

snap	flip	drop	truck	
crib	step	black	smell	
stuff	blocks	class	frogs	

No. Correct _____/12 (Goal 10)

2. Reading Tricky Words

we	on	me	see	
this	like	my	do	
the	yes	you	for	
she	now	he	was	

No. Correct _____/16 (Goal 12)

3. Word Reading Fluency

skip	glad	hop	frog	4
red	grass	cut	stick	8
dress	that	swim	chop	12
with	black	press	dog	16
truck	stop	gum	flag	20
then	wet	plug	trap	24
club	rock	snap	stuff	28
tell	drop	this	stuck	32
spell	trip	not	swing	36
class	slip	grab	brick	40

60 seconds _____ words correct (Goal 10)

Section 5
Long Vowels & Silent Magic e

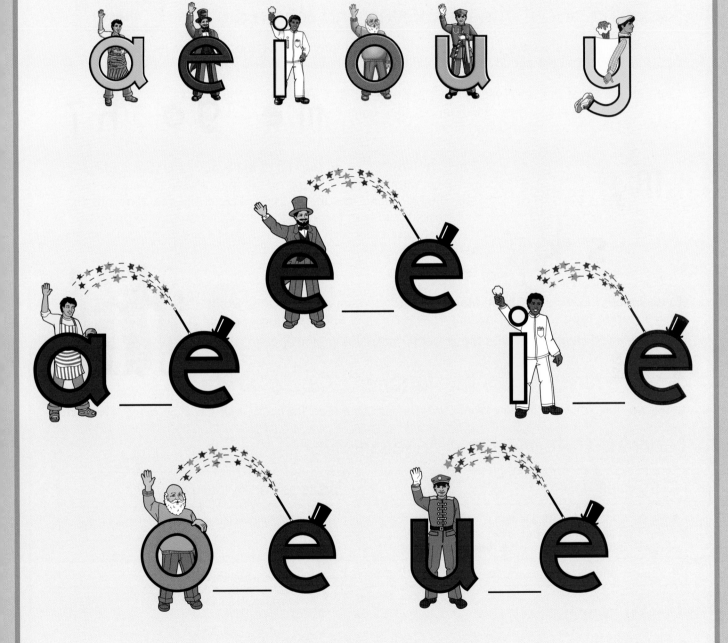

Lessons 149-162

The Vowel Men and Magic e

Section 5 The Vowel Men and Magic **e** with 14 lessons will help you teach your children to read and spell words with long vowels:

Unit 9 Lessons 149-150 The Vowel Men at the end of short words, e.g. **she, go, hi, my**

Unit 10 Lessons 151-154 Magic **e** and Mr. A, **a_e**

Unit 11 Lessons 155-157 Magic **e** and Mr. I, **i_e**

Unit 12 Lessons 158-160 Magic **e** and Mr. O, **o_e**

Unit 13 Lessons 161-162 Magic **e**, Mr. U, Mr. E, **u_e, e_e**, and Review

Learning about the Vowel Men and Magic e

This section continues many of the lively activities from previous sections, but also includes new activities specifically designed to make learning about these long vowel patterns fun and memorable.

Children learn that the Vowel Men like to be on the end of little words like **me** so they can shout out their names without yelling into another Letterlander's ear.

While Mr. I likes to be on the end of **hi** because it is such a friendly word, he normally avoids being on the end of words whenever he can. The Letterland reason: Mr. I gets dizzy at the end of a word and so he asks Yo-yo Man to say /**i**/ for him. Children love to dramatize this story, acting out Mr. I losing his balance and Yo-yo Man coming to the rescue.

To remember the story of **'Silent' Magic e**, children dramatize switching words such as **tap** to **tape** with Live Spelling. They learn that **'Silent' Magic e** is...

"The **e** you cannot hear with the power to make Vowel Men appear."

New Materials from the Teacher's Guide CD

In this section, you will find new *Word Cards* for each Unit (See *Teacher's Guide CD 2: Section 5 Word Cards*).

Learning Outcomes and Assessments

Outcomes	Assessments (See page 184)
● Read short words with a single vowel in the final position (e.g. **she, so, be**). Read words with a long vowel and final silent Magic **e** (**late, hide, tune**).	1.Word Reading Accuracy
● Spell Ce and CVCe words correctly.	2. Spelling Decodable Words

Tricky Words

● Children review earlier words and are taught to read and spell three additional Tricky Words in this Section:

what   **does**   **have**

Unit 9

The Vowel Men at the End

Preparation and materials
- *PCCs:* Review list plus **g, h, m, n, s, t, w, ck, sh**
- *BPCCs:* the Vowel Men Cards **a,e,i o,u**
- *Alphabet Songs* CD, # 29
- Optional: Props or costumes for the five Vowel Men (see Vol. 1, page 246)

✔ Small group/independent
- *Word Cards:* **can, we, We, go, to, the, pool, She, she, with, me, he, He, you, · ?** *TG CD 2*

Decodable Word Bank

he	she	no
me	we	go
		so

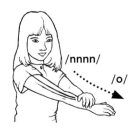

/nnnn/

/o/

Review

- **PCCs ă, ā, ĕ, ē, ĭ, ī, ŏ, ō, ŭ, ū** Use the 'Quick Dash' activity.

The Vowel Men

- **The Vowel Men Song** Distribute the *BPCCs* for the five Vowel Men to five children, and let them use any props or costumes you have for these characters. Have them stand in front of the class, and when each Vowel Man says his name in the song, the child holding the *BPCC* should raise it high in the air. Have the class raise their hands in the air like the Vowel Men, and shout out their names with the song.

- Make the word **'go'** on the pocket chart The Vowel Men like to shout out their names in words, just like in the song. Best of all, they like to be on the end of little words like this one so they can shout out their names in the Reading Direction without yelling in anyone's ear. Let's sound out this word... "/g/ /ō/, go!"

- Now let's change this word a bit so we can see why Mr. O likes to be on the end. Add the picture-side of Talking Tess's *PCC* to the end of **go** (making **got**, but leaving Mr. O's card in place for a moment.) If we left Mr. O in this word, he would be shouting in Talking Tess's ear. She wouldn't even be able to hear her telephone! So, let's put Oscar Orange in this word instead (change Mr. O to Oscar Orange.) Now what word have we **got**? Have the children sound out **got**. Change **got** to **not**. Have children sound out **not**. Now let's take away Oscar and Talking Tess so Mr. O can get another chance to shout out his name at the end. So now what's our new word? Sound it out, "/nnn//ō/, no!"

Live Reading

PCCs: ē, g, h, ī, m, n, ō, s, w, sh

Words: no, so, go, he, she, we, me, hi

- Distribute the *PCCs* and any props or costumes you have for Mr. O, Mr. E, and Mr. I. Arrange the children with **n** and **ō** to make the word **no**. Have Noisy Nick give his sound and have Mr. O raise one hand and pretend to shout his name /ō/ in the reading direction. Ask the children why this is a good word for Mr. O to appear in. **"He can shout his name without hurting anyone's ear."** Have the class rollercoaster this word. Present each word in the same way.

pool

Small group/independent activities

- **Picture-coding** (**Ind**) Provide each child with one of the large words you have prepared for picture-coding from the Decodable Word Bank, one word per page.

- **Pocket chart/table reading** Make the words below and have the children talk about why the Vowel Men like to be on the end of short words.

  PCCs: ĕ, ē, g, h, ī, m, n, ŏ, ō, s, t, w, sh, ck

  Words: **we, wet, bet, be, me, she, he, hi, nod, no, go, sock, so**

- **Sentence Building** Tell the children to pretend that it is a very hot day and they are asking a parent to take them to the pool. Show the word **pool** and elicit from the children that the two **o**'s need a wavy line underneath. Then build the first sentence, and have children read it. Have children rearrange the sentence to answer the question, as shown. Have children reread their answer. Form the next question for them to read and continue with the same steps.

  Word Cards: **Can, can, we, We, go, to, the, pool, She, she, with, me, he, He, you, · ?**

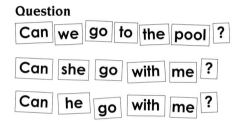

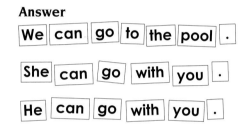

Yellow Yo-yo Man helps out Mr. I

Preparation and materials

- *PCCs:* Review list plus **y** (with Ice Cream)
- Optional Props: a yellow backpack or bag (any color) and an Ice Cream cone (a brown paper cone with a ball of paper for the Ice Cream.)
- Unit 9 *Word Cards:* **hi, try, fly, sky**, TG CD 2
- *Tricky Word Cards:* **we, he, she, I, no, so, my**, TG CD 2

Small group/independent

- *Word Cards:* **Can, can, we, in, the, to, My, my, you, not, But, · , ? , ! , ,**
- Additional *PCCs:* **b, h, p**
- Words for picture-coding

Review

- PCCs ā, d, ē, f, ī, k, l, m, ō, r, s, t, ū, y (with Ice Cream), **sh** Use the 'Guess Who?' activity.

Mr. I gets dizzy so Yo-yo Man helps out

- **Pocket chart reading** Make the word **my** on the pocket chart with the plain letter side of the *PCCs*. Tell children to stretch the word **my** and listen for the two sounds /**mmm**/ and /ī/.

  PCCs: **b, f, ī, l, m, y** (with Ice Cream)

  Words: **my, mi, my, fli, fly**

- Now let's look at our word. Turn **m** to the picture side. Munching Mike is making his usual sound /**mmm**/ but (turn **y** to the picture-side) Yo-yo Man is saying Mr. I's name /ī/ and look! He doesn't have yo-yos in his backpack now. What does he have? **"An Ice Cream cone!"**

- Let me explain what happened. Replace the Yo-yo Man *PCC* with Mr. I. Mr. I has a funny problem. He usually gets dizzy when he is on the end of a word with no letter coming next. Make Mr. I's card wobble in place a bit. He feels so dizzy that he's afraid he will fall down. So Mr. I asks Yo-yo Man to take his place, and say his name for him, just at the *ends* of words. And guess how Mr. I thanks Yo-yo Man? He gives him a great big Ice Cream cone every time Yo-yo Man saves him from getting dizzy by taking his place! Let's put these two sounds on our arms and rollercoaster them together. "/**mmmm**/ /**ī**/, **my**."

- Here's another word where Mr. I gets dizzy. Make **fli** (with Mr. I where the **y** should go). Wobble his card again and ask the children to explain what happens. "**Mr. I get's dizzy on the end of little words, so Yo-yo Man takes his place.**" Replace Mr. I with the Yo-yo Man with Ice Cream. Have children rollercoaster the sounds.

Live Reading

- Distribute the PCCs Give the child with Mr. I's card the Ice Cream cone you have made (see materials box above) and give Yo-yo Man a backpack. Make each word first with Mr. I at the end. Have Mr. I act dizzy and almost fall down, and then have Yo-yo Man come to the rescue. Mr. I thanks him, giving him his Ice Cream cone to put in his backpack. Yo-yo Man takes Mr. I's place and calls out "**I!**" The rest of the class rollercoasters the word. Let different children take the part of Mr. I and Yo-yo Man for each word.

    PCCs: d, f, k, l, m, r, s, t, sh, Mr. I, y (with Ice Cream)

    Words: my, try, shy, dry, fly, sky

- Write the words **hi** and **I** on the board. Luckily for Mr. I, these are two words where he does not get dizzy. Maybe that's because **hi** is such a friendly word, and **I** is such an important word (since everyone needs it to talk about themselves), and he loves standing beside his nice tall capital **I**.

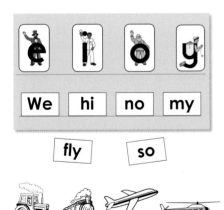

Word Sorting

    PCCs: ē, ī, ō, y (with Ice Cream)

    Word Cards: we, he, she, hi, I, no, so, my, try, fly, sky

- Place the *PCCs* for Mr. E, Mr. I, Mr. O, and Yo-yo Man (with Ice Cream) across the top of the pocket chart as shown. Show the first *Word Card* for the children to read. Let the class decide which Vowel Man (or Yo-yo Man) is in the word. Let a child place the card under that Vowel Man. With the rest of the cards ask children to read the card aloud and 'point with their eyes' to the correct Vowel Man. Then have a child place the *Word Card*. Let the child point to all the words in the column for all to read each time. Conclude the activity by rereading with cards with the *Tractors, Trains, Plains, and Helicopters* activity (Vol. 1, page 204).

Small group/independent activities

- **Picture-coding (Ind)** Print some of the words in the Decodable Word Bank, one word per page, for children to picture-code.

- **Pocket chart/table spelling** Display the *PCCs* and have children build the words with them as usual (Vol. 1, page 239).

    PCCs: ă, b, ē, f, h, ī, l, m, ō, p, r, t, y (with Ice Cream)

    Words: me, my, by, try, trap, fly, sky, hi, so

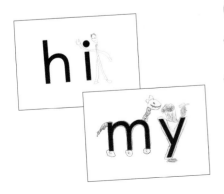

- **Sentence Building** Display the *Word Cards*. Call out each sentence for children to build. (Put the cards for **can** and **not** close together in the second sentence to show they make one word.) Let several individual children point to and read each sentence after it is built.

    Words: **Can, can, we, try, to, fly, in, the, sky, My, my, you, You, not, But,** ⟨ . ⟩, ⟨ ? ⟩, ⟨ ! ⟩, ⟨ , ⟩

    Sentences: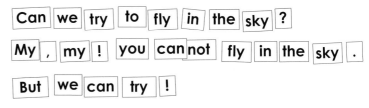

    | Can | we | try | to | fly | in | the | sky | ? |

    | My | , | my | ! | you | can not | fly | in | the | sky | . |

    | But | we | can | try | ! |

Unit 10

Unit 10: Lesson 151

Magic **e** makes Mr. A appear

✔ **Preparation and materials**
- *PCCs*: Review list plus **Magic e, a_e** (Mr. A with Magic **e**)
- *Big PCCs*: **Annie Apple, Mr. A**
- Props: Make, or locate a wand to represent **Silent Magic e**'s sparks (shown below)

✔ **Small group/independent**
- Make words for picture-coding, one per page, from the *Decodable Word Bank* below
- Additional *PCCs*: **g, h, l, r**
- Unit 10 *Word Cards*: **game, chase, drag, gate, flat, brave, wag, plate**

Decodable Word Bank

came	gate	lake	made	tape
game	late	make	trade	shape
name	plate	take		grape
		shake		vase
				chase
				brave

Review

- **PCCs ă, ā, c, d, m, n, p, s, t, y=ī** Use the 'Quick Dash' activity.

Magic **e**

- **Listen first** Display Mr. A's *Big PCC* up high on the board or pocket chart, and Annie Apple's *Big PCC* down low. Everyone stands up. Tell children this game is called Up High, Down Low. If they hear Mr. A's name in a word, they reach both hands high up in the air. If they hear Annie Apple's sound, they squat down low. Say each word and have them repeat it. Tell them to listen for the beginning sound in these words: actor, **a**pe, **a**corn, arrow, **a**pron, accident, **a**ce, **a**im. They can rubber-band stretch these next words to hear the middle sound: c**a**ke, m**a**de, had, s**a**ve, t**a**ke, pack, t**a**pe. Alternatively, have children do the Action Tricks for Mr. A and Annie Apple in response to the words.

- **Pocket chart reading** Make the word **tap** as shown on the following page with only Annie Apple's picture side showing. Hide Mr. A's *PCC* behind Annie Apple's *PCC*. Have the children rollercoaster the word.

    PCCs: **ă, ā, c, n, p, t, Magic e, a_e**

    Words: **tap, tape, can, cane**

- We have been talking about the Vowel Men and about how they are often on the end of little words like **go** and **me**. Now let's look at some other words where we will find the Vowel Men saying their names. It all started because the Vowel Men wanted to appear in more words. "Why not make up a Naming Game?" said Mr E. If I can think of a way to make any Vowel Man magically appear in a word, that could be a lot of fun! After a lot of hard work, he came up with a very special new kind of Magic **e**. He announced it to everyone in Letterland like this. Show the picture side of the Magic **e** *PCC* as you say:

    Introducing the **e** you cannot hear,
    with the power to make Vowel Men appear!

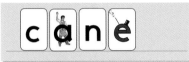

- So let's see how this Magic **e** works. We put it right here on the end of the word **tap**, and it sends its magic sparks over the top of one letter...(Wave your wand in front of the Annie Apple card as you switch the Mr. A card to the front.) ...and makes Mr. A appear! Now, when we rollercoaster this word, we hear Mr. A saying his name. Do we hear this new Magic **e**? No! It doesn't make any sound at all. It's a silent letter. But it does tell us that a Vowel Man has appeared and will be saying his name in this word. Let's put the sounds on our arm and rollercoaster down: "/t/ /ā/ /p/, **tape**." (Show the **a_e** PCC.) On this card you can see the magic sparks flying over one letter to make Mr. A appear. There is a blank here because different letters can go in that space.

- The great thing about this Naming Game is that we can always tell when the Vowel Men are playing it in a word. We just look out for one of Mr. E's Magic **e** at the end. Let's try another word. Make **can** on the pocket chart, with Mr. A behind Annie Apple, and use the Magic **e**, as before, to make Mr. A appear, silently changing the word to **cane**.

- **Live Reading** Let's use the Magic **e** in Live Reading words. Distribute the *PCCs*. Give the wand to the child with Magic **e** and have the child stand to the audience's right of the Live Reading area.

    PCCs: ă, ā c, d, m, n, p, s, t, Magic e

    Words: tap-tape, mad-made, Sam-same, can-cane

- Make **tap** with the Mr. A child hiding behind the Annie Apple child. After children sound out the word, have the Magic **e** child move into position at the end of the word, reach over the child with the **p**, and wave the magic wand over Annie Apple. Mr. A and Annie Apple then change places. Have the class sound out the new word **tape**. Make each pair of words in the same way, with different children playing the key roles of Mr. A, Annie Apple, and Magic **e**.

- **Demonstrate picture-coding** Show children how to picture-code with Magic **e** on a whiteboard as shown, to prepare them for picture-coding on their own.

Small group/independent activities

- **Picture-coding** Give children large copies of words from the Decodable Word Bank to picture code.

- **Pocket chart/table reading** Make the words with an empty space for the vowel (e.g. **l_ke, h_t**) and let children choose Mr. A or Annie Apple to go in the blank. Then have them arm-blend the word.

    PCCs: ă, ā g, h, l, m, n, p, r, t, Magic e

    Words: lake, hat, name, shape, trap, grape, nap

- **Sort Word Cards** Display the Annie Apple *PCC* and the **a_e** *PCC* side by side. Have children take turns placing words under the *PCC* that matches the word. Have the child read the word, then point to all the words in the column for all to read.

    Words: game, chase, drag, gate, flat, brave, wag, plate

More with Mr. A and Magic e

Preparation and materials

✔ **Preparation and materials**
- *PCCs:* Review list plus **f, m, w**
- Props: Magic **e**'s wand
- *Blends and Digraphs Songs* CD, # 29
- Project lyrics or copy to a chart, *TG CD 2*

✔ **Small group/independent**
- *Letterland Word Builders,* or other individual letter sets
- Unit 10 *Word Cards:* **trap, safe, game, drag, late, flat, made, grape, hat, wag**

Magic e

Draw your wand.
Shoot every spark.
Jump back one letter
to land on the mark.

It's always the same.
The Vowel Man says his name.
Whenever the magic lands on him,
the Vowel Man says his name.

It's always the same.
the Vowel Man says his name.

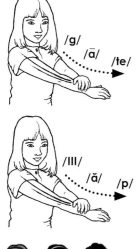

Review

- **PCCs ă, ā, b, c, d, g, l, p, s, t, v, y=ī, Magic e, a_e** Use the 'Guess Who?' activity. When you show the Magic **e** card, teach children the rhyme about Magic **e**. They can recite after you one line or phrase at a time and then the whole rhyme.

    Introducing the **e** you cannot hear,
    with the power to make Vowel Men appear!

- Show the **a_e** PCC. Tell children that the blank means different letters can be there. Ask what Mr. A says and then elicit from them that Magic **e** doesn't make a sound.

Magic e

- **Magic e Song** Play # 29 on the *Blends and Digraph Songs* CD. Read the lyrics to the children a few lines at a time as you point to the words. Then let them read the lines with you. After completing the lyrics, play the song again for all to sing.

- **Pocket chart review** Make the first pair of words on the pocket chart with only the plain letter sides showing: **gate, lap.**
    PCCs: ă, ā, b, c, d, f, g, l, m, p, s, t, v, w
    Words: gate, lap; wag, game; bad, safe; flag, cave

- When we see these words, we have to decide how to say the vowel sound. Point to the **a** in gate. Will it be Mr. A's name or Annie Apple's /ă/ sound? So, I look over to the end of the word and I see an **e**. That must be a Magic **e** (turn the PCC to the picture side). That Magic **e** is sending out its sparks over one letter and landing right here. Point to the **a**. So I am pretty sure that this is Mr. A. Let's see. Turn the PCC to the picture side. So, now we know Mr. A says his name. Let's rollercoaster our word: "/g/ /ā/ /t/, **gate.**" Use the word in a brief sentence.

- Now, let's look at this other word. No Magic **e**, and our vowel is in the middle, not on the end. We can be pretty sure it is going to be Annie Apple. Let's see if we are right. Flip to the picture side. Yes, it is and what's her sound? "/ă/" That's right. Let's rollercoaster this word: "/lll/ /ă/ /p/, **lap.**" Give a brief sentence.

- For the rest of the words, have the children predict who the vowel will be and explain how they know.

Word Building

- **Live Spelling** Distribute the PCCs. Give Magic **e** the magic wand. Have Magic **e**, Annie Apple, and Mr. A stand to the audience's left. Let other children with PCCs remain in their seats. Call out the first word for children to rubber-band stretch. Let children decide on who goes in each word. You might call on a child each time to decide on the vowel and then have the class do the Action for that vowel. When it is Mr. A with Magic **e** you could have Mr. A hold on to one end of Magic **e**'s wand as the two move into place on either side of the last consonant in the word.

    PCCs: ă, ā, c, d, m, p, s, v, w, Magic e
    Words: sad, cave, same, cap, save, map, came, mad, wave, made

Small group/independent activities

- **Reading with individual letter sets** Call out the letter names for the first word: **t, a, p, e**. Children put the letters in place and then talk about what sound to give the **a** and why. **"The Magic e makes the Vowel Man appear."** Then they rollercoaster the word together: **"/t/ /ā/ /p/, tape."** For the word **tap**, **"No Magic e so we probably hear Annie Apple."** Follow these steps with each word.

    Letters used: a, e, g, l, m, n, p, t, v

    Words: tape, late, tap, gate, mat, gave, name, nap

- **Word Sort** Display the Annie Apple *PCC* and the **a_e** *PCC* side by side. Give a *Word Card* to a child. The child places it under the *PCC* that represents the vowel sound. Then the child reads the word. As cards accumulate, the child who places the card then points to all the words in the row for the group to read.

    Word Cards: trap, safe, game, drag, late, flat, made, grape, hat, wag

- **Concentration Game** Turn over the *Word Cards* and mix them. Arrange them face down in rows. The first player turns over two cards to read. If both have the same vowel sound, the child collects them. If different, the child turns them back face down. Each child does the same in turn.

Unit 10: Lesson 153

Clever Cat and Magic **e**'s sparks **ē**

Review

- PCCs ă, ā, c, k, m, r, t, ck, y=ī, Magic e, a_e Use the 'Quick Dash' activity.

Magic **e** and Clever Cat

- **Pocket chart** Make the word **back** on the pocket chart with picture sides showing. Hide Mr. A behind Annie Apple and hide the **c** and **k** *PCCs* behind the **ck**.

    PCCs: ă, ā, b, c, k, ck, Magic e

    Words: back, backe (sic), bake

- Have the children rollercoaster the word **back**. Ask someone to tell why Clever Cat and Kicking King like to be on the end of a word. Next place the Magic **e** card on the end of **back**. Remove the **ck** *PCC* leaving the single letter *PCCs* for **backe** (sic).

- When Magic **e** comes along, it shoots its magic sparks over one letter. Wave the Magic **e** wand over Clever Cat. Clever Cat is a bit afraid that the sparks might burn her fur so she runs away. Remove the **c** *PCC* and slide **k** and Magic **e** over close to **a**. Now the sparks land on Annie Apple and make the Vowel Man appear! Remove Annie Apple to reveal Mr. A. Have the children rollercoaster the resulting word **bake**.

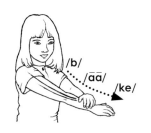

- Make **back** again as at the beginning and have the *children* explain what happens just as you did. Have them help move the cards as they explain the changes.

- **Live Reading** Do you think we could show the same thing with Live Reading?

  PCCs: ă, ā, c, k, m, r, t, ck, Magic e

  Words: tack, tacke (sic), **take, rack, racke** (sic), **rake, Mack, macke** (sic), **make**

- Pass out the *PCCs.* Give two children **ck** and your magic wand to the child with Silent Magic **e.** Line children up to make the word **tack** with the Mr. A child hiding behind Annie Apple. Children in the audience then rollercoaster the word. Next, add the child with Magic **e** on the end. Have Magic **e** wave the wand over Clever Cat who runs away. Give Kicking King his **k** PCC and have Magic **e** move close to Annie Apple. As Magic **e** waves the wand over Annie Apple, she changes places with Mr. A. Then the class rollercoasters the word **take.** Do the same steps in changing **rack** to **rake** and **Mack** to **make** with different children playing the key roles.

Spelling with Kicking King and Magic e

- **Chalkboard Spelling** Call out the word. Have children repeat and then stretch the word. Then call on a different child for each letter. The child tells you the Letterlander whose letter you should write. You may want to do a quick picture code for the vowels. After writing an Annie Apple word, ask a child why no Magic **e** is needed. **"Because it's Annie Apple, not Mr. A."** You could also ask after writing the words **sack** and **pack** why there is a **c** *and* a **k.** With **make** and **lake,** you could ask why Clever Cat is *not* in the word with Kicking King.

  Words: sack, make, pack, lake, wake

Small group/independent activities

- **Spelling with individual letter sets** Call out the words for children to repeat, rubber-band stretch and build with their own letters. Question them about the reasons for Magic **e** and why some words have **ck** while others just have **k.**

  Letters used: a, b, c, e, h, k, n, p, s, t

  Words: back, take, pack, cake, stack, snake, shake

- **Word Sort by Sound** Display the Annie Apple *PCC* and the **a_e** card side by side. Give out one *Word Card* at a time. As usual the child placing a word points to the words in the column for all to read. After children have placed two words under each *PCC,* begin calling out the words without showing the card to the children. Children stretch the word and decide which column. Before showing the word you might ask if there will be an **e** on the end. Let a child place the card and lead all in reading the column as before.

  Word Cards: trap, safe, take, drag, late, flat, lake, grape, hat, wag, name

- **Sentence Building** Display the *Word Cards* below in a random order. Tell the children that you want them to imagine that they have been making things out of clay and you are going ask them a question with *Word Cards.* Show the *Word Card* for **what** and say the word. Have them repeat the word. Have them stretch **what** and elicit from them that they do not hear the expected sounds for **h** or **a.** Put a wavy line under each of these two letters and write **what** on the board with a dotted **h.**

Word Cards: What, did, you, make, I, made, a, snake, cake, plate, shape, · ?

- Make the question below. Have children read it. Then have them construct an answer with the remaining words. Possible answers are listed below.

What did you make?	**I made a snake.**	**I made a cake.**
I made a plate.	**I made a shape.**	

Unit 10: Lesson 154

a_e Consolidating Mr. A with Magic e

✔ **Preparation and materials**
- *PCCs:* Review list plus **m**
- *Blends and Digraphs Songs* CD, # 29
- Project lyrics or copy to a chart, *TG CD 2*
- Props: Magic **e**'s wand
- *Tricky Word Cards:* **What, did, you, I, a, ? , ·** *TG CD 2*
- Unit 10 *Word Cards:* **long, snake, made, make,** *TG CD 2*

✔ **Small group/independent**
- Copies of 'Lesson 154 Word Sort,' *TG CD 2*
- *Word Cards:* Select 12 to 15 words for the 'Word Race'

Word Wall

what

Review

- PCCs ā, c, g, l, k, n, s, y=ī Magic e, ng, a_e Use the 'Guess Who?' activity.

Reviewing Mr. A with Magic e

- **Magic e Song** Review your written or projected lyrics to # 29 and then all sing along with the recording.

- **Live Reading: Consonants Go Marching** Have three children stand in front of the class and hold the three *PCCs* for **ake**. Pass out *PCCs* for the consonants listed below, and line these children up on the audience's left of the room where they can see the words being made. Have the consonants come forward one at a time and stand at the beginning to form a word with -**ake**.

Real		Nonsense
cake	name	gake
lake	same	nake
sake	gate	cate
came	late	sate
lame		

- Children rollercoaster the word and decide if it is a real word or a nonsense word. Write the word on the board as shown. Do the same with **ame** and **ate**.

  PCCs: ā, c, g, l, k, m, n, s, Magic e

  Rimes: (make with *PCCs* one at a time) -**ake**, -**ame**, -**ate**

  PCCs for initial positions: c, g, l, n, s

- Practice reading the lists of real and nonsense words with the *Tractors, Trains, Planes, and Helicopters* activity (Vol 1, page 204).

Sentence Writing

- **Tricky Word** Write **what** on the board. Use **what** in a sentence. Have children repeat the word and then stretch it. Talk about the **h** and **a** that do not make the expected sounds. Put a wavy line under **h** and a separate one under **a.** Practice air-writing and saying letter names three times, repeating the word after each spelling. Erase the word from the board. Children say the letter names and repeat the word while writing it on paper three times. Add **what** to your Word Wall.

- **Sentences on the pocket chart** Make the sentences below and have children practice reading them as you point to words. Turn the cards in the first sentence to the blank side. Point to the cards as the children recite the sentence twice from memory. Then have them write the sentence on their papers. Turn the cards back over for them to check their sentence. Do the same with the second sentence.

| What | did | you | make | ? |

| | | | | ? |

| I | made | a | long | snake | . |

| | | | | . |

Lesson 154 Written Word Sort

a	a_e
back	same
snap	cave
flag	lake

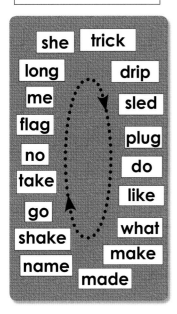

she | trick
long | drip
me | sled
flag | plug
no | do
take | like
go | what
shake | make
name | made

Small group/independent activities

- **Written Word Sort** Project a copy of the 'Lesson 154 Word Sort', or draw similar boxes and picture-codings on the board. Call out the first word. Children repeat it and then rubber-band stretch the word. Tell children to look at the top two boxes to find the vowel sound. Each child points on his or her paper to the box under Annie Apple or Mr. A with Magic **e**. Once children have chosen a box, point to the correct box on your page. Have children rubber-band stretch the word again, and write it in the box. After they have written the word, write it on your copy for all to check. Then do the same with the rest of the words.

  Words: back, same, cave, snap, lake, flag

- **Word Race** Lay out a number of *Word Cards* including words from this Unit and review words in a square or oval "race track" on a mat. Point to words in sequence around the track as children read them. Repeat a second and third time, going a little faster each time.

  Variations:
  1) time the group on each round, trying to beat the previous score;
  2) let individual children take a turn pointing and reading, alone or with a partner.

Unit 11

Mr. I with Magic e

Preparation and materials

- *PCCs:* Review list plus **b, f, n, p, r, t** and *BPCCs* **ĭ, ī**
- Props: Magic **e**'s wand
- *Blends and Digraphs Songs* CD, # 29
- Project lyrics or copy to a chart

Small group/independent

- Additional *PCCs:* **m, s, v, z**
- *Word Cards:* **hike, pin, live, nine, rid, pile, wide, flip, fin**

Decodable Word Bank

hide	kite	fine
ride	hike	pine
bike	pile	nine
like	smile	five
wide	wise	live
side	time	size

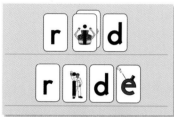

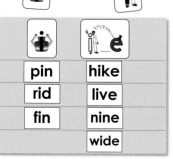

pin	hike
rid	live
fin	nine
	wide

Review

- PCCs **d, h, ĭ, ī, k, l, w, Magic e, ck, sh, a_e** Use the 'Guess Who?' activity.

Magic e makes Mr. I appear

- **Listen first** Display Mr. I's *Big PCC* up high on the board or pocket chart, and Impy Ink's *Big PCC* down low. Everyone stands up for the 'Up High, Down Low' game. If children hear Mr. I's name in a word they reach both hands high up in the air. If they hear Impy Ink's sound, they squat down low. Say each word and have them repeat it. Tell them to listen for the beginning sound in these words: **i**ce, **i**nsect, **i**sland, **i**f, **i**tch, **i**sland, **i**vy. Then tell them to rubber-band stretch these next words to hear the middle sound: d**i**p, b**i**te, w**i**de, s**i**ck, p**i**pe, f**i**t, t**i**me, w**i**fe. Alternatively, have children do the Action Tricks for Mr. I and Impy Ink.

- **Pocket chart reading** Make the word **rid**, as shown in the margin with only Impy's picture side showing. Hide Mr. I's *PCC* behind Impy Ink. Have the children rollercoaster the word. Use **rid** in a brief sentence.

   PCCs: **b, d, ĭ, ī, r, t, Magic e** Words: **rid, ride, bit, bite**

- Show the children the picture side of the Magic **e** *PCC*. What do you think will happen if we put Magic **e** on the end of **rid**? Let children predict, and then place the Magic **e** at the end of **rid** to make **ride**. Replace Impy Ink with Mr. I and have the children rollercoaster the word. Do the same with **bit** and **bite**.

- **Magic e Song** Review the lyrics by reading them with the children. Then play # 29 on the CD and sing along.

- **Live Reading** Line children up to make the first word, Have the class sound out the word. Use each word in a brief sentence. Change the letters to make the next word, etc.

   PCCs: **d, f, h, ĭ, ī, k, l, n, p, w, Magic e, ck, sh**
   Words: **hid, hide, wide, win, fin, fine, shine, ship, lip, lick, like**

Small group/independent activities

- **Picture-coding** Give children large copies of words from the Decodable Word Bank, to picture-code.

- **Pocket chart/table reading** Make each word with an empty space for the vowel (e.g. **b_ke, s_p**) and let children choose Mr. I, or Impy Ink to go in the blank and explain why. Then have them rollercoaster blend the word.

   PCCs: **b, f, ĭ, ī, k, l, m, p, r, s, t, v, z, Magic e, ck**
   Words: **bike, sip, kite, pick, five, smile, trip, size**

- **Sort Word Cards** Display the **ĭ**, and the **i_e** *PCCs* side by side. Have children take turns placing words under the *PCC* that matches the word. Have the child read the word, and then point to the words in the column for all to read.

   Words: **hike, pin, live, nine, rid, pile, wide, flip, fin**

More with Mr. I and Magic e

Review

- **PCCs d, f, ĭ, ī, l, m, w, Magic e, ch, ll, a_e, i_e** Use the 'Guess Who?' activity.

Word Building

- **Live Spelling** Distribute the *PCCs*. Give Magic **e** the magic wand. Have Impy Ink, Mr. I and Magic **e** stand to the left, facing the audience, ready to join the word when children decide on the vowel sound. Let other children with *PCCs* remain in their seats. Call out the first word for children to rubber-band stretch. Let them decide on the beginning and ending consonants, and then the vowel to go in each word. You might call on one child each time to decide on the vowel, and then have the class do the Action for that vowel. When it is Mr. I, you could have Mr. I hold on to one end of Magic **e**'s wand as the two move into place on either side of the last consonant, holding the wand above his or her head.

   PCCs: d, f, ĭ, ī, l, m, n, s, t, w, Magic e, ch, ll

   Words: win, side, chin, line, wife, still, dime, wide

Word Cards

- **Word Sort** Display the *PCCs* for Impy Ink and **i_e** at the top of the pocket chart. With the first two words, show the *Word Card* and have children read it together. Have them point with their eyes to the *PCC* that represents the vowel sound in the word. Have one child place the word.

   Word Cards: pile, pin, five, rid, wide, nine, fin, hike, slip

- Call out the next word, but do not show the card. Have children stretch the word, and point with their eyes to the matching *PCC*. Then call on one child to point to the correct *PCC*. Let this child stand facing the class. Tell the class you want to show them a new game called Mind Reader. You hold the *Word Card* above the child's head so that the child cannot see it but the rest of class can. Ask the child to 'read the children's minds' by spelling the word aloud. (Alternatively, the child could write the word on a small white board.) Then the child places the card on the pocket chart and points as everyone reads the words in the column. Let other children be Mind Readers with the rest of the words.

Small group/independent activities

- **Spelling with individual letter sets** Call out the words for children to repeat, rubber-band stretch and build with their own letters. After the first word, children leave letters in place and only change those needed to make the next word.

   Letters used: b, d, h, ĭ, ī, l, s, t, Magic e

   Words: side, slide, slid, hid, hide, hit, bit, bite

- **Written Word Sort** Project a copy of the 'Lesson 156 Word Sort' or draw similar boxes with picture-coded letters on the board. Call out the first word. Children repeat it and then rubber-band stretch the word. Tell children to look at the top two boxes to find the vowel sound. Each child points to the

Lesson 156 Written Word Sort

pin	bike
lip	time
chin	nine

box under Impy Ink, or Mr. I with Magic **e** on their Written Word Sort page. Once children have chosen a box, point to the correct box on your page. Have children rubber-band stretch the word again and write it in the box. After they have written the word, write it on your copy for all to check. Then do the same with the rest of the words.

> **Words: bike, pin, time, lip, chin, nine**

● **Sentence Building** Make the first sentence below. Display the other word cards in random order. Guide children in reading and rereading the sentence. Then say the second sentence and have children repeat it twice. Work with the children to change the first sentence into the second. Do the same with the third and fourth sentences.

> **Word Cards: I, like, to, ride, my, bike, take, hike, fly, kite, go, a, for, ▪**
>
> **Sentences: I like to ride my bike.**
> **I like to fly my kite.**
> **I like to take a hike.**
> **I like to go for a ride.**

Unit 11: Lesson 157

Mr. A and Mr. I with Magic e

Preparation and materials
- *PCCs*: Review list plus **g, h, k, m, n, p, s, t, w**
- Props: Magic **e**'s wand
- Unit 11 *Word Cards*: **kite, pin, wide, like, rid, dive, pile, slip** TG CD 2

✔ **Small group/independent**
- Additional *Word Cards*: **I, like, to, take, a, hike, safe, wag, late, take, hat, snake, grape**
- *Vowel Scenes* Poster with Magic **e**

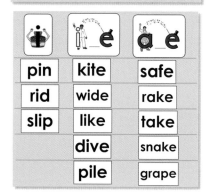

pin	kite	safe
rid	wide	rake
slip	like	take
	dive	snake
	pile	grape

Review

● PCCs ă, ā, b, d, ĭ, ī, l, w, ck, ll, a_e, i_e Use the 'Quick Dash' activity.

Word Building

● **On the pocket chart** I am going to make some words and let you work out what the vowel sound is going to be. Make all of the first set of words using the plain side of Mr. E for the extra Magic **e**. Ask children to look at **nap** and think about whether it is Annie Apple hiding behind the letter or Mr. A. Call on someone to predict who it will be and tell why. Then have the child flip the *PCC* to the picture side. Everyone can then rollercoaster the word. Do the same with the word **bake**. Ask children to predict the vowel characters in **wig** and **side**. Make the next set of words and do the same.

> **PCCs: ă, ā, b, d, ē, g, h, ĭ, ī, k, m, n, p, s, t, w, Magic e, ck, ll**
>
> **Word Set 1: nap, bake, wig, side**
>
> **Word Set 2: kite, hill, name, pack**

Word Cards

● **Word Sorting** Place the *PCCs* at the top of your pocket chart as shown.
● Show each *Word Card* and ask the children to read the word aloud and point with their eyes to the spot where it belongs on the pocket chart. Call on one child to place the card and lead others in reading the column of words as they accumulate.

> **Word Cards: kite, pin, wide, like, rid, dive, pile, slip**

Small group/independent activities

- **Display your Vowel Scenes Poster featuring Magic e words** Explain that we will soon be finding lots more words where Mr. E's Magic **e** makes different Vowel Men appear.

- **Word Sort by Sound** Display the *PCCs* listed below in a row. Call out each of these words without showing the *Word Card*. The children repeat the word and stretch it. Then choose one child to point to the *PCC* that matches the word. The child places the word under the *PCC*. All read the column as the words accumulate. After all the *Word Cards* are played, practice reading the words fluently with the *Tractors, Trains, Planes, and Helicopters* activity (Vol. 1, page 204).

PCCs: ă, a_e, ĭ, i_e

Word Cards: pin, kite, safe, wag, rake, rid, wide, take, like, hat, live, snake, pile, grape

- **Sentence Dictation** Build the sentence below with *Word Cards* and have children read it a few times. Then turn one card to its blank side and ask children to reread the sentence to identify the 'invisible word.'

| I | like | to | take | a | hike | . |

| I | | to | take | a | hike | . |

- **Ask one child to spell the missing word** (or write it on a small erasable board.) Confirm the spelling by turning the card back over. Do several words this way. Then turn over all the cards and have children repeat the sentence twice as you point to the blank sides of the cards ('reading the invisible sentence'). Have the children write the sentence on their papers (make the invisible sentence visible again). Help them as needed. Turn the *Word Cards* back to the word side to confirm the children's writing.

Unit 12

Old Mr. O with Magic e

Preparation and materials
- *PCCs*: Review list plus **c, d, l, m, n**, extra **p, r** and *BPCCs*: **ŏ, ō**
- Props: Magic **e**'s wand
- *Blends and Digraphs Songs* CD, # 29
- Project lyrics or copy to a chart

Small group/independent
- Unit 12 *Word Cards*: **hose, hop, rode, clock, stop, home, rod, close, drop, pole, cone** *TG CD 2*
- Words for picture-coding

Decodable Word Bank

those	note	rose
rope	rode	chose
hope	wrote	doze
nose	pole	hose
hole	bone	close
home	cone	
close	stove	

Review

- PCCs **b, h, n, ŏ, ō, p, s=z, t, z, Magic e, ck, o_e** Use the 'Guess Who?' activity.

Magic e makes Mr. O appear

- **Listen first** Display Mr. O's *Big PCC* up high on the board or pocket chart and Oscar Orange's *Big PCC* down low for the 'Up High, Down Low' game. If children hear Mr. O's name in a word they reach both hands high up. If they hear Oscar Orange's sound, they squat down low. Say each word and have them repeat it. They listen for these beginning sounds: **o**cean, **o**pen, **o**ffice, **o**ak, **o**strich, **o**live, **o**val, **o**dd, **o**bey. Tell them to rubber-band stretch these next words to hear the middle sound: n**o**se, s**o**ap, box, hop, r**o**ad, j**o**ke, sock, h**o**me, b**o**at. Alternatively, have children do the Action Tricks for Mr. O or Oscar Orange.

- **Pocket chart reading** Make the word **hop**, as shown in the margin with only Oscar's picture side showing. Hide Mr. O's *PCC* behind Oscar Orange. Have the children rollercoaster the word. Use **hop** in a brief sentence.

  PCCs: **d, h, n, ŏ, ō, p, r, t, Magic e**

  Words: **hop, hope, not, note, rod, rode**

- Show the children the picture side of the Magic **e** *PCC*. What do you think will happen if we put Magic **e** on the end of **hop**? Let children predict and then place the Magic **e** at the end of **hop** to make **hope**. Replace Oscar Orange with Mr. O and have the children rollercoaster the new word. Do the same with **not, note, rod** and **rode**.

- **Magic e Song** Review the lyrics by reading them with the children. Then play Track 29 on the CD and sing along.

- **Live Reading** Line children up to make the first word. Have the class sound out some of the words. Then have individuals sound out some words first followed by everyone sounding them out. Use each word in a brief sentence. Change the letters to make the next word, etc.

  PCCs: **c, d, h, l, m, n, ŏ, ō, p, r, s=z, Magic e**

  Words: **hop, hope, rope, rode, rod, home, hole, cone, close, hose**

> **Magic e**
> Draw your wand.
> Shoot every spark.
> Jump back one letter
> to land on the mark.
>
> It's always the same.
> The Vowel Man says his name.
> Whenever the magic lands on him,
> the Vowel Man says his name.
>
> It's always the same.
> the Vowel Man says his name.

Small group/independent activities

- **Picture-coding** Give children large copies of words from the Decodable Word Bank to picture-code.

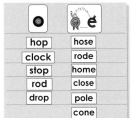

- **Pocket chart/table reading** Make each word with an empty space for the vowel (e.g. **r_pe, d_t**) and let children choose Mr. O or Oscar Orange to go in the blank space and tell why. Then have them rollercoaster blend the word.

  PCCs: **b, c, d, l, n, ŏ, ō, p, p, r, s=z, z, Magic e, ck**

  Words: **rope, bone, dot, lock, nose, drop, doze, pole, plop, close**

- **Sort Word Cards** Display the Oscar *PCC* and the **o_e** *PCC* side by side. Have children take turns placing words under the matching *PCC*. The child read the word and then point to the words in the column for all to read.

  Words: **hose, hop, rode, clock, stop, home, rod, close, drop, pole, cone**

Unit 12: Lesson 159

More with Mr. O and Magic e

Preparation and materials

- *PCCs:* Review list plus ☐, **d, h, m, ve**
- Props: Magic **e**'s wand
- Unit 12 *Unit Word Cards:* **rode, drop, hose, not, cone, those, rod, rock, bone,** *TG CD 2*

✓ Small group/independent

- *Letterland Word Builders,* or other letter sets
- Copies of 'Lesson 159 Written Word Sort' *TG CD 2*
- *Tricky Word Cards:* **a, a, Does, have,** ❓ *TG CD 2*
- Units 11 and 12 *Word Cards:* **bike, bones, clock, doze, home, hop nose, snake, rope, rose, stop,** *TG CD 2*

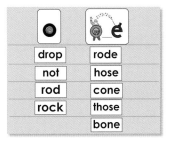

Review

- PCCs **ŏ, ō, p, r, s, t, v, z, Magic e, a_e, i_e, o_e** Use the 'Guess Who?' activity.

Word Building

- **Live Spelling** Distribute the *PCCs.* Give the Magic **e** child the magic wand. Have Magic **e**, Oscar Orange, and Mr. O stand to the audience left ready to join the word when children decide whether they need a vowel sound or vowel name. Let other children with *PCCs* remain in their seats. Call out the first word for children to rubber-band stretch. Let children decide on the beginning and ending consonants, and which vowel should go in each word. You might call on one child each time to decide on the vowel and then have the class do the Action for that vowel. When it is Mr. O, you could have Mr. O hold on to one end of Magic **e**'s wand as the two move into place on either side of the last consonant in the word, holding the wand above the head of the child with that consonant. Display your Magic **e** poster nearby.

  PCCs: **d, h, m, ŏ, ō, p, r, s, t, v, z, Magic e**

  Words: **home, hop, hope, rope, rode, rod, drop, doze, stove**

Word Cards

- **Word Sort** Display the *BPCCs* for Oscar Orange and **o_e** at the top of the pocket chart. With the first two words, show the *Word Card* and have children read it together. Have them 'point with their eyes' to the *PCC* that represents the vowel sound in the word. Have one child place the word.

  Word Cards: **rode, drop, hose, not, cone, those, rod, rock, bone**

- Call out the next word but do not show the card. Have children stretch the word and point with their eyes to the matching *PCC.* Then call on one child to point to the correct *PCC.* Let this child stand facing the class. Tell the class you want to play the Mind Reader game again. You hold the word card above the child's head so that the child cannot see it but the rest of class can. Ask the child to

'read the children's minds' by spelling the word aloud. (Alternatively, the child could write the word on a small white board.) Then the child places the card on the pocket chart and points as everyone reads the words in the column. Let other children be Mind Readers with the rest of the words.

Tricky Words

- Write **does** on the board. Use **does** in a sentence and talk about the **oe** that doesn't sound as expected. Put a wavy line under **oe**. Practice air-writing with the children and saying letter names three times repeating the word after each spelling. Children do the same while writing the word on paper three times.

- Practice the word '**have**.' Make **have** on the pocket chart with the picture sides of the *PCCs*. Remind children that the Vase Prop **e** holds up the vase of violets when it is on the end of the word.

    PCCs: ă, h, ve (Vase Prop **e**)

- Tell them that Vase Prop **e**'s are not usually Silent Magic **e**'s as well, but Vase Prop **e**'s are always silent. With no Magic there won't be any Vowel Man, so we still hear Annie Apple's sound in this word. Write **have** on the board and write the silent **e** as a dotted line. Have children practice air-writing and writing on paper or white board three times each, as with **does** above. Add **does** and **have** to your Word Wall.

Small group/independent activities

- **Spelling with individual letter sets** Call out the words for children to repeat, rubber-band stretch, and build with their own letters. After the first word, children leave letters in place and only change those needed to make the next word.

    Letters used: c, c, d, e, h, k, l, n, o, p, r, s

    Words: hop, hope, rope, rode, rod, rose, nose, close, clock, cone

- **Written Word Sort** Project a copy of the 'Lesson 159 Word Sort'. or draw similar boxes with picture-coded letters on the board. Call out the first word. Children repeat it and then rubber-band stretch the word. Tell children to look at the top two boxes to choose: vowel sound (ă) or vowel name (ā). Each child points on their paper to the box under Oscar Orange or Mr. O with Magic **e**. Once children have chosen a box, point to the correct box on your page. Have children rubber-band stretch the word again and then write it in the box. After they have written the word, write it on your copy for all to check. Then do the same with the rest of the words.

    Words: rope, hot, poke, pop, job, home

- **Sentence Building** (This is a variation of Silly Questions, Volume 1, p 261.) Give all the children **yes** and **no** cards. Make sure everyone can read their cards. Warm up with some oral questions that they can answer (e.g. **Does a cat have claws? Does a dog have wings?**) Make the first of the sentence questions below. Display the other word cards in random order. Guide children in reading and rereading the question. Have them respond with their **yes** or **no** card. Build several of the suggested sentences for them to answer. Have them take turns reading the questions. Have them read some sentences to themselves and respond before reading aloud. (Whispering the words when reading to themselves is expected.) You might let the children try to alter some of the sentences.

    Tricky Word Cards: a, a, Does, have, ?

    Unit Word Cards: bike, bones, clock, doze, home, hop nose, snake, rope, rose, stop

Possible Questions:

Does a snake have a nose?   Does a snake have bones?

Does a clock have a nose?   Does a rose have bones?

Does a rope doze?   Does a bike stop?

Does a snake doze?   Does a home hop?

Unit 12: Lesson 160

Mr. I and Mr. O with Magic e

Preparation and materials

✔ **Preparation and materials**
- *PCCs:* Review list plus **b, d, g, h, k, m, n, p, s, t, w**
- Props: Magic **e**'s wand
- Units 11 and 12 *Word Cards:* **doze, pin, nine, clock, pole, rid, like, those, pile stop, rod, rose, ride** *TG CD 2*

✔ **Small group/independent**
- Units 11 and 12 *Word Cards:* **hike, hop, pin, bone, rid, nose, drop, wide, pole, five, slip, rope, nine, hot, fish, fins**
- *Tricky Word Cards:* **a, a, Does, have** *TG CD 2*

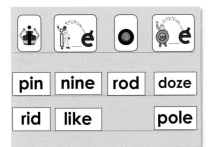

Review

- PCCs ĭ, ī, ŏ, ō, **w, ck, ll, i_e, o_e** Use the 'Quick Dash' activity.

Word Building

- **On the pocket chart** I am going to make some words and let you work out which vowel you hear.

- Make the first set of four words below with plain letter sides using the plain side of Mr. E in place of the second Magic **e**. Ask children to look at **sip** and think about whether it is Impy Ink hiding behind the letter or Mr. I. Call on someone to predict who it will be and tell why. Then have the child flip the PCC to the picture side to confirm the choice. Everyone can then rollercoaster the word. Do the same with the word **kite**. Ask children to predict the vowel characters in **lock** and **cone**. Make the next set of words on the pocket chart and do the same.

  PCC: ă, ā, b, c, d, ē, g, h, ĭ, ī, j, k, l, m, n, ŏ, ō, p, s, t, w, Magic e, ck, ll
  Word Set 1: sip, kite, lock, cone   Word Set 2: bike, sit, job, home

Word Cards

- **Word Sort** Place the *PCCs* at the top of your pocket chart as shown.

- Show each card and ask the children to read the word aloud and point with their eyes to the spot where it belongs on the pocket chart. Ask one child to place the card and lead others in reading the column of words as they accumulate.

  Word Cards: doze, pin, nine, clock, pole, rid, like, those, pile, stop, rod, rose, ride

Small group/independent activities

- **Word Sort by Sound** Display the picture side of the *PCCs* listed below in a row. Call out the words *without showing* the Word Card. The children repeat the word and stretch it. Then choose one child to point to the *PCC* that matches the word. The child places the word under the *PCC*. All read the column as the words accumulate.

  PCCs: ĭ, i_e, ŏ, o_e

Word Cards: hike, hop, pin, bone, rid, nose, drop, wide, pole, five, slip, rope, nine, hot

- After all the *Word Cards* are played, practice reading the words fluently with the *Tractors, Trains, Planes, and Helicopters* activity (Vol 1, page 204).

- **Sentence Dictation** Build the sentence below with *Word Cards* and have children read it a few times. Then turn one card to its blank side and ask children to reread the sentence to identify the 'invisible word.'

    Sentence:

Does	a	fish	have	fins	?					

- Ask one child to spell or write the missing word. Confirm the spelling by turning the card back over. Do several words this way, also the question mark. Then turn over all the cards and have children repeat the sentence twice as you point to the blank cards ('reading the invisible sentence'). Children write the sentence on their papers. Turn the cards over to confirm their writing.

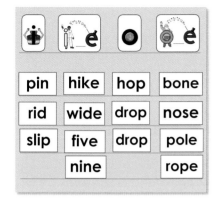

pin	hike	hop	bone
rid	wide	drop	nose
slip	five	drop	pole
	nine		rope

Unit 13

Mr. U and Mr. E with Magic e

✓ Preparation and materials

- *PCCs*: Review list plus **c, f, l, n, t**; *BPCCs*: **ŭ, ū**
- Props: Magic **e**'s wand
- *Blends and Digraphs Songs* CD, # 29
- Project lyrics or copy to a chart
- *Vowel Scenes* Poster with Magic **e**

✓ Small group/independent

- Unit 13 Word Cards: **tube, use, cube, luck, rule, mud, tune, June, pup** *TG CD 2*

Decodable Word Bank

cute	use	Pete
June	flute	complete
cube	tune	delete
tube	these	

Review

- PCCs **b, ĕ, ē, j, ŭ, ū, s, s=z, Magic e, th, a_e, i_e, o_e** Use the 'Guess Who?'.

Magic e makes Mr. U appear

- **Listen first** Display Mr. U's *Big PCC* up high on the board or pocket chart and Uppy Umbrella's *Big PCC* down low. Everyone stands up for the 'Up High, Down Low' game, reaching up on hearing Mr. U's name, or squatting down low for Uppy Umbrella's sound. Alternatively, they do the Action Trick for Mr. U or Uppy Umbrella. Say each word and have them repeat it. Tell them to listen for the beginning sound in these next words: **u**se, **u**ncle, **U**nited States, **u**p, **u**sual, **u**nicorn, **u**nder, **u**niform. Then tell them to rubber-band stretch these next words to hear the middle sound: c**u**be, m**u**le, l**u**ck, h**u**ge, f**u**n, t**u**be, c**u**p, t**u**ne. (Some speakers may pronounce some of Mr. U's words with an /oo/ sound as in **zoo** rather than as in **you**. Tell children that sometimes Mr. U only says part of his name.)

- **Pocket chart reading** Make the word **cub**, as shown in the margin with only Uppy Umbrella's picture side showing. Hide Mr. U's *PCC* behind Uppy Umbrella. Have the children rollercoaster the word and use it in a brief sentence.

    PCCs: **b, c, t, ŭ, ū, s, s=z, Magic e**
    Words: **cub, cube, tub, tube, us, use, pet, Pete**

- Show the children the picture side of the Magic **e** *PCC*. What do you think will happen if we put Magic **e** on the end of **cub**? Let children predict and then place the Magic **e** at the end of **cub**. Replace Uppy Umbrella with Mr. U and have the children rollercoaster the new word. Do the same with the other words above. (Note: change Sammy Snake to Sleep Sammy with **us/use**.)

- **Magic e Song** Review the lyrics by reading them with the children. Then play Track 29 on the CD and sing along.

- **Live Reading** Line children up to make the first word. Have the class sound out some of the words, then some individuals, followed by the class sounding out the same word. Use each word in a brief sentence. Change the letters to make the next word, etc. Display the *Vowel Scenes Poster* for Magic **e** nearby.

  PCCs: b, c, ē, f, j, l, n, t, ŭ, ū, s=z, Magic e, th

  Words: cut, cute, cube, cub, tub, tube, tune, June, flute, these

Small group/independent activities

- **Picture-coding** Give out words from the Decodable Word Bank to picture-code.

- **Pocket chart/table reading** Make each pair of words with an empty space for the vowel (e.g. **t_be, m_d**) and let children choose Mr. U or Uppy Umbrella to go in the blank and tell why. Then have them rollercoaster blend the word.

  PCCs: b, c, ē, ŭ, ū, s=z, Magic e, sh

  Words: tube, mud; cub, tune; June, shut; these, net

- **Word Sort** Display the Uppy Umbrella *PCC* and the **u_e** *PCC* side by side. Have children take turns placing words in the correct column. Then have the child read the word and then point to the words in the column for all to read.

  Word Cards: tub, use, cube, luck, rule, mud, tune, June, pup

tub	use
luck	cube
mud	rule
pup	tune
	June

Unit 13: Lesson 162

All the Vowel Men with Magic e

✔ Preparation and materials

- *PCCs:* Review list plus **d, ĭ, ī, m, n, r, s=z**
- Props: Magic **e**'s wand
- Units 10-13 *Word Cards:* **kite, rope, game, close, lake, these, bike, shape, tube, stove, June, smile**
- Project or enlarge the decodable booklet 'Peter Puppy's Presents' and make copies

✔ Small group/independent

- Units 10-13 *Word Cards:* **bone, cake, nine, those, wide, use, snake, made, these, pole, side, cube, grape, rode**
- *Word Cards:* **fish, fin**; *Tricky Word Cards:* **Does, a, have**

Review

- **PCCs ă, ā, d, ĕ, ē, j, l, w, ck, th, a_e, e_e, i_e, o_e, u_e** Use the 'Quick Dash' activity.

Word Building

- **On the pocket chart** I am going to make some words and let you work out which vowel you can hear. Make each word with the plain letter sides of the *PCCs*. Ask children to decide which Letterlander is hiding on the other side of the vowel card. Ask how they can tell which one will be there. Then have a child flip the *PCC* to the picture side to confirm. Everyone can then rollercoaster the word.

  PCC: ă, ā, d, ĕ, ē, ĭ, ī, j, m, n, ŏ, ō, r, s=z, ck, th, ŭ, ū, Magic e

  Words: map, made, wide, win, June, run, rock rode, these, then

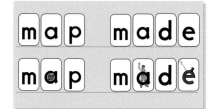

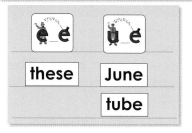

Word Cards

- **Word Sorting** Place the *PCCs* listed below across your pocket chart.
- Show each card and ask the children to read the word aloud and point with their eyes to the spot where it belongs on the pocket chart. Call a different child to place each word and lead others in reading the column of words as they accumulate.

  PCCs: a_e, e_e, i_e, o_e, u_e

  Word Cards: kite, rope, game, close, lake, these, bike, shape, tube, stove, June, smile

Read the Decodable Booklet: 'Peter Puppy's Presents'

- Project or enlarge the booklet or write the title on the board. Provide copies for each child. (There are a few words in this booklet that children may need help with. The children may like to add a wiggly line under the tricky parts on their copies.) Read the title with the children, look at the first few pages, and discuss the pictures. Read the pages together and then reread several times with different groups of children reading each page.

Small group/independent activities

- **Word Sort by Sound** Display the picture side of the *PCCs* listed below in a row. Call out the words *without showing the Word Card*. The children repeat the word and stretch it. Then choose one child to point to the *PCC* that matches the word. The child places the word under the *PCC*. All read the column as the words accumulate. After all the *Word Cards* are listed, practice reading the words with the *Tractors, Trains, Planes, and Helicopters* activity.

  PCCs: a_e, e_e, i_e, o_e, u_e

  Word Cards: bone, cake, nine, those, wide, use, snake, made, these, pole, side, cube, grape, rode

- **Reread Peter Puppy's Presents** with the group and then pair children up to partner read.

- **Sentence strips** Read sentence strips from pages 2-5 of the booklet with the children in a random order. Have children compare the strips to the pages of the booklet and arrange them in sequence. Then read the strips from pages 6-8 and do the same. Have the children reread all the sentence strips.

- **Play the game called What is Missing?** Have children hide their eyes. Remove one sentence strip and leave a gap where it belongs. Then have children reread the remaining sentence strips and try to remember what the missing sentence is about. Then show the missing sentence and have children read it. Do the same with a few other sentences

It was Peter Puppy's birthday.

All the Vowels gave him gifts.

Can you guess who gave him these gifts?

Who gave Peter Puppy a big kite?

Impy Ink and Mr. I gave him a big kite.

Who gave Peter Puppy a stack of pancakes?

Annie Apple and Mr. A gave him

a stack of pancakes.

The best gift was a dog bone.

Who do you think gave him that?

It was Oscar Orange and Mr. O.

Section 5 Assessments

You can measure your children's mastery of the outcomes for this Section with the following two assessments

    1. Word Reading Accuracy Children read the list of 12 decodable words below.

    2. Spelling Decodable Words Children write words to match 8 pictures.

Assessment Pages

    Teacher's Guide: Student reads from this page.

    Teacher's Guide CD: 'Section 5 Assessment' (copymaster including Score Sheet and Spelling Decodable Words)

Score Sheet

Section 5 Assessment

Child_____ Teacher _____ Date_____

1. Word Reading Accuracy

game	me	bike	cone
she	no	tube	lake
wide	rope	my	try

No. Correct ____/12 (Goal 10)

2. Spelling Decodable Words

cake rope fire cube slide waves flute bone

No. Correct ____/8 (Goal 6)

Assessment Instructions

(1) Word Reading Accuracy (Individuals) The child reads the 12 words below. Encourage the child to 'sound them out.' If the child says the word in a segmented fashion (e.g. **/g/ /ā/ /m/** for 'game'), you may say, Put it together, or, Blend it. Only count the word as correct if the child is able to say it finally without segmentation (e.g. "**game**"). After about five seconds on a word, have the child move on to the next word. On the Score Sheet put a line through any words missed, or write the substitution above the word. The goal is at least 10 of 12 words correct.

(4) Spelling Decodable Words (Group) Give each child a copy of the page (*TG CD 2*) and project or enlarge a copy to demonstrate. Name the first picture and have children repeat it. Ask the children to rubber-band stretch the word on their own, and spell it in the box. When everyone is ready, do the same with each picture. On the Score Sheet, copy misspellings or put a line through words missed. The goal is at least 6 of 8 words correct.

Section 5 Assessment Student Page

1. Word Reading Accuracy

game	me	bike	cone
she	no	tube	lake
wide	rope	my	try

No. Correct _____/12 (Goal 10)

Section 6
The Vowel Men Out Walking

Lessons 163-172

The Vowel Men Out Walking

The first 10 lessons focus on 'Vowel Men Out Walking' to help you teach your children to read and spell words with a long vowel next to a silent vowel such as **ai**, **ea**, and **oa**. Once the concept is in place the number of new words the children can decode grows at an exciting pace. There are three Units in this section.

Unit 14: Lessons 163-165 **ai** and **ay**

Unit 15: Lessons 166-167 **ea** and **ee**

Unit 16: Lessons 168-172 **oa**, **ie**, **ue** and review

Children learn that two Vowel Men often go out walking in Letterland. When they do, "the first one says his name but his friend won't do the same." The Letterland reason: because the second Vowel is the lookout man. He is silent because he is busy looking out for Robots who may try to capture them. (Section 7 focuses on **r**-controlled vowels.)

Learning about the Vowel Men out Walking

This section continues with variations on the lively activities from previous sections, but also includes new activities specifically designed to make learning about these long vowel patterns fun and memorable.

Children learn a Vowels Out Walking Song and sing it with actions and games that help them remember the sounds of these letters in words.

There are seven vowel pairs in this section, but children learn them easily because they all work the same way. They are reminded of these seven pairs of vowels out walking, by the Vowels Out Walking Poster shown below.

Children build a 'train' of new words in many of these lessons and practice reading these words fluently.

They review the new patterns with Live Word Sorting.

New Materials from the Teacher's Guide CD

For this section, you will find new *Word Cards* for each Unit, and 'Written Word Sort' pages for Lessons 171 and 172 on the *Teacher's Guide CD 2*.

Learning Outcomes and Assessments

Outcomes	Assessments (See page 202)
• Read words with a long vowel followed by a silent vowel (e.g, **leap**, **boat**)	1. Word Reading Accuracy
• Spell VV words correctly.	2. Spelling Decodable Words

Tricky Words

• Children are taught to read and spell five additional Tricky Words in this Section:

all   **give**   **some**   **they**   **your**

Unit 14

Mr. A and Mr. I out walking

✔ **Preparation and materials**
- *PCCs*: Review list plus **ai**
- Props: A red apron, or cap for Mr. A, a white apron, or cap for Mr. I
- *Blends and Digraphs Songs* CD, # 30
- Project lyrics or copy to a chart

✔ **Small group/independent**
- Prepare words from the *Decodable Word Bank*, one per page for children to picture-code
- Additional *PCCs*: **b, p, s**
- Unit 14 *Word Cards*: **train, bait, wait, mail, aim, chain, main, trail, plain, nail**, *TG CD 2*

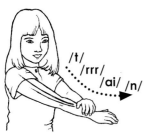

/t/ /rrr/ /ai/ /n/

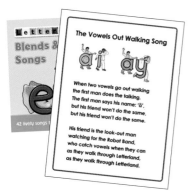

Review

- PCCs ă, l, m, n, r, t, w, a_e, e_e, i_e, o_e, u_e Use the 'Guess Who?' activity.

Introduce a and i out walking

- Show the **ai** *PCC* picture side and tell the children that the Vowel Men like to go out for walks in Letterland together. When Mr. A and Mr. I go out walking, Mr. A waves to everyone and says his name /ā/ as you can see right here. But look at Mr. I. Is he waving and saying his name? **"No."** Can you do what he is doing? Children put their hands up above their eyes like Mr. I. Mr. I is the lookout man. He is busy looking out for Robots who like to sneak up on them and capture them while they are out walking!

- Let's get two of you to be Mr. A and Mr. I. Have two children hold the **ai** *PCC*. If you have the costume items listed above, give them these. Have them begin on one side of the class and walk in the audience's reading direction across the room as they hold the *PCC* together. Mr. A, of course, should be waving with his right hand and saying /ā/. Mr. I should be a half step ahead of Mr. I with his hand to his forehead on the lookout.

- Now let's everyone pair up. One partner can be Mr. A and the other Mr. I. Everyone walk in place and do your part as Mr. A or Mr. I. Then have children switch places and roles with their partners and repeat.

- Show the **ai** *PCC* plain side. Now when you see these two together you will know why they only make one sound. What sound? "/ā/". Yes! Tell your neighbor what Mr. A is doing. Then listen while your neighbor tells you what Mr. I is doing.

Word Building

PCCs: **l, m, n, r, t, w, ai**

Words: **wait, rain, train, nail, mail**

- **Pocket chart reading** Let's make some words with these Vowel Men Out Walking. Build each word and have children tap the sounds down their arms and then rollercoaster them to blend. Tell them, Remember to tap just one time for the /ā/ sound of **ai**.

Sing Along

- **The Vowels Out Walking Song** Read the words to the children as you point to the lyrics you have prepared. Then play the song (Track 30) and sing along. The second time through the song the lyrics say "the first man says his name: /ē/." You may want your children to sing "/ā/" again just like the first time.

• You might then play this game as you play the song again: Have one child be a vowel stealing Robot. Mr. A and Mr. I hold their *PCC* together and turn their backs to the class. The Robot hides somewhere in the classroom. Then Mr. A and Mr. I turn around and begin to walk around the room, Mr. A waving and saying "A!" while Mr. I leads him as he searches for the Robot. The class can help by telling them if they are getting "warmer" or "colder" but they are not allowed to point. The Robot is not allowed to move from the hiding place. When Mr. I tags him he must return to his seat.

Decodable Word Bank

wait	aim	brain
rain	raise	drain
train	bait	stain
nail	mail	plain
main	chain	Spain
trail	gain	

Small group/independent activities

• **Picture-coding** Give children large copies of words from the Decodable Word Bank, to picture-code.

• **Pocket chart/table reading** Make the words below for the children to rollercoaster blend. Use the picture side of the *PCCs* for the vowels and the plain side for the consonants. Let individuals be Blending Leaders by blending a word first. Then the group blends it. Say a brief sentence with each word.

   PCCs: ă, b, l, m, p, n, r, s, t, w, ai

   Words: **ran, rain, train, bat, bait, wait, pal, pail, sail**

• **Make a Word Card train** Since **train** is one of our words with Mr. A and Mr. I, let's make a train across the table as we read our word cards. Each child takes a turn reading a *Word Card* and adding it to the lengthening train. As each word is added, the child placing the card points as the group reads the whole train of words.

   Word Cards: **train, bait, wait, mail, aim, chain, main, trail, plain, nail**

Unit 14: Lesson 164

More with Mr. A and Mr. I

Preparation and materials
• *PCCs*: Review list
• *Beyond ABC* book, p 38-39
• Unit 14 *Word Cards*: **trap, waits, aim, brat, chain, flag, black, trail, plan, plain, snap, nail,** *TG CD* 2

Small group/independent
• Character name cards, *TG CD* 2: Talking Tess, Firefighter Fred
• Unit 14 *Word Cards*: **waits, train, rain, bait, fish,** *TG CD* 2
• *Tricky Word Cards:* **for, the, the, in, with, his, a,** • *TG CD* 2
• *Letterland Word Builders* or other letter sets.

Review

• PCCs ă, d, g, l, m, n, p, r, t, w, ai Use the 'Quick Dash' activity.

Read About Mr. A and Mr. I out walking

• **Beyond ABC book** Read the story to the children (page 38) and explore the picture with them identifying items with the sound of **ai** in the middle.

Word Building

• **On the pocket chart** I am going to make some words and let you work out what vowel we hear. Make each word with the plain letter sides of the *PCCs*. Ask children to decide which Letterlander(s) will be on the other side of the vowel

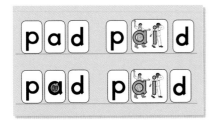

PCC. Do we hear a vowel sound? or a vowel name? Ask how they can tell what they will find on the other side. Then have a child flip the *PCC* to show the picture side. Everyone can then rollercoaster the word.

PCCs: ă, d, g, l, m, n, p, r, t, w, ai

Words: pad, paid, pal, pail, rail, ran, man, main, wag, wait

Live Spelling

- Distribute the *PCCs*. Have the children with the *PCCs* for Annie Apple and for **ai** stand to the audience left of your live spelling area so that the class can choose which is needed to represent the vowel in each word. Children rubber-band stretch each word, choose the beginning consonants then choose the vowel(s). Then if it is Mr. A and Mr. I, they walk across the room with Mr. A waving and saying his name and Mr. I on the lookout. They take their place in the word. Finally, children identify the final consonant. Have the vowels return to their place on the left after each word is spelled.

  PCCs: ă, g, l, m, n, p, r, t, w, ai

  Words: tail, wag, main, trail, pat, rain, wait, mat, train

Word Cards

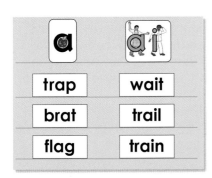

  Word Cards: trap, wait, aim, brat, chain, flag, black, trail, plan, plain, snap, nail

- **Word Sorting** Place the Annie Apple *PCC* and the **ai** *PCC* at the top of your pocket chart. Read the first *Word Card* and place it under the *PCC* that matches its vowel sound or vowel name. Have children take turns doing the same with six to eight cards. Each time a card is placed have the child who places it point to all the words in the column for everyone to read.

Small group/independent activities

- **Spelling with letter sets** Call out words for children to rubber-band stretch and build. (For children needing more support, let the group build the words together with *Picture Code Cards*.)

  Letters Used: a, i, l, m, n, p, r, t, w

  Words: pan, pain, rain, ran, main, mail, wait, plan, plain

- **Word Sort by Sound** Place the two *PCCs* on the table or pocket chart. Read the first *Word Card* to the children but do not show it. Have children repeat the word and rubber-band stretch it listening for the vowel sound. Then have one child point to the *PCC* that represents the vowel spelling for the word. The child places the card. After the first card, the child placing the card leads the group in reading the column of *Word Cards*.

- **Sentence Building** Build the first sentence in the pocket chart for the children. Read it to them and then read it with them a few times pointing to the words. Then have them shut their eyes to play the 'Disappearing Words' game. You remove one of the **ai** words, leaving a space, and then have them open their eyes. The children reread the sentence to identify the word. One child then spells the word aloud, or writes it before you return it to the sentence. Do the same with the other **ai** words and then with the second sentence.

  Sentence 1: | Talking | Tess | waits | for | the | train | in | the | rain | . |

  Sentence 2: | Firefighter | Fred | waits | with | his | bait | for | a | fish | . |

Yo-yo Man helps out

Preparation and materials
- *PCCs*: Review list plus **ay**
- Unit 14 *Words Cards*: **trap, trail, tray, rain, say, brat, wait, day, flag, mail, plan, way,**

✔ **Small group/independent**
- Name card for Golden Girl
- Unit 14 *Words Cards*: **stay, play, day, May, hay, today, horse** *TG CD 2*
- *Tricky Word Cards*: **will, and, all, we, give, the, to, ?**
- Large words for picture-coding
- *Letterland Word Builders* or other letter sets.

Decodable Word Bank

day	pay	way
hay	play	today
lay	say	
may	stay	

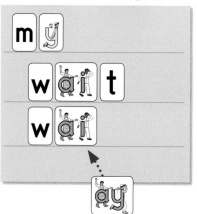

Review

- PCCs **ă, d, g, l, m, n, p, r, s, t, w, ai** Use the 'Guess Who?' activity.

Introduce **a** and **y** out walking

- **On the pocket chart** Make the word **my** (below left) with the *PCC* showing Yo-yo Man with an Ice Cream cone in his backpack. Ask children to recall why Yo-yo Man is making Mr. I's sound in this word. **"Mr. I gets dizzy at the end of words so Yo-yo Man takes his place."** Make the word **wait**. Have children blend it. Now I want to make the word **way**. I could just take the **t** off. Let's rollercoaster those two sounds. **"/w/ /ā/, way."** But Mr. I has a bit of a problem. Just like in **my**, when he is on the end of a word he often gets dizzy. Wobble the **ai** *PCC* back and forth a bit. He feels like he might just fall down when he's on the end. He wouldn't be much help as the lookout man like that, would he? Luckily, Yo-yo Man comes along to help out Mr. I again. Replace the **ai** *PCC* with the **ay** *PCC*. Yo-yo Man takes Mr. I's place as the silent lookout man. Mr. A still waves and says his name but Yo-yo Man says nothing because now *he* is too busy looking out for the **r**obots! Show the plain side of **ay** and ask children to say the sound three times as you push the card forward. Make the other words and have the children rollercoaster the sounds.

  PCCs: d, l, p, t, w, ai, ay

  Words: wait, way, paid, pay, play

Live Spelling

- Distribute the *PCC*s. Have two children hold the *PCC* for **ai** and stand in front of the class, and one child hold the **ay** *PCC*s ready to take Mr. I's place. Children rubber-band stretch each word, and decide on the Letterlanders needed. If it is Mr. A and Mr. I, the two children with this card take their place in the word. If **ay** is needed, Mr. A leaves Mr. I and joins Yo-yo Man in holding the **ay** card on the end of the word. As children choose **ai** or **ay**, elicit from them that the **ai** is needed when there is another sound after the /ā/ but **ay** is needed when the /ā/ is the last sound.

  PCCs: d, l, m, n, p, s, t, ai, ay

  Words: main, may, day, pay, play, plain, pail, sail, say, stay

- Explain, as you complete the Live Spelling: So, when we hear /ā/ at the end of a word who will it be? **"Mr. A and Yo-yo Man."** And if we hear /ā/ in the middle of a word, who will it be. **"Mr. A and Mr. I."**

Word Cards

Word Cards: **trap, trail, tray, rain, say, brat, wait, day, flag, mail, plan, way**

- **Word Sorting** Place the *PCCs* for Annie Apple, **ai**, and **ay** at the top of your pocket chart. Read the first *Word Card* and place it under the *PCC* that matches. Have children take turns doing the same with the first six cards or so. Each time a card is placed have the child who places it point to all the words in the column for everyone to read.

- **Sort by Sound** Then for the last six cards call out the word without showing the card. Have all the children stretch the word to hear: vowel sound or vowel name? Have a child come forward and point to the *PCC* it belongs under. Ask the children to explain each time how they know where the card goes. The child places the word and leads the class in reading that column.

Small group/independent activities

- **Picture-coding** Give children large copies of words from the **ay** Decodable Word Bank, to picture-code, e.g. **day** and **stay**.

- **Spelling with letter sets** Call out words for children to rubber-band stretch and build.

  Letters needed: **a, d, g, i, l, n, p, r, t, w, y**

  Words: **plan, play, rain, train, day, wag, way, wait**

- **Tricky Words** Write **all** on the board. Use **all** in a sentence. Have children repeat the word and then stretch it. Talk about how **a** does not make the expected sound. Put a wavy line under **a.** If children are curious to know the story for this sound, see the Letterland Advanced Teacher's Guide, page 10, on Giant All.

- Practice **all**. Lead children in air-writing the word while saying the letter names three times, repeating the word after each spelling. Erase the word from the board. Children say the letter names and repeat the word while writing the word on paper three times. Add **all** to your Word Wall.

- Write **give** on the board. Talk about the silent **e**, quietly propping up the vase. This is not a Magic **e** so it does not make the Vowel Man appear. Rewrite the **e** with a dotted line. Have the children practice **give** as they did **all** above. Add **give** to your Word Wall.

- **Sentence Building** Build the first sentence for the children. Read it to them and then read it with them a few times, pointing to the words. Then have them shut their eyes to play the 'Disappearing Words' game. You remove one of the **ay** words leaving a space and then have the children open their eyes. The children reread the sentence to identify the word. One child then spells the word aloud or writes it before you return it to the sentence. Do the same with the other **ay** words, and then with the second sentence.

  Sentence 1: | Golden | Girl | will | stay | and | play | all | day | . |

  Sentence 2: | May | we | give | hay | to | the | horse | today | ? |

Unit 15

Mr. E and Mr. A out walking

Preparation and materials
- *PCCs*: Review list plus **ea**
- *Beyond ABC* book, p 40-41
- *Blends and Digraphs Songs* CD, # 30
- Project lyrics or copy to a chart

✔ Small group/independent
- Write *Decodable Word Bank* words, for children to picture-code
- Additional *PCCs*: **d, f, r**
- Unit 15 *Word Cards*: **seat, mean, teach, clean, each, leaf, treat, dream**, *TG CD 2*

Decodable Word Bank

beans	leap	seat
clean	leash	tea
dream	mean	teach
each	meat	team
eat	neat	reach
heat	peach	read
jeans	peas	real
leaf	sea	treat
lean	seal	

The Vowels Out Walking Song

When two vowels go out walking
the first man does the talking.
The first man says his name: 'ē,'
but his friend won't do the same,
but his friend won't do the same.

His friend is the look-out man
watching for the Robot Band,
who catch vowels when they can
as they walk through Letterland,
as they walk through Letterland.

Review

- **PCCs b, ĕ, j, l, m, n, p, s, s=z, t, ai, ay, ch, ea** Use the 'Quick Dash' activity.

Introduce e and a out walking

- Show the '**ea**' *PCC* picture side and tell the children that Mr. E and Mr. A like to go out walking, just like Mr. A and Mr. I*. Look at the picture. Who do you think is waving and saying his name? "**Mr. E.**" And what is Mr. A doing. "**He is looking out for robots.**" Exactly. Turn the card to the plain side. So what sound do we hear when we see these two letters in words? "**/ē/**". Yes! Show the plain side of the **ea** *PCC* and push it forward three times as children repeat the sound.

- Let's have everyone on this side of the class be Mr. E and wave and say your name together. Everyone on this other side be Mr. A and put your hand up and look all around without saying a thing. Then have the sides switch roles and repeat the actions.

  Now tell your neighbor what Mr. E is doing. Then listen while your neighbor tells you what Mr. A is doing.

- **Beyond ABC book** Read the story (page 40) to the children and explore the picture together identifying items with **ea** and perhaps writing them on the board.

Word Building

- **Pocket chart reading** Let's make some words from our story with these Vowel Men Out Walking. Build each word and have children tap the sounds down their arm and then rollercoaster them to blend. Have someone explain how the word relates to the story or illustration in *Beyond ABC*. (For **beat** for example, "**The boy beat the drum in the picture.**")

    PCCs: **b, j, l, m, n, p, s, s=z, t, ch, ea**

    Words: **eat, meat, seal, jeans, peach, beat**

Sing Along

- **The Vowels Out Walking Song** Sing the first five lines. With the first verse push the **ai** *PCC* forward as Mr. A says his name. Do the same with the **ea** *PCC* with the second verse Let one of the children point to the words as you all sing.

- You may want to play this game introduced in Lesson 163 as you play the fuller song. Have one child be a Robber Robot. Mr. E and Mr. A hold their *PCC* together, and turn their backs to the class. The Robot hides somewhere in the classroom. Then Mr. E and Mr. A turn around and begin to walk around the room, Mr. E waving and Mr. A leading him as he searches for the Robot. The class can help by telling them if they are getting "warmer" or "colder" but they

are not allowed to point. The Robot is not allowed to move. When Mr. A tags him he must return to his seat.

Small group/independent activities

- **Picture-coding** Give out words from the Decodable Word Bank to picture-code.
- **Pocket chart/table reading** Make the words below for the children to blend. Use the vowel *PCC*s picture sides, and consonant plain sides. Let individuals be the Blending Leaders, followed by the group blending the word. Say a brief sentence with each word.

  PCCs: d, ĕ, f, l, n, r, t, ch, ea

  Words: net, neat, red, read, leaf, teach, reach

- **Make a Word Card train** Hand out one *Word Card* at a time. The child reads it and places it on the table to make a train of cards and points to each word in order as the group reads the words.

  Word Cards: seat, mean, teach, clean, each, leaf, treat, dream

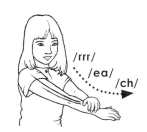

/rrr/
/ea/
/ch/

---

* Note this pair of vowels can also represent the **ĕa** sound, e.g. **pleasant** and **ready**. This sound is explained in a brief story about Eddy Elephant joining Mr. E and Mr. A out walking in later volumes.

Unit 15: Lesson 167

Mr. E and his Brother

Preparation and materials
- *PCCs*: Review list plus **s, ee**
- *Blends and Digraphs Songs* CD
- *Beyond ABC book*, p 42-43

✔ **Small group/independent**
- Additional *PCCs*: **ă, Magic e, ŏ**
- *Unit 15 Word Cards*: **feet, tree, feel, leaf, shell, team, sled, read, need, eat, leg, queen, needs, clean, jeans**, *TG CD 2*
- *Tricky Words*: **The, some**
- Words to picture-code.

Review

- **PCCs b, ĕ, d, f, j, l, n, p, t, w, sh, th, ll, qu** Use the 'Guess Who?' activity.

Introduce e and e out walking

- Show the children the **ee** *PCC* picture side. Did you know that Mr. E has a brother who looks just like him? He is also called Mr. E. And what do you think happens when they go walking? What is the first Mr. E is doing and saying? **"Waving and saying his name."** And what is the second Mr. E doing? **"Looking out for robots."** Yes,(show the plain letter side) so when we see these two letters in words what do you think we will hear? **"/ē/"** Yes, the first Mr. E saying his name. Push the *PCC* forward three times as children repeat the sound.

- **Play and sing** or chant the Vowels Out Walking Song (Track 30). Perhaps all the children could pair up and all march in a circle clockwise as they sing. Each inside partner can be Mr. E waving and saying /ē/ while the outside partner looks out for **r**obots. Then have everyone change sides and roles and march to the song again.

- **Beyond ABC** Read the **ee** story (page 42) to the children and have them hunt for pictured items with the **ee** spelling. Are they noticing how many Vowels Out Walking words there are in books, and how valuable it is to know how the Vowel Men always behave in them? Suddenly loads of words that used to be too difficult become easy to read!

Decodable Word Bank

sweet	sleep	seem	jeep
see	keep	bee	meet
green	week	free	queen
need	feel	feed	weed
tree	seed	heel	

Word Building

- **Live Readng** Distribute PCCs. Arrange children to make each of these words from the **ee** story in *Beyond ABC*. Have children rollercoaster the words and ask them to tell how that word relates to the story or picture in the book. (For example, **"Mr. E and his brother need to keep their feet moving because it is freezing."**)

  PCCs: **d, f, j, l, p, s, t, w, ee, th**

  Words: **feet, sweep, sleet, deep, jeep, teeth**

Small group/independent activities

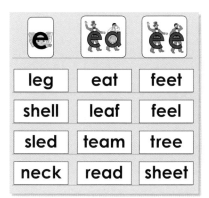

- **Picture-coding** Give children large copies of words from the **ee** Decodable Word Bank to picture-code, e.g. **week** and **free**.

- **Pocket chart/table reading** Make the words below for children to blend. Use the picture sides for the vowels and the plain sides for the consonants.

  PCCs: **ă, b, ě, Magic e, d, f, l, n, ŏ, ee, ll, qu,**

  Words: **fell, feel, fed, feed, need, bed, bee, queen, bone, fade**

- **Word Sort** Place the three *PCCs* on the table or pocket chart. Children take turns placing a card under the right *PCC*, based on the vowel sound and spelling. Then the child points to the words in the column for all to read.

  PCCs: **ě, ea, ee**

  Word Cards: **feet, leaf, shell, team, sled, tree, feel, read, neck, sheet, eat, leg**

- **Tricky Words** Write **some** on the board. Use **some** in a sentence. Have children repeat the word and then stretch it. Remind them that Oscar's Bothersome Little Brother says /ŭ/. Put a wavy line under **o** or picture-code it with a baby. Remind them that Silent **e** can be burned out. Rewrite the **e** with a dotted line and a thin trail of smoke streaming up from it.

- Practice **'some.'** Lead children in air-writing the word while saying letter names three times, repeating the word after each spelling. Erase the word from the board. Children say the letter names and repeat the word while writing the word on paper three times. Add **some** to your Word Wall.

- **Sentence Building** Say the sentence below and have the children repeat it twice. Have them tap the table from left to right as they say each word. Then display the *Word Cards* and have them build the sentence, taking turns placing the words in sequence. Each time a child places a word, the child points to each word in order as the class reads the partial sentence. After rebuilding the sentence, have everyone close their eyes and move one word from its spot to another part of the sentence. Then see if the children can correct it.

  Sentence: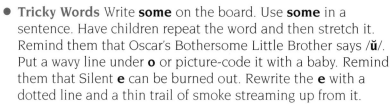

  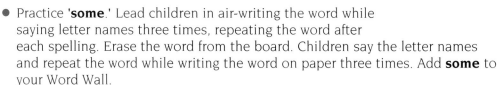

Word Wall

some

Unit 16

Mr. O and Mr. A out walking

Preparation and materials
- *PCCs*: Review list plus **oa**
- *Beyond ABC book*, p 44

✔ **Small group/independent**
- Unit 16 *Word Cards*: **float, goat, road, goal, load, soap, coat, boat**, *TG CD 2*
- Words to picture-code.

Decodable Word Bank

boat	goat	load
coat	oak	soak
soap	loaf	toad
road	foam	
float	goal	

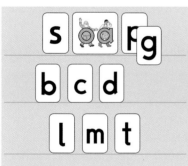

Review

- **PCCs b, c, d, ŏ, g, l, r, m, p, s, t, o_e** Use the 'Quick Dash' activity.

Introduce O and a out walking

- Show the **oa** *PCC* picture side, and tell the children that Mr. O and Mr. A like to go out walking just like some other Vowel Men they know about. Have children explain what these two Vowel Men do and say when they go out walking. Now will another whole batch of words become easy to read? **"Yes!"**

- Now let's everyone on this side of the class be Mr. O and wave and say your name together and everyone on this side be Mr. A and put your hand to your forehead and look all around without saying a thing. Then have the sides switch roles.

  Now tell your neighbour what Mr. O is doing. And listen while your neighbor tells you what Mr. A is doing.

- **Beyond ABC book** Read the **oa** page to the children (page 44) and have them hunt for pictured items with **oa**.

Word Building

- **On the pocket chart** Build each of these words from the **oa** story in *Beyond ABC*. After the class blends each word ask someone to tell how that word relates to the story or picture in the book. (For example, **"Someone was washing their socks with soap."**)

  PCCs: b, c, d, g, l, m, p, s, t, oa

  Words: boat, goat, toad, soap, goal, moat, coal

Small group/independent activities

- **Picture-coding** Give children large copies of words from the **oa** Decodable Word Bank to picture-code.

- **Pocket chart/table reading** Make the words below for blending. Use only the vowels' picture sides.

  PCCs: b, c, d, g, ŏ, l, r, t, oa

  Words: got, goat, goal, rod, road, load, lot, cot, coat, boat

- **Make a Word Card train** Let's make a train across the table as we read our Word Cards. Each child takes a turn reading a card and adding it to the lengthening train. As each word is added, the group reads the whole train of words.

  Word Cards: float, goat, road, goal, load, soap, coat, boat

Mr. I and Mr. E out walking

Preparation and materials

✔ **Preparation and materials**
- PCCs: Review list plus **l, p, t, ie**
- Unit 16 *Word Cards:* **pie, drip, coat, lie, drop, float, tie, goal, trip, tried, shop**, *TG CD 2*

✔ **Small group/independent**
- Additional Unit 16 *Word Cards:* **goat, die, soak, tied, chip, toad, fried, hope, boat**, *TG CD 2*
- *Tricky Word Cards:* **Have, they, your, my, I, the, will, [•] [?]** *TG CD 2*
- *Letterland Word Builders* or other letter sets.

Decodable Word Bank

tie	pie	tried	dried
lie	tied	fried	

drip	pie	drop	coat
trip	lie	shop	float
	tie		goal
	tried		

Review

- PCCs **c, d, ĭ, ŏ, r, ch, ai, ay, ch, ea, ee, oa**, Use the 'Guess Who?' activity.

Introduce i and e out walking

- Show the **ie** PCC picture side, and tell the children that Mr. I and Mr. E like to go out walking just like some other Vowel Men they have learned about. Have children explain what these two Vowel Men do and say when they go out walking.*

- Now let's everyone on this side of the class be Mr. I and wave and say your name together and everyone on this other side be Mr. E and put your hand up to your forehead and look all around without saying a thing. Then have the sides switch roles.

- Now tell your neighbor what Mr. I is doing. Then listen while your neighbor tells you what Mr. E is doing.

Word Building

- **Live Reading** Distribute *PCCs* and arrange children to form the words below. The class rollercoaster blends each word.

  PCCs: **c, d, l, p, t, ch, ie, oa**

  Words: **pie, tie, tied, lied, lie, load, coal, coach, toad**

Word Cards

- **Word Sorting** Place the *PCCs* along the top of the pocket chart. Show the *Word Card*. Have children say the word and call on one child to place the card under the *PCC* that it goes with. As the words accumulate, the child that places the card points to each card in that column for the whole class to read.

  PCCs: **ĭ, ie, ŏ, oa**

  Word Cards: **pie, drip, coat, lie, drop, float, tie, goal, trip, tried, shop**

Small group/independent activities

- **Reading with individual letter sets** Call out the letters in order for the children to build the first word but do not tell them the word. For each subsequent word, tell which letters need to be changed. After building each word, children touch each letter or pair of letters as they say the sounds together, then sweep their finger under the word as they blend the sounds. After they read the word, use it in a brief sentence. Then have them cover the word with their hand, spell it aloud, and then say the word again.

  Letters used: **a, d, e, f, i, l, m, o, p, r, t**

  Words: **pie, tie, tied, tried, fried, road, load, loaf, foam**

---

* Note: Children may find exceptions, eg. **Annie** (and other names), **field, believe, chief**. In Letterland terms this is because Mr. I and Mr. E sometimes like to take turns with the talking.

trip	pie	shop	goat
chip	die	drop	soak
	tied		toad
	fried		

- **Word Sorting by Sound** Place the four *PCCs* along the top of the pocket chart or table, as shown. Review the sound of each *PCC.* Say the first word but do not show the card. Have children repeat the word. Call on one child to rubber-band the word first and then have the rest of the children repeat the sounds. The first child then points to the *PCC* that represents the sound of the vowel in the word. Give the child the word to place under the *PCC.* The child then points to the word (and any others in the column) for all to read.

  PCCs: ĭ, ie, ŏ, oa

  Word Cards: **pie, trip, goat, die, shop, soak, tied, chip, toad, drop, fried**

- **Tricky Words** Write **they** on the board. Use **they** in a sentence. Have children repeat the word and then stretch it. Talk about the **e** that sounds like it should be Mr. A. This is not the Mr. E you know, but a very old man called Mr. Mean-E who tries to trick us by saying /ā/. Put a wavy line under **e** or picture-code it with stick man with a cane and a gray beard. (This *PCC* and story are in the Advanced Letterland materials.) Her Mr. Mean-E is out walking with Yo-Yo Man.

- **Practice** <u>they</u>. Lead children in air-writing the word while saying letter names three times, repeating the word after each spelling. Erase the word from the board. Children say the letter names and repeat the word while writing the word on paper three times. Add **they** to your Word Wall.

Word Wall

they

y<u>ou</u>r

- **Practice** <u>your</u>. Write **your** and and use it in a sentence. Show children that it is spelled like **you** with an **r** added. Put a wavy line under the **ou** and practice **your** just as you did with **they**. Add **your** to your Word Wall.

- **Sentence Building** Build Sentence 1. Read it to and then with the children as you point to the *word cards*. Then mix up the *Word Cards* and have children reconstruct the sentence, taking turns adding each word in turn. Do the same with the Sentence 2.

  Sentence 1: **Have they tried my pie?**

  Sentence 2: **I hope your boat will float.**

Mr. U and Mr. E out walking

Preparation and materials
- *PCCs*: Review list plus **ue**
- **Small group/independent**
  - Unit 16 *Word Cards*: **boat, tie, die, soak, glue, blue, lies, float, true**, *TG CD 2*
  - Words to picture-code

Decodable Word Bank

glue	clue	rescue
true	blue	

Review

- PCCs **b, ĕ, c, d, g, k, l, r, s, t, ie, oa** Use the 'Quick Dash' activity.

Introduce **i** and **e** out walking

- Show the '**ue**' *PCC* picture side. Here are the last two Vowel Men out walking that we will study. I bet you can tell me about these two. What is Mr. U saying? Yes, he is waving and saying his name, /ū/. And what is Mr. E doing? Yes, he is silent because he is too busy looking out for robots. Now, with Mr. U walking along so fast we sometimes don't hear his whole name. In most words it just comes out /oo/ (as in zoo). Can you say that with me when I push these two letters forward three times? /oo/ /oo/ /oo/

Word Building

- **Pocket chart reading or Live Spelling** Let's make some words with Mr. U and Mr. E out walking. Build each word and have the children blend them on their arm rollercoasters. Use each word in a brief sentence. When you build the last word **rescue**, put a space between the syllables as shown at the left. Have children blend the first syllable (**res**) and say it. Then have them blend the second syllable (**cue**). Push the syllables together for children to read the whole word. Tell them that in this word Mr. U is careful to say his name clearly (**you**) because he is so pleased to be part of a **rescue**.

  PCCs: **b, ĕ, c, g, l, r, s, t, ue**

  Words: **blue, glue, clue, true, rescue**

Small group/independent activities

- **Picture-coding** Give children large copies of various words from the **ie** and **ue** Decodable Word Banks to picture-code.

- **Spelling with letter sets** Review the sounds of the *PCCs* for **ue, ie, oa** and leave them visible on the table. Call out the word and have children repeat it and then rubber-band stretch it to hear all the sounds. Children build the word and blend it to check their spelling. Then have them cover the word, spell it aloud, and repeat the word. They leave the letters of the word in place and follow the previous steps to segment the next word. Then they change the letters as needed to make the new word, etc.

  Letters needed: **a, b, c, d, e, f, g, i, l, o, r, t, u**

  Words: **tied, tried, true, toad, goat, glue, clue, blue, load, lie, lied, fried**

- **Word Sort** Display the picture side of the three *PCCs* in a horizontal row. Have children take turns placing the *Word Cards* and leading the reading of the words in the column.

  PCCs: **ie, oa, ue**

  Words: **boat, tie, die, soak, glue, blue, lies, float, true**

Review ai, ay, ea

Preparation and materials

- *PCCs*: Review list
- *Vowel Scene Poster*: Vowels Out Walking
- Unit 14 *Word Cards*: **tail, play, main, stay, aim, wait, way, say**, *TG CD 2*
- Unit 15 *Word Cards*: **read, clean, real, reach, heat**, *TG CD 2*
- Copies of *The Vowel Men Out Walking: A Play*, *TG CD 2*

Small group/independent

- Copies of 'Lesson 171 Written Word Sort', *TG CD 2*
- Unit 14 *Word Cards*: **may, play, train**, *TG CD 2*
- Unit 15 *Word Cards*: **team** *TG CD 2*
- *Tricky Word Cards*: **not, on, the, The,** ▪ , *TG CD 2*
- *Letterland Word Builders,* or other letter sets

Review

- **PCCs ai, ay, ee, ea, ie, oa, ue** Use the 'Guess Who?' activity.

The Vowel Men out walking

- **Vowel Scene Poster: Vowels Out Walking**
Display the poster and have children identify the sound of each pair of Vowel Men and think of a word that contains the pair. Have children point out the Robots hiding in the scene. Keep the poster on display in the classroom to remind children of these pairs of vowel letters with just one sound per two letters.

Live Word Sorting

- Distribute the *PCCs* to three pairs of children. Have them stand in front of the class with the first Vowel Man in each pair holding the *PCC* and the second one pretending to look out for robots. Mix up the *Word Cards* listed below in a random order. Call another child to the front and give him or her a *Word Card* to read. Then let the child deliver the *Word Card* to the pair of Vowel Men that match its sound and spelling. The first one calls out his name and the second Vowel Man then holds the *Word Card* for everyone to read. When a Vowel Man has accumulated more than one *Word Card*, he shows all of his words in turn for the class to read every time he receives a new word.

  PCCs: ai, ay, ea

  Unit 14 Word Cards: tail, play, main, stay, aim, wait, way, say

  Unit 15 Word Cards: read, clean, real, reach, heat

Readers' Theater Play: 'The Vowel Men Out Walking'

- Read Part One (Prologue and Scenes 1 and 2) of *The Vowel Men Out Walking: A Play* to the children. Then assign roles and read it as a play. The children could practice their roles for fluency. After Lesson 172 they could produce it as a radio play or memorize their lines for a little performance.

Small group/independent activities

- **Spelling with letter sets** Review the sounds on the *PCCs* for **ai, ay, ea** and leave them visible on the table. Call out the word and have children repeat it and then rubber-band it to hear all the sounds. Children build the word and blend it to check their spelling. Then have them cover the word, spell it aloud, and repeat the word. They leave the letters of the word in place and follow the previous steps. Then they change the letters as needed to make the new word, etc.

  Letters needed: a, b, d, e, i, l, m, s, t, w, y

  Words: day, deal, meal, mail, may, way, wait, sail, seat, beat, bait

ai	ay	ea
plain	stay	real
brain	tray	dream
nail	lay	beat

Lesson 171 Written Word Sort

- **Written Word Sort** Children point to the pairs of Vowel Men at the top of each column of the 'Lesson 171 Written Word Sort' page, and give the sounds. Call out the words below. Children repeat the word, rubber-band stretch the word, and point to the column where they think the word belongs. After you agree, they write the word in the column. When all the words have been written, have the children read their columns of words to a partner.

  Words: stay, real, dream, plain, tray, brain, lay, beat, nail

- **Sentence Writing** Read the sentence below to the children and have them repeat it twice. Display the *Word Cards* in random order and have the children build the sentence. Then turn the cards over to the plain side. Have them read the 'invisible sentence' as you point to the words. Then have them 'make the sentence visible' by writing it on their own paper. Turn the cards back over for children to check their sentence.

  Sentence: | The | team | may | not | play | on | the | train | . |

Unit 16: Lesson 172

Review ee, ie, oa, and ue

Preparation and materials
- *PCCs*: Review list
- Unit 15 *Word Cards*: **deep, green, need, feet**, *TG CD 2*
- Unit 16 *Word Cards*: **boat, loan, road, tie, lie, tried, glue, clue, true, blue**, *TG CD 2*
- Copies of *The Vowel Men Out Walking: A Play*, *TG CD 2*

✔ Small group/independent
- Copies of 'Lesson 172 Written Word Sort', *TG CD 2*
- Unit 16 *Word Cards*: **blue, boat, tied**
- *Tricky Word Cards*: **The, is, not, up,** | ! | *TG CD 2*
- *Letterland Word Builders*

Review

- **PCCs: ai, ay, ee, ea, ie, oa, ue** Use the 'Quick Dash' activity.

Live Word Sorting

- Distribute the *PCCs* to four pairs of children. Have them stand in front of the class with the first Vowel Man in each pair holding the *PCC* and the second one pretending be the lookout man. Mix up the *Word Cards* listed below in a random order. Call another child to the front and give the child a *Word Card* to read. Then let the child deliver the card to the pair of Vowel Men that match its sound and spelling. The second Vowel Man (the lookout) then holds the *Word Card* for everyone to read. When a lookout man has accumulated more than one card, he shows all of his words in turn for the class to read each time he receives a new word.

  PCCs: ee, ie, oa, ue

  Unit 15 Word Cards: deep, green, need, feet

  Unit 16 Word Cards: boat, loan, road, tie, lie, tried, glue, clue, true, blue

Readers' Theater Play

- Read Part Two (Scenes 3-5) of *The Vowel Men Out Walking: A Play* to the children. Then assign roles and read it as a play. The children could practice their roles for fluency, then produce it as a radio play (tape record and play it back for them), or memorize their lines for a little performance for another class or for parents.

Small group/independent activities

- **Spelling with letter sets** Quickly review the sounds of the *PCCs* for **ee, ie, oa, ue** and leave them visible on the table. Call out the word and have children repeat it and then rubber-band stretch it to hear all the sounds. Children build the word and blend it to check their spelling. Then have them cover the word, spell it aloud, and repeat the word. They leave the letters of the word in place and follow the previous steps, changing the letters as needed to make the new word, etc.

  Letters needed: a, b, d, e, e (or tile for 2nd **e**)**, f, g, h, i, l, n, o, r, t, u**

  Words: lie, tie, teeth, toad, true, blue, glue, green, loan, float

- **Written Word Sort** Children point to the pairs of Vowel Men at the top of each column and give the sound. Call out the words below. Children repeat the word, rubber-band stretch the word, and point to the column where they think the word belongs. After you confirm their choice, they write the word in the column. When all the words have been written have children read the columns of words to a partner.

  Words: seem, blue, pie, goat, peep, true, lie, soap, foam, sheet, glue, tied

- **Sentence Writing** Read the sentence below to the children and have them repeat it twice. Display the *word cards* in random order and have the children build the sentence. Then turn the cards over to the plain side. Have them read the 'invisible sentence' as you point to the words. Then have them 'make the sentence visible' by writing it on their own paper. Turn the cards back over for children to check their sentence.

  Sentence: | The | blue | boat | is | not | tied | up | ! |

Section 6 Assessments

You can assess your children's mastery of the outcomes for this Section with the following two assessments:

1. Word Reading Accuracy Children read a list of 12 decodable words.

2. Spelling Decodable Words Children spell 6 words that you dictate.

Assessment Pages

Teacher's Guide: Student reads the word list below.

Teacher's Guide CD 2: Section 6 Assessment (Score Sheet).

Assessment Instructions

(1) Word Reading Accuracy (individual administration) The child reads the 12 words below. Encourage the child to 'sound them out.' If the child says the word in a segmented fashion (e.g. /**h**/ /**ē**/ /**t**/ for 'heat'), you may say, Put it together, or, Blend it. Only count the word as correct if the child is able to say it finally without segmentation (**"heat"**). After about five seconds on a word, have the child move on to the next word. On the Score Sheet put a line through any words missed, or write the substitution above the word. The goal is at least 10 of 12 words correct.

(2) Spelling Decodable Words (group administration) Provide paper and pencil for each child. Ask the children to rubber-band stretch the word on their own and then write it. When everyone is ready, do the same with each word. On the Score Sheet, copy misspellings or put a line through words missed. The goal is at least 4 of 6 words correct. (Note **ea** spellings are not tested as they have the same sound as **ee** spellings.) Words tested: **rain, say, soap, blue, lie, tree.**

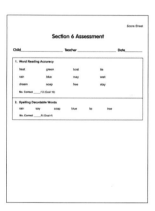

Section 6 Assessment Student Page

1. Word Reading Accuracy

heat	green	boat	tie
rain	blue	may	wait
dream	soap	free	stay

No. Correct _____/12 (Goal 10)

Section 7
The Vowel Stealers

Lessons 173-180

The Vowel Stealers

Section 7 The Vowel Stealers includes 8 lessons to help you teach your children about those tricky r-controlled vowels: **ar, er, ir, or**, and **ur**.

> **Unit 17**: Lessons 173-176 **Arthur Ar** and **Orvil Or**
>
> **Unit 18**: Lessons 177-180 **Ernest Er**, **Urgent Ur**, and **Irving Ir**

Learning about the Vowel Stealing Robots

This section continues many of the lively activities from previous sections, but also includes new activities specifically designed to make learning about **r**-controlled vowels fun and memorable.

The five Vowel Stealing Robots are Letterland's law-breakers. They alert children to the power of the letter **r** to alter the behavior of any vowel they discover 'behind a **r**obot's back'. The robots' alliterative names cue each new sound, while the *Picture Code Cards* provide visual clues (**Ar**thur **Ar**'s rad**ar** c**ar**, **Or**vil **Or**'s boat by the sh**or**e, **Er**nest **Er**'s running shoes, showing he is the fast**er** runn**er**, **Ur**gent **Ur** with his boots of c**ur**ly, p**ur**ple f**ur**, and **Ir**ving **Ir** with his ink-stained d**ir**ty sh**ir**t). What with each vowel captured and being dragged off in the Robot's sack, they clearly won't be making their usual sounds!

Children learn to spot these sneaky robots by becoming Reading Detectives, always on the lookout for those **r**'s with vowels behind their backs. Each child shows the power of the letter **r** to control the vowel by drawing the two letters connected by a simple outline of a sack. The robots are, in fact, great motivators for children to get in the habit of looking ahead as they process print, because they love catching the robots in the act! The same strategy will continue to stand them in good stead when it comes to decoding larger units of sound such as **–air, -ear, -eer, -oar**, and **–our** where the **r** controls two vowels.

Lively songs and stories will strengthen your teaching of this Section on **r**-controlled vowels, and also the *Vowel Stealer Poster* with its further visual clues. These include: **ar**—st**ar**s in the d**ar**k sky, **or**—the edge of the sh**or**e, **er**—the f**er**ns, **ur**—the c**ur**b in the c**ur**ving road, and **ir**—the b**ir**d and a f**ir** tree. (Note that the robots never bother to mend their nets. That means that the vowels always manage to free themselves so they can still turn up in lots of other words!)

New Materials from the Teacher's Guide CD

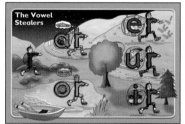

You will find in this section new *Word Cards* for each Unit (on the *Teacher's Guide CD 2*), a short Reader's Theater Play, featuring the law-breaking robots and the days of the week, and a score sheet for Section 7 Assessment.

Learning Outcomes and Assessments

Outcomes	Assessments (See pages 220–221)
• Read words with **r**-controlled vowels: **ar, er, ir, or, ur**	1.Word Reading Accuracy
• Read high-frequency words with irregular spellings.	2. Cumulative Tricky Word Assessment

Tricky Words

• Children are taught to read and spell two additional Tricky Words in this Section:

    are   **going**   (Previous Tricky Words are also reviewed.)

Unit 17

Introducing Arthur Ar

✔ Preparation and materials
- *PCCs*: Review list plus **c, f, k, m, n, sh, ar**
- *Beyond ABC* book, pages 26-27
- Write the sentences on the board for Word Detectives (or project)

✔ Small group/independent
- Write or print words from the *Decodable Word Bank*, one per page for children to picture-code.
- *Letterland Word Builders*, or individual letter sets
- Unit 17 *Word Cards*: **dark, barn, park, smart, bark, yard, car, harm, star**, *TG CD 2*

Decodable Word Bank

art	start	star
car	part	bark
far	jar	dark
farm	hard	yard
barn	card	sharp
park	smart	shark
arm	harm	alarm

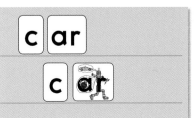

Review

- **PCCs ă, ā, b, d, h, j, y, ai, ay, a_e** Use the 'Guess Who?' activity.

Arthur Ar

- **Introduce Arthur Ar, the Apple Stealer** Before revealing the *PCC*, share this. We all know about Red Robot and how he likes to run away with things that begin with his sound, but did you know that there are five other Robots in Letterland that sometimes capture the vowels? Let me show you one of these trouble-makers. Show the **ar** *PCC* picture side and write his name to show how it is spelled. This is Arthur Ar, and as you can see he has captured Annie Apple. Just look at her! How do you think she feels about that? She is very unhappy because now she is too upset to make her usual sound. What we will hear instead is Arthur Ar calling out his own last name "**Ar!**", using his tiny mobile phone hidden on his outstretched arm to report to his ring leader, Red Robot. Every time he captures a talking apple he reports it to Red Robot by saying his last name. Can you say it with me?..."**Ar! Ar!**"

All the robots have torn sacks which they can't be bothered to fix, so all the vowels eventually escape!

- Now the tricky thing about the Vowel Stealing Robots is catching them in a word! They are trouble-makers for us because they make different sounds. Turn to the plain letter side. Point to the **a**. When you see this letter, you may think it will be Annie Apple making her usual 'a' sound sound, but you need to be a good detective and spot the next letter, because it is a Vowel Stealing Robot! Point to the **r**. Ah! ha! It's you, Arthur Ar, and you're running away with that talking apple and saying your own name, **Ar**. Well, you didn't fool us! Let's show Arthur Ar that he didn't trick us by saying his name three times as I push his card forward. "**Ar, Ar, Ar.**"

- Let's see if we can find out more about this Letterland Apple Stealer.

- **Beyond ABC book** (pages 26-27) Share the story and picture and let the children discover more words with the /**ar**/ sound and perhaps write them on the board. (A full list is on page 47 of *Beyond ABC*.)

Word Building

- **On the pocket chart** Make the word **car** with the plain letter sides of the *PCCs*. Let's be detectives and see if there is a Vowel Stealing Robot in this word. Do you see one? Where? Yes, there right after Annie Apple. Good detective work! Turn **ar** to the picture side. We caught you at your robber trick, Arthur Ar! So, is Annie Apple going to be saying her usual sound? "**No.**" Not while she is stuck behind that Robot's back in his net. What sound are we going to hear instead? /**ar**/. So let's put these two sounds on our arm rollercoaster and blend them. "/**k**/ /**ar**/, **car.**"

- Make the rest of the words one at a time with plain letters sides, and for each word let a child be the 'chief detective.' The Chief Detective comes forward and flips the **ar** card to the picture side to show Arthur Ar that he hasn't fooled anybody. Then the Chief shows the class how to rollercoaster the word. The Chief repeats this as the class joins in.

  PCCs: b, c, d, f, h, j, k, m, n, y, ar, sh

  Words: car, card, hard, barn, far, farm, jar, yard, shark

- **Word Detectives** Write the sentences below on the board or project them. Tell the children that this is an even more challenging detective job because Arthur Ar is hiding in several words in these sentences. Have children come forward and picture-code each **ar**, roughly as shown at the left. (If you write the sentence large and spread out, several children may be able to picture-code at the same time.) You may want to make copies of the sentences for each child to picture-code. If time is limited, just have children draw the robber bag from the top of the **r** going around Annie Apple. Then read the sentences with the children several times.

  Arthur Ar parks his radar car in the dark yard.

  The smart farmer sets his alarm to start his day on time.

Small group/independent activities

- **Picture-coding** Give each child one large **ar** word from the Decodable Word Bank to picture-code.

- **Reading with individual letter sets** Have children first place the letters **a** and **r** together and then touch under the two letters and say /ar/. Then say, Place an **f** (or /fff/) at the beginning of the word. Now, let's touch the first letter and say the sound (/f/) and then the **a-r** together and say /ar/. Now, slide your fingers underneath and blend the sounds ("**ffffar, far**"). Guide children in building and blending the remaining words in the same way. (Option: After reading the word, children spell it aloud with eyes shut.)

  Letters: a, c, d, f, h, j, m, r, s, t, t

  Words: far, farm, arm, art, start, star, jar, hard, card, car

- **Word Card Train** Give each child a *Word Card*. Then one at a time, they read their words and place them in a train line. Each time a child places a word, that child points to each word in the train from left to right for all to read.

  Word Cards: dark, barn, park, smart, bark, yard, car, harm, star

More with Arthur Ar

Preparation and materials

- *PCCs*: Review list plus **b, c, n, p, t**
- Poster: *The Vowel Stealers*
- *Blends and Digraphs Songs* CD, #33
- Project lyrics or copy to a chart, *TG CD 2*
- Props: A net shopping bag, a backpack, or a towel for Arthur Ar's robber sack

Small group/independent

- *Letterland Word Builders,* or individual letter sets
- Unit 17 *Word Cards*: **park, dark, stars**, *TG CD 2*
- *Tricky Word Cards*: **are, Are, going, in, the, the, to, see, Yes, we**, *TG CD 2*

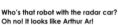

The Apple Stealer's Song

Who's that robot with the radar car?
Oh no! It looks like Arthur Ar!

Arthur Ar thinks he's very smart,
but we know where he got
those apples in his tarts!

Catch him, catch him, before he goes too far.
Catch Arthur Ar in his radar car.

Review

- **PCCs ă, ā, Magic e, k, ŭ, ai, ar, ay, a_e, sh** Use the 'Quick Dash' activity.

Reading Detectives

- **Listening for Arthur Ar** Display the **ar** *PCC*. Remind children how they showed they were good detectives with their *eyes* in the previous lesson, by finding Arthur Ar running off with Annie Apple. Tell them that good detectives also use their *ears* to catch Arthur Ar when they are spelling words. Have children close their eyes and listen for Arthur Ar saying /ar/ at the beginning of the words below. They can signal with a 'thumbs up' if they hear him, 'thumbs down' if not (or whatever signal you would like them to use). Then have them rubber-band stretch the second group of words and listen for the /**ar**/ sound in the middle, or at the end of each word.

    At the beginning? **ar**gue, book, **ar**m, cave, **ar**tist, **ar**my, ape, **ar**tichoke

    At the middle or end? j**ar**, sock, p**ar**t, day, m**ar**k, shake, h**ar**d, st**ar**

- **Using our ears and eyes** Display the Vowel Scene Poster entitled "The Vowel Stealers." Have children look for things pictured near Arthur Ar that contain his /**ar**/ sound. As they are identified, write these words for children to see the spelling: e.g. st**ar**s, rad**ar** c**ar**.

Sing Along

- **The Apple Stealer's Song** Play Track 33 of the *Blends and Digraph Songs* CD. Read your displayed version of the lyrics as you point to the words a few lines at a time. (In US schools you may want to explain that a **tart** is a pie.) Then let them read the lines with you. After completing the lyrics, play the recording again for all to sing. Option: have children highlight **ar** in the lyrics you have displayed, or print copies for each of them to highlight.

Word Building

- **Live Spelling** Distribute the *PCC*s. Have two children share the **ar** card. Arthur Ar faces in the reading direction with his robber sack over his shoulder. Annie Apple holds onto the sack with one hand as if captured, and holds the *PCC* in the other hand. These two stand to the audience's left and wait to come rushing in together when signalled by the class.

- Call out the first word. Have children rubber-band stretch it to segment the sounds. Children decide which letters are needed. (Call on individuals sometimes and sometimes the whole class.) When ready for **ar** to be added to the words, the class could make siren noises as if the police are looking for Arthur Ar. (If this is too noisy, you could just have children raise their hands and make circles in the air as if they were the flashing lights of a patrol car.) For the next words they decide who needs to sit down and who needs to be added to the word. If there is no **ar** sound the **ar**-children return to the left to await another **ar** word.

PCCs: ă, ā, b, c, Magic e, k, n, p, t, ar, ai, sh

Words: cap, car, cane, barn, bait, shake, sharp, shark, bark

Small group/independent activities

- **Spelling with individual letter sets** Call out words for children to rubber-band stretch and build. (For children needing more support, let the group stretch the words and build them together with *Picture Code Cards*.) If only one or two letters are to be changed, have the children leave the previous word in place as they stretch the next word. If more than two letters will be changed have them clear their board and start from scratch.

  Letters: a, b, c, d, e, h, i, k, m, n, o, p, r, t

  Words: back, bank, barn, boat, home, harm, arm, chain, chart, art, dart

- **Tricky Words** Write **are** on board. Use it in a sentence. Elicit from children that the **ar** is saying Arthur Ar's last name and that he has had to overpower the silent Magic **e** on the end, as well, to make sure it could not make Mr. A appear in Annie's place! Draw a sack around the **e** as well, and show the wand being broken by Arthur Ar and the top hat falling off.

- **Practice 'are'** Lead children in air-writing the word while saying letter names three times, repeating the word after each spelling. Erase the word from the board. Children then say the letter names and repeat the word while writing the word on paper three times. Add **are** to your Word Wall.

- Write **'going'** on the board. Cover up the **–ing** and have children read **go**. Then cover up **go** and ask children to say **–ing**. Explain that we add **–ing** on to lots of words that tell what we are doing, i.e. walking, running, sitting, talking, playing. Have the children practice writing and spelling **going** as they did **are** above. Add **going** to your Word Wall.

- **Sentence Building** Build the Question sentence below and read it *to* the children and then *with* them several times. Take away the *Word Cards* and say the Answer sentence. Have the children repeat it two or more times. Display the *Word Cards* for the Answer sentence in random order and have children build that sentence. As in previous lessons, have each child add a word in turn and lead the group in reading the words placed so far.

  Question: Are we going to the park in the dark?

  Answer: Yes, we are going to see the stars.

- **Word Hunt Challenge** Good detectives keep a sharp lookout for Arthur Ar wherever there are words! Let them collect some examples. (They don't have to be able to read these words, but will probably *want to* with your help.) How many classmates' first, middle and last names can the children discover with **ar** in them? How many places can they find on a map? They could collect street names, shop names, words on signs, in shop windows, and of course words in notices around the school.

  Note: Children may find exceptions, especially words with **rr**. The Letterland explanation: Two **r**obots together rarely rob. They are too busy racing each other! Examples: a**rr**ow, ca**rr**y, ma**rr**y, be**rr**y, me**rr**y, mi**rr**or, so**rr**y, tomo**rr**ow.

Word Wall

are

going

Introducing Orvil Or

Preparation and materials

✔
- *PCCs*: Review list plus **c, f, h, k, m, n, or**
- *Vowel Stealers* Poster
- *Beyond ABC* book, pages 28-29
- Props: A net shopping bag, or backpack, or a towel for Orvil Or's robber sack
- Write/project the Word Detective sentences on the board
- Prepare Word Bank words for children to picture-code

✔ **Small group/independent**
- Additional *PCCs*: **b, th**
- *Word Cards* Unit 17: **horn, park, north, card, start, for, short, sharp, born**, *TG CD 2*

Decodable Word Bank

<u>or</u>	<u>ore</u>	<u>oor</u>
or	store	floor
for	sore	door
born	shore	poor
fork	score	
corn	more	<u>our</u>
horn	core	four
storm	chore	your
north	snore	pour
pork		fourteen
torn		
worn		<u>oar</u>
sports		oar
		roar
		soar

Review

● **PCCs** ă, ā, p, s, s=z, t, ar, oa, sh, o_e Use the 'Guess Who?' activity.

Orvil Or

● **Introduce the Orange Stealer** You've become good detectives. You've been catching Arthur Ar by keeping a sharp lookout and listening carefully. Display the plain side of the *PCC* for Orvil Or. Now we have a new Robber for you to go after, Reading Detectives! When you see this **o** with an **r** after it (point to the **o**) you might want to say Oscar Orange's sound, but don't do it! There is another Vowel Stealing Robot right next to that **o**. Do you want to see what he looks like?

● Show the plain letter side. Here is that tricky, sneaky, Robot. His name is Orvil Or. Write it out so everyone can see how it is spelled. We had better memorize his name. Let's say it three times. **"Orvil Or"** (x 3). We need to be on the lookout for Orvil Or, or else we might be fooled and say the wrong sound. Every chance he gets, Orvil Or takes a talking orange and runs off with it. He reports back to Red Robot on a tiny mobile phone, just like Arthur Ar, except Orvil Or reports with his own last name, Or. Turn back to the plain letter side. So, whenever you see an **o**range right behind a **r**obot's back, do you know what to say? Let's say it three times as I push his card toward you. **"Or, Or, Or."**

● **Beyond ABC book** Let's read more about Orvil Or so we can make sure he doesn't trick us. You might hear his sound in this story a lot. Then we'll see what things we can discover in the picture with his sound. Share the story and picture and let the children discover more words with the /**or**/ sound. (A full list is on page 47 of *Beyond ABC*.)

Word Building

● **Live Reading** Distribute *PCCs*. Begin with two children holding the **or** *PCC*. Orvil Or holds his sack over his shoulder as he faces in the reading direction and Oscar Orange holds onto the sack with one hand as if captured, and holds the **or** *PCC* with the other hand. Line children up to make the words below from the *Beyond ABC* pages. After the class rollercoasters the word, ask someone to tell how the word relates to the story or illustration. (For the extra **s** in sports use the plain side of the Sleepy Sammy *PCC*.)

    PCCs: **c, f, h, k, m, n, p, s, s=z, t, or, sh**

    Words: **or, corn, fork, horns, storm, snort, sports, shorts**

● **Word Detectives** Write the sentences on the board or project them and read each one *to* and then *with* the children. Tell the children they need to be good detectives and find Orvil Or in these sentences. Have children come forward and picture-code each **or** roughly as shown at the left. (If the sentence is large and spread out, several children may be able to picture-code at the same time.) You may want to print copies of the sentences for each child to picture-code. If time is limited, just have children draw the robber bag from the top of the **r** going around Oscar Orange.

    Orvil Or was born in the north.
    These shorts are worn for sports.

 park | horn
card | north
start | born

Small group/independent activities

- **Picture-coding** Give each child a sheet with one large **or** word from the Decodable Word Bank to picture-code.
- **Pocket chart/table reading** Make the words below for children to rollercoaster. Use each word in a brief sentence after the children decode it.

  PCCs: **b, c, f, k, n, p, s, s, t, or, th**

  Words: **or, for, fork, born, corn, north, torn, sports**
- **Word Sort** Review the **ar** and **or** sounds. One at a time, children read a *Word Card* and place it under the *PCC* that matches the sound. Every child that places a word gets to lead the group in reading the column where it was placed.

  PCCs: **ar, or**

  Word Cards: **horn, park, north, card, start, for, short, sharp, born**

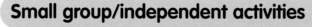

Unit 17: Lesson 176

More with Orvil Or

Review

- **PCCs Magic e, ŏ, ō, o=ŭ, y, oa, or, o_e, sh** Use the 'Quick Dash' activity.

Listen first

- **Listening for Orvil Or** Display the **or** *PCC*. It's time to be detectives with our ears listening for Orvil Or in words so we'll know how to spell those words. Have children close their eyes and listen for Orvil Or saying /or/ at the beginning of the words below. They can signal with a 'thumbs up' if they hear him, 'thumbs down' if not. Then have them rubber-band stretch the second group of words and listen for the /**or**/ sound in the middle or at the end.

  Note: Many words have divergent spelling with the same sound. These spellings will be addressed later in the lesson. Here children are listening to but not seeing the words.

  At the beginning? order, sudden, **or**gan, **or**chard, exit, office, **or**dinary, **or**chestra

  At the middle or end? st**or**e, sh**or**t, game m**or**e, f**our**, snap, d**oor**, munch, f**or**t

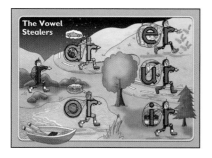

- **Using our ears and eyes** Display your *Vowel Stealers Poster* and point out Red Robot, the Ringleader, **r**unning between the **r**ed **r**ocks. Review the now familiar Apple Stealer, Arthur Ar, and notice how he is thinking about making a quick escape in his rad**ar** c**ar** as the sky turns d**ar**k and the first st**ar**s appear. Point out that Orvil Or keeps his getaway boat by the sh**or**e and that he has m**or**e oranges st**or**ed in his boat. Also call attention to the **oars** he uses to move it along. Write these /**or**/ words for children to see that Orvil Or is an especially tricky Robot to catch because he sometimes captures more than one vowel, as in the word o**ar**. We'll learn more about his spelling tricks a little later.

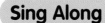

Sing Along

- **The Orange Stealer's Song** Play Track 34 of the *Blends and Digraph Songs* CD. Read the lyrics to the children as you point to the words a few lines at a time. Then let them read the lines with you. Play the recording again for all to sing. (Option: have children highlight **or** in the lyrics you have displayed, or make copies for each of them to highlight.)

Word Building

- **Chalkboard Reading** Write the word **more** and quickly picture-code it as shown below. Explain that Magic **e**'s magic sparks don't work in **ore** words because Orvil Or abs**or**bs the sparks into his robot arm. Write the other -**ore** words below **more**, one at a time. Have children rollercoaster them. Then review the list before moving on to the next column.

- Picture-code **door, four,** and **oar** as shown and explain, Orvil Or is in such a rush to capture vowels that he sometimes catches an extra one. But one or two, it doesn't matter to him. He keeps on rep**or**ting back his name **"Or"** as he has always done bef**or**e. Write the words under each picture-coded word and guide children as they rollercoaster the words. Review each column. (Note: not all –**our** words say /**or**/.)

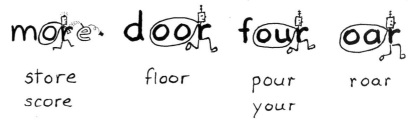

more	door	four	oar
store	floor	pour	roar
score		your	

Small group/independent activities

- **Word Card Train** Display the Orvil Or *PCC.* Remind children that Orvil Or sometimes captures two vowels. Tell them that all the *Word Cards* in this train will have Orvil's /**or**/ sound.

  Give each child a *Word Card.* One at a time, they read their words and place them in a train line. Each time a child places a word, that child points to each word in the train from left to right for all to read.

  Word Cards: four, your, more, store, score, door, floor, oar, roar

- **Sentence Building** Build the sentence and read it *to* the children and then *with* them several times. Take up the *Word Cards* and say the sentence together. All repeat it twice. Display the words in random order and have children build the sentence. As in previous lessons, have each child add a word in turn and lead the group in reading the words placed so far.

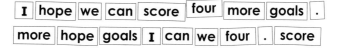

- **Word Hunt Challenge** Now is a good time for catching Orvil Or in words in the environment, and in the names of people and places, on signs, on maps, etc. The children may discover for themselves how Orvil Or keeps on turning up in far away places like **New York, Georgia, Florida, Oregon,** and even up at the **North Pole**!

  Note: Children may find exceptions, particularly when trouble-maker Walter Walrus is about: e.g. **word, work, world, worm, worth** and **worst**.

Unit 18

Introducing Ernest Er

Preparation and materials
✔ **Preparation and materials**
- *PCCs:* Review list plus **f, g, h, m, n, s, s, t, ŭ, er,**
- *Vowel Scenes Poster: The Vowel Stealers*
- *Beyond ABC* book, p 30-31
- *Blends and Digraphs Songs*, #38
- Project lyrics or copy to a chart

✔ **Small group/independent**
- Write or print words from the **er** *Decodable Word Bank*, one per page for children to picture-code
- *Letterland Word Builders*, or individual letter sets
- Unit 18 *Word Cards:* **her, brother, mother, ever, better, over, other, summer,** *TG CD 2*

Decodable Word Bank

faster	bother	sister
runner	better	over
other	letter	summer
brother	ever	winter
mother	never	

Review

- **PCCs ă, b, ĕ, ĭ, ī, ō, o=ŭ, r, v, ar, or, th** Use the 'Guess Who?' activity.

Ernest Er

- **Introduce the Er/Ur/Ir Brothers** Display the *Vowel Stealers Poster*. Here we have all the Robots in Letterland. Let's name the ones we have already met. Point to Red Robot, Arthur Ar, and Orvil Or as children name them. Here are three more Robots that are all the same color and they sort of look alike. That's because they are brothers, the **Er Brothers**. They all say their last name the same way /**er**/, but, look! They spell it three different ways because each one captures a different vowel! Write the names of **Ernest Er**, **Irving Ir**, and **Urgent Ur** for the children to compare. Today we are going to learn about this one. Point to Ernest Er. His name is Ernest Er. Circle his name. We had better be good detectives and memorize his name. Say it with me three times. "**Ernest Er.**" (x 3)

- Let's see what is in the picture that has his sound. Oh, here are some **ferns**. You may have seen this plant around homes or offices. Write **ferns** for all to see.

- Show the *PCC* of Ernest Er. So which vowel does Ernest Er like to capture? Yes, Eddy Elephant. And just like the other Robot Robbers, he reports his capture on his tiny mobile phone. He calls out his last name, "**Er.**" Turn to the plain letter side. So when we see these letters together, we'll show Ernest Er that he can't trick us. We'll always say /**er**/. Let's practice. Say it each time I push the card forward. "**Er, Er, Er.**"

- **Beyond ABC book** (page 30) Let's listen for Ernest Er's last name in words as we read about him. You will hear his name at the end of lots of words and we'll find out why shortly. In the second paragraph you may want to stop occasionally and ask children to name words where they heard /**er**/. Let them discover more words in the picture with the /**er**/ sound. (A full list is on page 47 of *Beyond ABC*.)

Word Building

- **Live Reading** Distribute *PCCs*. Begin with two children holding the **er** PCC. Ernest Er holds his sack over his shoulder as he faces in the reading direction and Eddy Elephant holds onto the sack with one hand as if captured, and holds the **er** PCC with the other hand. Line children up to make the words below.

   PCCs: **ĕ, h, n, ō, s, s, t, v, er** Words: **her, never, ever, over, enter, sister**

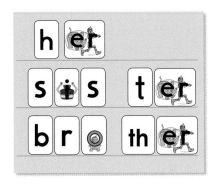

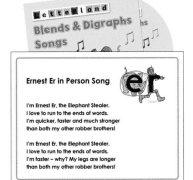

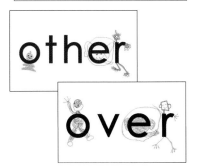

- **On the pocket chart** Make the word **her** and have children rollercoaster the two sounds. Then explain, Ernest Er turns up a lot in this one little word, **her**, but you wont see him in many other little words. Instead you will often find Ernest Er at the end of long**er** words. Because he is a fast**er** runn**er**, he turns up in more long**er** words than eith**er** of the oth**er** robot broth**er**s. Write out **faster** and **runner** for the children to see how Ernest Er beats his broth**er**s to the ends of these long**er** words.

- **Family Words** Leave a space between the syllables (i.e. **sis ter**). Have children rollercoaster the first syllable and say **"sis,"** then the second syllable and say **"ter."** Then push the syllables together and have them say the two parts together, **"sister."** Handle the other two syllable words below in the same way. Point out that Ernest Er is in several words that name family memb**er**s. Write **sister, mother,** and **brother** (review Oscar's Bothersome Little Brother briefly). Write **father** on the board and tell children the word. Have them decide which letter doesn't say its usual sound. (**a**) Draw a wavy line under the **a**. Continue with the other two syllable words.

  PCCs: ă, b, ĕ, f, g, h, ĭ, m, n, ō, o=ŭ, r, s, s, t, ŭ, v, er, th

  Words: **her, sis-ter, broth-er, moth-er, oth-er, num-ber, un-der**

Sing Along

- **Ernest Er in Person Song** Explain that if they listen closely they can find out *why* Ernest Er is fast**er** than his oth**er** broth**er**s. Listen to the song and then discuss. Read the lyrics *to* the children and then a few times *with* them. They could highlight each time **er** appears in the lyrics. Have everyone sing the song again as you point to the words. Leave the lyrics where children can read or listen to them later as they follow with the recording.

Small group/independent activities

- **Picture-coding** Give each child one large **er** word from the Decodable Word Bank to picture-code.

- **Spelling with individual letter sets** Display the Ernest Er *PCC*. Review his sound. Children stretch the word **her** and orally segment the two sounds. They build the word and then blend it to check. For the two-syllable words use the steps below. (It may help to demonstrate the first few words with your own set of letters as children follow with their letter sets.)

  1. Help them repeat the word as a whole (e.g. "**sister**").
  2. Then say the word as separate syllab**er**s ("**sis-ter**").
  3. Repeat the first syllable ("**sis**").
  4. Build the first syllable with letters.
  5. Say the second syllable ("**ter**") and build the second syllable.
  6. Read the word to check. ("**sister**").

  Letters: e, e, f, g, h, i, l, n, o, r, s, s, t, ŭ, v

  Words: **her, sister, number, never, singer, longer**

- **Word Card Train** Give each child a *Word Card*. When needed, help them read it by covering up the last syllable as they blend the first. Then cover the first syllable as they blend the last. Then make sure they say the whole word. After each word is read, the children place them in a train line. Each time a child places a word, that child points to each word in the train from left to right for all to read.

  Word Cards: **her, brother, mother, ever, better, winter, other, summer**

- **Word Hunt Challenge** Ernest Er in names. Let the children discover which four Letterlanders contain **er** in their names (Clev**er** Cat and…?). Has anyone in the class got **er** in their first, middle or last name! Has anyone spotted this Vowel Steal**er** in the word Lett**er**land? Or twice in Lett**er**land**er**s! Or in street names, or towns? If they are al**er**t they will obs**er**ve him in lots of words!

Unit 18: Lesson 178

Introducing Urgent Ur

✔ **Preparation and materials**
- *PCCs*: Review list plus **b c, d, f, g, h, l, n, r, t, ur, Magic e**
- *Vowel Scenes Poster*: *The Vowel Stealers*
- *Beyond ABC* book, p 32-33
- *Blends and Digraphs* Songs, #39
- Project lyrics or copy to a chart

✔ **Small group/independent**
- Make words for picture-coding, one per page, from the *Decodable Word Bank* below
- *Letterland Word Builders*, or individual letter sets
- Unit 18 *Word Cards*: **fur, curve, burn, curb, nurse, disturb, Thursday, Saturday**, *TG CD 2*

Decodable Word Bank

fur	curb	disturb
turn	nurse	lurk
burn	curve	urn
hurt	Thursday	
curl	Saturday	

Review

- PCCs ă, s, s=z, ŭ, ū, ay, er, th, ue, ve, u_e, y=e Use the 'Quick Dash'.

Urgent Ur

- **Introduce Urgent Ur, the Umbrella Stealer** Display the *Vowel Scenes Poster* showing The Vowel Stealers. Have children name the Vowel Stealers from previous lessons. Today we are going to learn about another of the Er Brothers. Point to Urgent Ur. His name is Urgent Ur. Write it out to show the spelling. He looks a little different from his brothers because he runs about in purple fur boots. Who do you think is faster, Urgent Ur or Ernest Er? Yes, Ernest Er is faster. And we can always tell Urgent Ur because he has what kind of boots? Ah, yes, purple fur boots!

Write out **purple** and **fur**. And can you see what vowel he likes to capture? "**Uppy Umbrella.**" Right, now, look at Uppy. Does she like being captured? Can you make a face like the one Uppy Umbrella is making? We had better be good detectives and memorize this robber's name or else he's likely to trick us. Say it with me three times. "**Urgent Ur**" (x 3). Let's see what we can spot near Urgent Ur on the poster that may have an **ur** sound. Here at the edge of the street is a c**ur**b. And if he trips on that c**ur**b he might get h**ur**t. He might even need a n**ur**se! Write **curb**, **hurt** and **nurse** to show the spellings.

- Show the *PCC* of Urgent Ur Whenever Urgent Ur captures a talking umbrella, I bet you know what he does. He reports his capture on his tiny mobile phone. He calls out his last name, **"Ur."** It sounds just like his brothers' last names but he insists on spelling it differently. Turn to the plain letter side. So when we see an **u**mbrella behind that **r**obot's back, we'll show Urgent Ur that he can't trick us. We'll always say /**ur**/. Let's practice. Say it each time I push the card forward. "**Ur, Ur, Ur.**"

- **Beyond ABC book** Let's listen for Urgent Ur's last name in words as we read about him. You may want to stop occasionally and ask children to name words where they could hear /**ur**/. Share the story and picture and let the children discover more words with the /**ur**/ sound. (A full list is on page 47 of the book.)

Word Building

- **Live Spelling** Let's Live Spell some words with Urgent Ur. Give the **ur** *PCC* to two children to hold. Have them stand in front of the class. Pass out the other *PCCs* to seated children. Stretch the words with the class and have children decide on which Letterlanders need to come up and stand before/after Urgent Ur. Once the children with the needed *PCCs* have formed the word, guide the class in blending the sounds to check the spelling.

PCCs: b, c, h, l, n, t, y (saying e), **ur Words: burn, turn, hurt, curb, curly**

- **On the pocket chart** Make the word **fur** and have children rollercoaster the two sounds (**/f/ /ur/** "**fffffur, fur.**") Continue with the other words. Make the last three words separated by syllables (e.g. **Thurs day**). Have children blend one syllable at a time, then put them together. When you make **burger** have children explain why Ernest Er makes it to the end of this word instead of Urgent Ur. "**He's faster than this brother**."

    PCCs: ă, b, c, d, f, g, h, n, r, s, s=z, t, ay, er, th, ur, ve, Magic e (plain side)

    Words: fur, turn, curve, nurse, Thurs-day, Sat-ur-day, bur-ger

Sing Along

Urgent Ur in Person Song

When umbrellas vanish
(and this will occur),
the burglar in question
will be me, Urgent Ur!

On Thursdays and Saturdays
watch me, Urgent Ur,
come plodding along
in my boots
of curly fur.

- **Urgent Ur in Person Song** Listen to the song. Then read the lyrics *to* the children and then a few times *with* them. Children could highlight each time **ur** appears in the lyrics. Have everyone sing the song again as you point to the words. Leave the lyrics where children can read them during independent time, or listen to the song at a listening center as they follow with the lyrics.

Small group/independent activities

- **Picture-coding** Give each child one large **ur** word from the Decodable Word Bank to picture-code.
- **Spelling with individual letter sets** Display the Urgent Ur *PCC*. Review his sound. Have children stretch the word **turn** and orally segment the three sounds **/t/ /ur/ /n/**. Have them build the word and blend it to check their spelling. It may be helpful to demonstrate the first few words, with your own set of letters. For two-syllable words, follow the steps below:

    1. Have them repeat the word as a whole (e.g. "**Thursday**").
    2. Then say the word as separate syllables ("**Thurs day**").
    3. Repeat the first syllable ("**Thurs**").
    4. Build the first syllable with letters. ("**thurs**")
    5. Say the second syllable. ("**day**")
    6. Build the second syllable.
    7. Read the word to check. ("**Thursday**").

    Letters: a, a, b, c, d, h, l, n, r, s, t, u, y

    Words: turn, burn, curb, curl, hurt, Thurs-day, Sat-ur-day

- **Word Card Train** Give each child a *Word Card*. Help them read the longer words by covering up the last syllable as they blend the first. Then cover the first syllable as they blend the last. Make sure they then say the whole word. After each word is read, the children place them in a train line. Each time a child places a word, that child points to each word in the train from left to right for all to read.

    Word Cards: fur, curve, burn, curb, nurse, disturb, Thursday, Saturday

- **Word Hunt Challenge** This umbrella-stealing robot turns up in relatively few useful words apart from those featured in the *Beyond ABC* book. So it may not be worth while taking time trying to find more. But has anyone stopped to notice that he actually helps Arthur Ar to spell his first name, Arth**ur**?

Introducing Irving Ir

Decodable Word Bank

girl	first	twirl
bird	dirt	swirl
thirst	shirt	whirl
stir	skirt	third
sir	squirt	thirteen
	birthday	

Review

- **PCCs ĭ, ī, s, s=z, ay, er, th, ur, ve, y=e, Magic e, ie, i_e** Use the 'Guess Who?' activity.

Irving Ir

- **Introduce Irving Ir, the Ink Stealer** Display the Poster. Have children name the Vowel Stealers from previous lessons. There is just one more of the Er/Ur/Ir Brothers that we need to know about so we won't get tricked. Point to Irving Ir. His name is **Irving Ir**. Write his name so everyone can see how it is spelled. Who does Irving Ir like to capture? **"Impy Ink."** Right. Now look at Impy and what do you see squirting right out of his bottle onto Irving Ir? Impy is so mad he squirts ink right on Irving Ir's shirt. We'll hear more about that in our story and song. We had better be good detectives and memorize this last robber's name or else he's likely to trick us. Say it with me three times. **"Irving Ir"** (x 3).

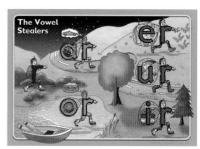

The Vowel Stealers

- Do you think there might be something on the poster near Irving Ir that has his spelling for the **ir** sound? Here is a **fir** tree. And what is this flying around the **fir** tree? Yes, it is a **bird**. It may be chi**rp**ing and if it goes all the way around the tree it will be making a...**cir**cle. Write these **ir** words to show their spelling.

- Show the *PCC* of Irving Ir Whenever Irving Ir captures a talking ink bottle, what do you think he does? Yes, he reports his capture on his tiny mobile phone. He calls out his last name, "Ir." It sounds just like his brothers' last names but <u>he</u> spells it differently! Turn to the plain letter side. So when we see an **i**nk bottle behind a **r**obot's back, we'll show Irving Ir that we can't be tricked by him, or any of his brothers. We'll always say /ir/. Let's practice. Say it each time I push the card forward. **"Ir, Ir, Ir."**

- **Beyond ABC book** Let's listen for Irving Ir's last name in words as we read about him. You may want to stop occasionally and ask children to name words where they heard /**ir**/. Let the children discover more items in the scene that include the /**ir**/ sound. (A full list is on page 47 of *Beyond ABC*.)

Word Building

- **Live Spelling** Let's Live Spell some words with Irving Ir. Give the **ir** *PCC* to two children to hold. Have them stand in front of the class. Pass out the other *PCCs* to seated children. Stretch the words with the class and have children decide on which Letterlanders need to come up and stand before or after Irving Ir. Once the children with the needed *PCCs* have formed the word, guide the class in blending the sounds to check the spelling.

  Letters: b, d, t, s, ir, sh, th
  Words: bird, third, thirst, dirt, shirt

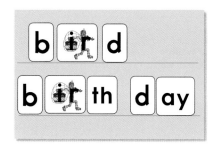

- **Pocket chart reading** Make the word **bird** and have children rollercoaster the three sounds (/**b**/ /**ir**/ /**d**/, "**bird**.") Continue with the other words. Make the last two words with a space between the syllables (e.g. **birth day**). Have children blend one syllable at a time, then put them together.

  PCCs: **b, d, g, l, n, s, t, ay, ee, ir, sh, th**

  Words: **girl, bird, sir, stir, birth-day, thir-teen**

Sing Along

- **Irving Ir in Person Song** (Track 40) Listen to the song. Then read the lyrics *to* the children and then a few times *with* them. Children could highlight each time **ir** appears in the lyrics. Have everyone sing the song again as you point to the words. Leave the lyrics where children can read them during independent time, or use in a listening center as they follow the lyrics.

Small group/independent activities

- **Picture-coding** Give each child one large **ir** word from the Decodable Word Bank to picture-code.

- **Spelling with individual letter sets** Display the Irving Ir *PCC*. Review his sound. Have the children rubber-band stretch the word **girl** and orally segment the three sounds. Have them build the word and then blend it to check. For the multi-syllable words use the steps below. (It may be helpful to demonstrate the first few words with your own set of letters as children follow with their letter sets.)

  1. Help them repeat the word as a whole (e.g. "**birthday**").
  2. Then say as the word separate syllables ("**birth-day**").
  3. Repeat the first syllable ("**birth**"). Stretch the syllable and jiggle out the sounds.
  4. Build the first syllable with letters.
  5. Say the second syllable. ("**day**"). Stretch the syllable and jiggle out the sounds.
  6. Build the second syllable.
  7. Read the word to check. ("**birthday**").

  Letters: **a, b, d, e, e, f, g, h, i, k, l, n, o, r, s, t, t, v**

  Words: **sir, shirt, skirt, dirt, third, girl, swirl, thir-teen, birth-day**

- **Word Card Train** Give each child a *Word Card*. When needed, help them read it by covering up the last syllable as they blend the first. Then cover the first syllable as they blend the last. Make sure they say the whole word. After each word is read, the children place them in a train line. Each time a child places a word, that child points to each word in the train from left to right for all to read.

  Word Cards: **bird, third, thirst, girl, skirt, shirt, squirt, birthday, thirteen**

- **Word Hunt Challenge** The number of useful words for children to find spelled with this th**ir**d Ir brother is too low for a really rewarding word hunt. However a brief look at names may be interesting. Make sure they don't overlook the name of this Letterlander: Golden G**ir**l.

All the Vowel Stealers

Review

- **PCCs ĕ, g, ō, v, ar, er, ir, or, ur, sh** Use the 'Quick Dash' activity.

Er/Ir/Ur

- **Display the PCCs** for **er, ir,** and **ur.** Review the robots' names and their shared sound (spelled with three different vowels).
- **The Er/Ur/Ir Brothers' Song** Listen to the song. Then read the lyrics together a few times. You may want to have children highlight each time **er, ir,** and **ur** appear in the lyrics. Have everyone sing the song again as you point to the words. Leave the lyrics where children can read them during independent time, or use in a listening center as they follow with the lyrics.

Word Building

- **Live Reading** Distribute the *PCCs.* Have two children hold the **er** *PCC* and two more each hold the **ur** and **ir** *PCCs.*). Line the children up to form the words. Have the class rollercoaster each word.

   PCCs: b, d, ĕ, g, h, l, n, ō, t, v, er, ir, sh, ur

   Words: over, ever, never, hurt, turn, burn, bird, girl, shirt

Word Cards

- **Live Word Sort** Distribute the *PCCs* to five pairs of children. Have them stand in front of the class. The vowel child holds the *PCC* and holds on to the robot's sack. Mix up the *Word Cards* listed below in a random order. Call a child to the front. Give the child a *Word Card* to read and deliver to the matching children. The robot child then holds the *Word Card* for everyone to read. When a robot has been given more than one card, each time he receives a new word he shows all of his words in turn for the class to read.

   PCCs: ar, er, ir, or, ur

   Word Cards Unit 17: farm, fork, yard, smart, storm, more

   Word Cards Unit 18: mother, hurt, stir, Saturday, brother, turn, first, after, birthday

Reading Theater Play: 'The Police and the Vowel Stealers'

- Read the play *to* the children and then *with* the children. Have them practice one character's part in pairs. Then read the whole play with these pairs reading their parts together. To perform it for parents or another class, 10 additional children could be the 5 robots. Each pair could sneak on stage, where the police can't see them, carrying a poster listing words with their spelling. There could be a pause before the Vowel Stealer exits, for him to point to his words and get the audience to echo-read them with him.

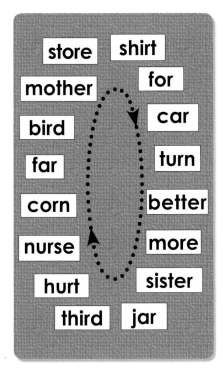

Small group/independent activities

- **Word Race** Lay 12-14 *Word Cards* from Units 17 and 18 in an oval pattern on a mat. The group reads the words in sequence as you point. Tell children this is a race track and challenge them to read a bit faster on the second and third turn. If time allows, let individual children have a run around the track of words.

- **Sentence Building** Build the sentence below on the table. Have children read it as you point to the words. Have them be detectives and pick out words that include an Er/Ur/Ir Brother. Discuss which brother is in each of these words. Mix up the *Word Cards* and have children reconstruct the sentence as in previous lessons each one adding a word at a time and rereading the words placed thus far.

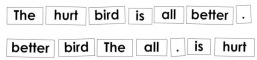

- **Sentence Writing** Tell children they are going to write the sentence. Explain that the tricky part is knowing which robot brother to put in the words since they all sound alike. Discuss how to remember that Ernest Er goes at the end of **better**. (He's a faster runner so he gets to the end of more words first.) Ask children to try remembering **bird** and **hurt** by thinking of the Vowel Stealers Poster (Irving Ir with the **fir** tree and the **bird**, and the **curb** where Urgent Ur might get **hurt**). Let them reread the sentence a few times in preparation for writing. When they are ready, turn the cards to the plain sides.

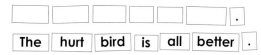

Let a child point to the blank side of the card as they all 'read' the 'invisible sentence.' Everyone writes the sentence and then reads it aloud. Turn over the *Word Cards* so everyone can check their papers.

- **Word Hunt Challenge** The best detectives can identify vowel-stealing robots even when there is more than one in a word! If a child happens to discover one in a book or a topic word, treat is as a great find! Help them to decode these words if needed. Examples: **adventurer, barber, border, burner, carpenter, curlers, dirtier, explorer, farmer, furthermore, gardener, lecturer, murderer, northerner, nursery, performer, sharpener, starter, surviver.**

Section 7 Assessments

You can assess your children's mastery of the outcomes for this Section with the following two assessments:

1. **Word Reading Accuracy** Children read the list opposite of 12 decodable words.

2. **Cumulative Tricky Word Assessment** Children read all irregular Tricky Words opposite, taught in sections 3-7. (Note: This final Tricky Word Assessment includes only 11 words. Many of the words usually considered to 'sight words' (e.g. **has, her, those**) are now decodable words to children who have been through these seven Step-by-Step Sections.)

Assessment Pages

Teacher's Guide: Student reads the words shown in the boxes opposite.

Teacher's Guide CD: Section 7 Assessment (copymaster Score Sheet)

Assessment Instructions

(1) **Word Reading Accuracy** (Individual) The child reads the 12 words opposite. Encourage the child to sound them out. If the child says the word in a segmented fashion (e.g. /**p**/ /**ar**/ /**k**/ for '**park**'), you may say, Put it together, or, Blend it. Only count the word as correct if the child is able to say it finally without segmentation (e.g. "**park**"). After about five seconds on a word, have the child move on to the next word. On the Score Sheet put a line through any words missed or write the substitution above the word. The goal is at least 10 of 12 words correct.

(2) **Cumulative Tricky Word Assessment** (Individual) The child reads from the columns of words below. Tell the child that these are Tricky Words so some letters may not sound right. Have the child read the words. After about five seconds on a word, have the child move on to the next word. On the Score Sheet put a line through any words missed, or write the substitution above the word. The goal is at least 8 of 11 words correct.

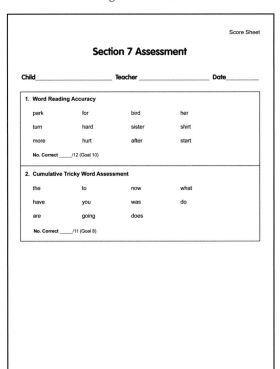

Score Sheet

Section 7 Assessment

Child_____ Teacher _____ Date_____

1. Word Reading Accuracy

park	for	bird	her
turn	hard	sister	shirt
more	hurt	after	start

No. Correct _____/12 (Goal 10)

2. Cumulative Tricky Word Assessment

the	to	now	what
have	you	was	do
are	going	does	

No. Correct _____/11 (Goal 8)

Section 7 Assessment Student Page

1. Word Reading Accuracy

park	for	bird	her	
turn	hard	sister	shirt	
more	hurt	after	start	

No. Correct _____/12 (Goal 10)

2. Cumulative Tricky Word Assessment

the	to	now	what	
have	you	was	do	
are	going	does		

No. Correct _____/11 (Goal 8)

Small Group Intervention

The Five Steps

1. Letter Sounds
2. Beginning Sounds in Words
3. Blending and Word Recognition
4. Segmentation and Spelling
5. Sentences and Stories

Continuing Your Intervention Lessons from Volume 1

● **The Five Step Intervention Plan** from Volume 1 aims to consolidate learning from Section 2 which is completed in this volume (Lessons 88-107). The Five Step Plan is fully explained in Volume 1, pages 192-218. For the letter sounds taught in lessons 88-106, use the lists below in your intervention planning and instruction. (Lists A, B, and C are in Volume 1, pages 216-217).

When children have mastered the objectives of the Five Step Plan, see the **Next Steps Plan** (page 223) for intervention which correlates with Sections 3-7 in this Volume.

Letter Sound, Word, and Sentence Lists for Intervention Using the Letterland Sequence

Set D: Using letters from Lessons 88-107

Number	Vowels	Consonants	Words	Sentence
D1	ĭ ŏ ŭ	b f g j m n r w x ll	job jog Jim run rug wig fix will	Jim will run <u>and</u> jog.
D2	ă ĕ	h n s t v w y ve	van have yes yet wet vet	Yes, <u>they</u> have a van.
D3	ă ĭ ŏ	f g n p r x z	fox fix zig zag ran fan zip rip nap fog	<u>The</u> fox ran in a zig zag.
D4	ă ĭ ŭ	d j t y ck qu	quit quick quack duck yack Jack	<u>The</u> duck <u>made</u> a quick quack.
D5	ă ĕ ĭ	j m n s=z t w ll th	Jan jet will well this jam wet tell tan	Will Jan go on this jet?
D6	ă ĭ ŏ=ŭ silent e*	c d g h l m n s ve	love done some come have give	Will you have some jam?
D7	ă ĭ ŭ	b n p r t z ck qu th	rub run quick quit zip zap that quack	That quick cat can zip <u>by</u> <u>so</u> fast.
D8	ĕ ĭ	f g l p s t v x	vet fix pet leg get pig let six set	<u>The</u> vet will fix <u>my</u> pet's leg.

* Use the plain letter side of the Magic **e** *PCC*.

Next Steps: Small Group Intervention for Sections 3-7

- **Next Steps** is the plan for Intervention for children who have mastered the skills and strategies of the Volume 1 **Intervention Plan**, but still need extra practice to build automaticity in letter sounds and fluency in reading words. This **Next Steps Plan** begins with the five *Word Family Units* in Section 3: Onsets and Rimes.

- This plan can be used with Sections 4-7 as well. Emphasis is also given to Tricky Words (irregular, high frequency words), spelling, reading and writing sentences, and to reading stories and books.

Getting Started

What is the difference between the Five Step Intervention Plan and the Next Steps Plan?

- The Intervention program detailed in Volume 1 is called the Five Step Intervention Plan (see Vol 1, page 192). The Five Step Plan is designed to help students in the very beginning stage of learning letter sounds, learning to blend sounds to read words, and to segment words into phonemes.

- The Intervention described here in Volume 2 is designed for students who know most letter sounds **a-z**, but who may still need to build fluency with letter sounds. It is also designed to build fluent word recognition, fluent spelling of regular one syllable words, fluent reading and spelling of irregular high-frequency words, and fluent reading and writing of basic sentences and simple stories.

When are children ready to move out of the Five Step Plan and into the Next Steps Plan?

- When children know most of the basic letter sounds **a-z** and can blend and segment three-sound short vowel words with ease, they may be ready to move out of the Five Step Intervention Plan. If these children still need more practice than the majority of the class to master fluent reading of words and the other skills taught in sections 3-7 of this guide, then they will benefit from small group instruction using the Next Steps Plan.

More specific assessments and criteria are provided in the table below to help you decide when your children may be ready to begin Next Steps. You may also have children who have not been in the Five Step Plan who may benefit from Next Steps instruction.

Assessment (and where to find it)	MID-YEAR SCORES		
	Continue in Five Step Plan	**Use Next Steps Intervention**	**Regular curriculum only**
Letter Sounds Fluency (*TG CD 2*)	less than 20 cspm	20-30 cspm	31 cspm or above
Word Recognition Fluency (*TG CD 2*)	less than 6 cwpm	6-8 cwpm	9 cwpm or above
Segmentation Accuracy (Assessment 5, Volume 2, pages 39 and 41)	less than 15	15-17 sounds	18

cspm: correct sounds per minute   **cwpm:** correct words per minute

Teaching with the Next Steps Plan

- The Next Steps Plan is intended for use with very small groups, preferably 2-5 children per group. The lessons take approximately 30 minutes. There are two types of lessons. On one day you teach the <u>Reading Lesson</u> and on the next day the <u>Spelling Lesson</u>. Continue to alternate every day. Both plans include six related steps. The Steps and the activities for Reading and Spelling Lessons are provided in the table below. A full description of the activities begins on page 225.

Step #	Step Description	Reading Lesson Activity	Spelling Lesson Activity
1	Letter Sound Review	Quick Dash: Letter to sound review or, Fast Sounds: Letter Sound Fluency Practice	Secret Sounds: Written sound-to-letter review
2	Word Building	Building Words to Read	Spelling with Letter Sets
3	Word Sorting	Word Family Houses: Sorting words by phonic patterns	Word Family Race: Written Word Sort
4	Word List Fluency	Reading Word Lists for Fluency	Reading Word Lists for Fluency
5	Tricky Word Practice	Reading Tricky Words	Spelling Tricky Words
6	Sentences/Stories	Building and Changing Sentences to Read	Writing Sentences

How do I plan my lessons?

- You can use a copy of the 'Next Steps Lesson Log' (*TG CD 2*). Your Next Steps lessons are coordinated with the 18 instructional Units that comprise sections 3-7 of this *Teacher's Guide*. The lists on pages 236-238 show the words and sentences that are used in each Unit. You will want to plan your lessons using words and sentences from the Unit that your intervention group is working on. You will also want to include some review words from previous Units.

With which Unit do I begin my Next Steps lessons?

- Begin all children in Unit 1. You will move your students to the next Unit level when they are ready, which may be after a few days or may take several weeks. Intervention groups may not keep pace with the same Units you are teaching in your whole class lessons.

How do I decide when to move my group to the next Unit?

- There are word lists for each Unit located on the CD accompanying this guide entitled *Next Steps Word Lists*. Practicing fluent reading of these lists is a daily part of both the Reading and Spelling Lessons in the Next Steps Plan. For each Unit 1-5 there are three lists:

    List A: Current Words Grouped by Rhyming Word Families

    List B: Current Words in Random Order

    List C: Cumulative List (current words plus review words)

    Note: No List C for Unit 1.

- For each Unit 6-18 there are two lists:

    List A: Current Words in Random Order

    List B: Cumulative List (current words plus review words)

- When your children can read the final List (B or C) for the Unit at approximately 12 correct words per minute, they are ready to move on to the next Unit. (The criteria are set a bit higher for this task than for the Word Reading Fluency Assessment since here the particular words will have already been practiced a good deal.)
- Other criteria to consider are:
    1) Can the children read and spell the Tricky Words used in the Unit?
    2) Can they read and write the sentences used in the Unit?

Reading Lesson

Step 1: Letter Sound Review

✔ **Preparation and materials**
- *Picture Code Cards (PCCs)* Use *PCCs* that correspond to words in your lesson. Add others your students need
- Fast Sounds pages (*TG CD 2*)

Do I choose the 'Quick Dash' or the 'Fast Sounds' activity, or both?

- If your children have not reached the goal of 30 correct sounds per minute by mid-year (40 cspm by the end of the year) on the Letter Sound Fluency, you will want to use both the Quick Dash with *Picture Code Cards* and the additional practice on basic sounds provided by the Fast Sounds activity.
- If your children have reached this goal, then you will only need the 'Quick Dash' activity. It will provide review of recently introduced sounds and sounds to be used in the lesson.

Quick Dash

- Display 6-10 *Picture Code Cards (PCCs)* on the table or pocket chart. It is preferable to show the plain letter side, but if children are unsure of some of the sounds, display the picture side of those *PCCs*.
- Point to each *PCC* in order and have children say the sound. If some children are hesitant or non-responsive with a sound, turn to the *PCC* to the picture side and briefly discuss the Letterlander or the phonic fable that explains the sound. Turn back to the plain side and have children say the sound. Continue practicing sounds with the plain letter sides.
- Point to the *PCCs* in order, repeat three times, a bit faster each time. Then point in random order to the cards and have the children give the sounds.

Variations

Taking Turns
Have a child respond individually as you point to several of the *PCCs*.

Quick Dash Leader
Let a child do the pointing to the letters as described above.

Fast Sounds: Letter sound fluency practice

- Enlarge a copy or give each child a copy of the 'Fast Sounds' (*TG CD 2*) page.
- If using an enlarged copy, you point to each letter as everyone says the sounds. If using individual copies, children point to the letters on their own copies as all say the sounds.
- Lead the children in saying the sounds going from left to right, row by row. Set your pace based on your children's needs. You can start on any row. Read four to eight rows. Then repeat the rows two to four times, increasing the pace slightly each time.
- To meet the needs of children with varying rates of fluency, set the pace of the first reading of the rows so that your slowest child can keep up. For more challenge, set the pace of the final reading to just a bit faster than the usual pace of the fastest child.

Variations

Beat the Clock

Have each child read a row or two of letter sounds on their own, followed by the next child reading the next row, etc. After a practice round or two, time the group on how long it takes to read the rows, with each child reading their own row(s) in turn. Share the number of seconds with the children. Then time the group again to see if they can do the same rows (each reading their assigned rows) in less time. The group may want to try a third time, or set a reasonable goal for a certain number of seconds, and repeat the rereading until the goal is met.

Sounds in Rhythm

Say three sounds in a row in a steady rhythm, pause one beat, then say the next three, etc. Repeat a few times, slightly increasing the tempo each time. You may find that other rhythms work well, also.

Step 2: Word Building

- There are two ways to carry out this step. You can build the words with *PCCs* for the children to read, or you can guide the children in building and then reading the words with individual sets of letters.

Building Words to Read

Teacher Builds Words: Table Reading

- This activity is the same as Pocket chart/table reading, as used in Whole Class and Small Group lessons throughout the Letterland Step-by-Step for Kindergarten program. The procedure is described briefly below and in more detail in Volume 1, on page 239. You could also substitute Chalkboard Reading for this activity on some days (Volume 1, page 240).
- Use 6-10 words from the current Unit and previous Units.
- Make the word with the plain letter sides of *PCCs*.
- Point to each letter or digraph as children place the sounds on their arm rollercoasters.
- Sweep across the letters from left to right as the children blend the sounds on their rollercoasters.
- Use the word in a brief sentence.
- Change the *PCCs* to make a new word and repeat the above procedures.

Preparation and materials
- *Picture Code Cards* (*PCCs*) Use *PCCs* that correspond to words in your lesson
  - *or* -
  Letterland Word Builders or other letter sets

Variation

Blending Leader

For some words, have one child demonstrate how to rollercoaster blend the word, and then have the group repeat the process.

Mystery Word: Reading with Letterland Word Builders

- This activity is also used in Small Group activities through the **Letterland Step-by-Step for Kindergarten** program. You will find a brief description of the procedure below and a fuller one in Volume 1, on pages 241-242. In Volume 1 the "Mystery Word" title is not used. It is added here to provide interest to the activity for the children.

- Use 6-10 words from the current unit and previous units.

- Provide children with *Letterland Word Builders* or other individual sets of letters.

- Introduce the activity the first few times with this explanation: The Letterlanders really like putting their sounds together to make words for us to read. They like to help us play the Mystery Word Game as well. A mystery is something unknown that we have to work out by using the clues we have. In this game the clues are the Letterlanders' sounds.

- I will name the letters (or sounds or Letterlander names) in order. You put your letters in that order. Then point to your letters as we say the sounds. Next you will slide your finger under the letters and blend the sounds together to say the Mystery Word. Remember to keep the mystery word a secret until we have all had a chance to blend it.

- After children say the word, use it in a brief meaningful phrase or sentence.

- If the next word only differs by one (or two) letters from the current word, tell children which letter(s) to replace and have them sound out and blend the word. If the next word differs by more, have children remove all the letters and start again.

Variation

Blending Leader

For some words, have one child demonstrate how to point to letters, say the sounds and then blend into a word. Then have the group repeat the process.

Step 3: Word Sorting

Word Family Houses

Preparation and materials
- Word Family House page, *TG CD 2*
- Next Steps *Word Cards* for the Unit *TG CD 2*

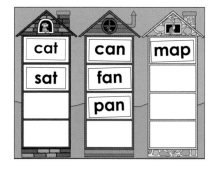

- This is a variation on the Word Sorting activity used in this *Teacher's Guide* in Sections 3-7. In this version of the activity, all the children are sharing one Word Family House sheet and taking turns placing *Word Cards* on it. You can slide the sheet around the table so that each child can reach it easily.

- Place three *Word Cards* (one from each rhyming word family or phonic pattern) in a horizontal row on the top floors of the three Word Houses.

- Make a deck of the rest of the cards including any of the special Instruction Cards you wish to use. The special Instruction Cards are intended to add interest to the game. You might use different ones on different days to provide some surprise.

- The houses in this picture are Word Family Houses. The words in each house go together because they rhyme, or have the same vowel sound/spelling. When you draw a card, read it and decide which house it belongs in.

Note: In some Units there may only be two patterns to sort. In this case you can make the third column a miscellaneous column where children can place *Tricky Words* or review words from previous Units that you have selected and included in the deck. Put the question mark card in the top slot on the page.

● Each child in turn, takes a card from the deck and reads it. Then the child places the card below a card that has the same pattern. The child points to each word in the 'family' as everyone reads the words. For special instruction cards, help the child read the card and carry out the instructions.

Variations

Tractors, Trains, Planes, and Helicopters

Once the Word Family House is filled with the *Word Cards* as above, practice reading the words with the children using the *Tractors, Trains, Planes, and Helicopters* activity. In this activity, explained fully on page 80, you point to each word in a column first with a slow pace (tractors) as children repeat the words. Then repeat with a faster pace each time (trains, then planes). Finally, point to words quickly in a random order imitating the maneuverability of a helicopter.

Full House Game

Give each child in your small group a copy of the *Word Family Houses* page. You will need a set of *Small Unit Word Cards* for each child, all mixed into one large deck including the special instruction cards.

- Give each child one *Word Card* from each of the three rhyming word families to place at the top level of their houses.

- Children take turns drawing cards and placing them in their own Word Family Houses. Each time a *Word Card* is placed, the child reads all of the cards "in their house".

- If children misplace or misread a word, use questioning to guide them to self-correct.

- If the child draws a card for a house that is already full, the child replaces one of the words with the new one and reads all the words in the family. The extra card is placed faced up in a discard stack. Any child can take the top card from the discard stack, rather than taking a 'new' card when it is that child's turn.

- The objective is for a child to have three "full houses." You may stop when one child has a full house, or keep playing until all have full houses.

Step 4: Word List Fluency

Preparation and materials
- Word Lists A, B, or C for the Unit (*TG* CD 2)
- If timing individuals, Robot Reading Racer charts (*TG* CD 2)

Reading Words in Lists

● For this activity you will use the *Word Family Word List* for Units 1-5. For each Unit in Section 2 of this *Teacher's Guide* there are two or three word lists (see page 224 for further explanation of the lists).

● Units 1 and 6-18 have two lists (A and B). Units 2-5 have three lists (A, B, and C).

● Begin practicing with your students on list A. When they can read List A at a rate of approximately 12-15 **c**orrect **w**ords **p**er **m**inute (**cwpm**), move on to List B. If there

List A

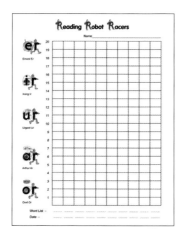

Next Steps Fluency Word Lists

Unit 1 List B

hat	man	lap	pan	cat
fan	nap	hat	ran	map
can	mat	cap	rat	lap
bat	that	can	tap	ran
nap	van	man	fat	cap
sat	lap	fan	rat	map

List B

Reading Robot Racers

is a List C, move to this list when children can read List B at 12-15 cwpm. When they can read the final list for the Unit (B or C) at 12 words per minute, move on to the next Unit.

Practice Activities

- **Leader Reader** Model being the Leader Reader by reading two rows of words *to* the children while they point to the words and listen. Then reread the two rows *with* the children, reading along and pointing. Let children take turns being the Leader Reader on the same rows, or subsequent rows. Everyone points while the Leader Reader reads. Then all reread the same rows together. Encourage children to increase the pace whenever you think the group is ready.

- **Aloud, Softer, Softest, No Sound** Practice reading and rereading two to four rows of words at a time. On the first reading, everyone reads the words together in a normal voice. On the second reading in a softer voice, and still softer on the third reading. Finally, everyone reads by mouthing the words, but without making any sound.

- **Reading in Rhythm** Read the words going from left to right, row by row, with the group. The pace for reading the words will depend on the capability of the children. Begin with a pace they can be comfortable with. On subsequent repetitions, increase the pace to challenge but not overwhelm them. Read with a steady rhythm. You might want to establish a simple rhythm pattern such as 'word, word, word, [pause); word, word, [pause].' (This rhythm fits the five words per row of the lists.) Keep the same rhythm pattern, but increase the pace a little bit each time you reread.

Assessment: Reading Racer

- In this assessment activity you will time each child separately in reading a word list. The child should continue to practice with the words in a Unit until reaching 12 correct words per minute (cwpm) on the final list (B or C). You will have children read for one minute and then determine the number of words read correctly. The correct words per minute (cwpm) is recorded on the Reading Robot Racer chart by the teacher. Then the child colors in the bar graph. Children should have at least two chances to be timed on the same day. Multiple timings usually allow the child to see progress on their chart even if the goal is not met. You may want to time the child first on List A, then a few days later on List B (and, for Units 2-5, finally a few days after that on List C). If you believe the child is ready, you may skip List A.

  - You will need a copy of the word list for yourself and one for the child. You may want to put your copy in a clear protective sleeve and mark it with a dry-erase marker, so it may be reused.

  - Time the child reading the selected word list for 60 seconds. Put a slash through any words missed. Draw a line under the last word. Record the number of words read correctly (cwpm) on the Robot Racer chart.

  - Review the correct pronunciation of any missed words with the child. Discuss the result with the child in a positive manner. You may want to ask the child to set a reasonable goal for the next reading.

  - Time the child again on the same list and record the result. (This may be done immediately, or you may let the child practice rereading the list with a partner before being timed again, while you time another child.)

  - If the child does not meet the goal of 12 cwpm, provide more practice with the above activities, and time again on another day. (If the child is very close to the goal, you may want do a third timing the same day.)

Step 5: Tricky Word Practice

- In each Unit, one to three *Tricky Words* are introduced. (See lists, pages 236-238.) In the various steps of the lessons children practice reading and spelling these words, use them in building sentences with *Word Cards*, and write them in sentences as well. For children who need more practice reading and spelling these words, use one of the activities below.

Reading Practice

- This research-backed method of mastering tricky words is called Constant Time Delay.
- Choose 2-5 *Tricky Word Cards* to practice from the current Unit or previous ones.
- Show the card and say the word.
- Count to three silently while the children study it.
- Point to the word to signal for the children to say it.
- Do the same with each *Tricky Word*.
- Go back through the words without saying the word yourself, but still waiting three seconds and pointing to the word for children to read it.
- If children miss a word or some seem unsure, tell them the word, point out a feature of the word (e.g. "**was**, the **s** says /**z**/"). Then wait three seconds and point to the word for children to read.
- Repeat all the words until children accurately read them two rounds in a row.
- On subsequent days review the cards. If children do not know them, follow the steps above again.

Tricky Word Phrases: Essential Words Phrase Game

- One advantage of this game is that it provides practice with a larger selection of high-frequency words than those listed for the 16 Units. (A number of words in the Essential Words Phrase Game are easily decoded and therefore not listed as *Tricky Words* in the Units. Nevertheless they are equally valuable to practice, given the aim of early fluency in all these high-frequency words.)

Set I

- This game can be found on the *TG CD 2* that accompanies this Volume 2: *Step-by-Step Teacher's Guide*. Full instructions are provided on the pages that you can print out from the CD. This game uses high-frequency words in phrases of two or three words (e.g. "**they said**," "**one of the**").
- You choose just a few phrases to begin with.
- As children master these phrases, gradually add additional phrase cards. In all, the game includes 60 of the most frequent words in English and includes a second set of cards that use the same words, for practicing in different combinations and phrases.

Set II

Step 6: Sentences and Stories

Preparation and materials
- Larger *Unit Word Cards* and *Tricky Word Cards* including punctuation needed for your sentence *TG CD 2*
- Letterland Take-Home-Booklets or other appropriate level reading

"The hat is on the cat."

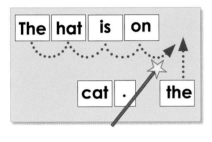

Sentence Building

- Lay out the *Word Cards* needed to build your sentence on the table in a random order.
- Point to the words and have children read them.
- Say the sentence that you want the children to build.
- Have children repeat the sentence as they 'line it out.' Children line the sentence out by touching the table, beginning at their left and moving to the right each time they say a word in the sentence. Do this at least two times.
- Ask one child to choose the first *Word Card* needed to build the sentence and place it at the far left.
- Have that child point to the first word and then the space just to the right as all say the first two words of the sentence.
- Call on another child to select the next word, and place it. Then lead the class in saying the first three words as the child points to the first two words and the space to the right, etc.
- After the sentence is fully built, have children read the whole sentence as one child points to the words.

Variations

Timed Sentence Building
Once the sentence has been built, display the words in random order again. Let children take turns placing the words in proper sequence, one word at a time. The last child points to the words for the children to read the sentence. Time the group on this process. Then time them as they repeat the sentence building, trying to beat the initial time.

Robbing Robots Game
Once the sentence is built, play this game (fully explained in Volume 1 on page 214). Briefly, have the children shut their eyes. Remove one word from the sentence and put it out of sight. Children reread the sentence to discover the word stolen by the Robot. Have a child spell the missing word before you return it to the sentence.

Story Reading

- Reread one of the *Letterland Take-Home Booklets*, *Letterland Vowel Readers* with the children, or any other material that provides appropriate level practice for them.
- Once children can comfortably read the story, have them read in pairs to maximize practice. After they read with one partner, have them read the same story with a different partner.

Spelling Lesson

Step 1: Letter Sounds

✓ Preparation and materials
- Picture Code Cards (*PCCs*) Use *PCCs* that match words in your lesson. Add others needed by your students
- Writing materials

Secret Sounds: Sound-to-letter review with handwriting

- Keep the *PCCs* out of sight. Provide children with writing materials.
- Tell the children that the Letterlanders like to play a game called 'Secret Sounds'. I will keep the pictures of the Letterlanders hidden and say their sound. You repeat the sound and then write the letter or letters. Then I'll make the Letterlander appear so you can check your answer.
- After children write each letter, show the Letterlander.
- If anyone wrote the wrong letter(s), have them correct it. Repeat the missed *PCC* after doing a few others.
- If anyone formed the letter incorrectly, demonstrate the letter formation. Have the group practice with air-tracing, or tracing on the table. Have them all write the letter again. Repeat the missed *PCC* after doing a few others.

Step 2: Word Building

✓ Preparation and materials
- *Letterland Word Builders,* or other letter sets

Spelling with Letter Sets

Children segment words to spell
- Say the word, use it in a brief phrase or sentence, repeat the word.
- One of the children segments the word with rubber-band stretching. Then the other children repeat the stretching.
- Children build the word with their letters. Use questioning to guide self-correction of any errors.
- After all the children have built the word correctly, they point to their own letters and say the sounds in unison. Then they slide their fingers under the letters from left to right and say the word.
- If the next word differs from the previous word by only one (or two) letters, have children keep the letters in place as you say the next word. If it differs by more, have children remove the letters.

Step 3: Word Sorting

✓ Preparation and materials
- Copies of the 'Word Family Race' page, TG CD 2

Word Family Race

- This is a variation on the 'Written Word Sort' activity used throughout Sections 3-7 of the *Teacher's Guide*. Provide each child with a blank copy of the Word Family Race page (*TG CD 2*). You may want to laminate the pages, or place them in clear sheet protectors and use with dry-erase markers.
- Have children write the rimes for the three word families across the top row, (e.g. **at, an, ap**) or in later Units the phonic elements being used (e.g. **ai, ee, ar**).

- You are going to write some words that include the letters you have written at the top. We will pretend this is a Word Family Race. Whichever word family gets four words first is the winner.

- Call out the word, use it in a brief phrase or sentence, then repeat it. Children repeat and then rubber-band stretch the words to segment the sounds (e.g. **"map, mmmaaaap, /mmm/ /ă/ /p/"**).

- Children point to the box where they think the word belongs. When you okay it, they write the word.

- If children choose the wrong column or misspell a word, guide them with questions to self-correct.

- **Optional Step 1:** After all the children have written the word, have everyone spell the word aloud and say the word again. Then have them cover the word with their hand, or close their eyes and spell it aloud and finally say the word again.

- **Optional Step 2:** After children write the word, have them read all the words in that column together.

- Just for fun, children will want to predict which Word Family will win the race and probably change their predictions as the game proceeds. They may even want to root for one 'team' (Word Family) or another.

- You can stop when one Word Family 'wins', or continue until all 'cross the finish line.'

- To conclude the activity, children read all the words to a partner. For extra practice, have them read down each column and then read all the words again by reading across the rows, from left to right.

Variation

Children call out words

Make a deck of *Word Cards* with the words needed for this activity. Place the deck face down on a small tray or mat so that it can be slid around the table. Let children take turns choosing a card and calling it out for everyone to write on their Word Family Race page. Then the child places the *Word Card* face down and all the children write the word. Next the child that chose the word, turns it face up for all to check their spelling. Once children learn this process, you can have them do it independently as you take one child at a time aside to time them on reading word lists, or stories, as described below.

Step 4: Word Lists

✔ **Preparation and materials**
- Word lists A, B, or C for the Unit, *TG CD 2*
- If timing individuals, *Robot Reading Racer* charts, *TG CD 2*

Reading Words in Lists

- This is the one activity that is used in both the Reading Lesson and the Spelling Lesson. Look back to pages 225 and 232 for full instructions.

Step 5: Tricky Words

- Use the first activity for introducing new *Tricky Words* or practicing particularly difficult ones. Use the second activity to practice spelling *Tricky Words* that the children have worked on previously.

Introducing Words: 3-by-3 Strategy

- Use this strategy when children are unfamiliar with a *Tricky Word*. It is called the 3-by-3 Strategy because children form the letters in the word in three different modes (air-tracing, invisible writing, and visible writing). For each mode, they spell the word by saying the letter names and repeat it in three different ways (aloud, whispering, silent mouth movements). This strategy will help children remember the word for both reading and spelling. Limit use of this strategy to one or two words per day. If children have difficulty recognizing or spelling a *Tricky Word* on subsequent days, repeat the 3-by-3 Strategy. For many words, children may only need to use this strategy in one lesson, followed by further practice with the strategies below.

- Write the word in very large letters on the board. Say the word and have children repeat it.

- Use the word in a brief sentence and then say the word again. Children repeat the word.

- Discuss the 'tricky part(s)' of the word with the children, that is any letters that are not making their usual sound (e. g. the **e** in **the**, the **o** in **to**).

- Make a wavy line under the tricky part.

- Practice the word with the children using the 3-by-3 Strategy below:

  1. Air-Tracing While looking at word on the board, children use their whole arm to trace large letters in the air. Arms should be completely straight, no bending of elbow or wrist, in order for children to make use of the large muscles of the shoulder and arm to form the letters. As children air-trace they say the names of the letters (e.g. "**t-h-e**"). Then they pretend to underline the word in the air from left to right as they say the word ("**the**"). Children do this three times:
  1) **Aloud**, saying the names of the letters in a normal voice;
  2) **Whispering** the names of the letters;
  3) **Making mouth movements**, silently forming the letter names with their mouths.

  2. Invisible Writing Erase the word from the board. Then children trace the letters with their fingers on the table (or carpet), as they repeat the letter names. Then they make an invisible underline as they say the word. Just as with air-tracing they do this three times:
  1) **Aloud**; 2) **Whispering**; 3) **Making mouth movements**.

  3. Visible Writing Children write the word saying the letter names and then underlining and saying the word. Each time they write the word again they cover the previously written word(s) in order to rely on their memories. As above, they do this three times:
  1) **Aloud**; 2) **Whispering**; 3) **Making mouth movements**.

Spelling Practice

- Choose 2-5 *Tricky Word Cards*.

- Show children the *Tricky Word Card* and have them say the word. Tell them to look at the word to get ready to write it.
- After five seconds remove the *Word Card* from sight. Say the word and have children write it.
- Show the word for children to check.
- If anyone misses the word, have the group use the 3-by-3 Strategy to practice it.
- Place the missed word back in the deck to write again after writing at least one other word.

Step 6: Sentences and Stories

Sentence Writing

- Make the sentence with *Word Cards*.
- Point to the words as the group reads the sentence.
- Let several children take turns pointing to the words as the group rereads the sentence.
- Turn the *Word Cards* to the plain side but keep them in order.
- Tell the children that they are going to read an Invisible Sentence. Say the sentence with the class as you point to the blank cards.
- Point to any word somewhere in the sentence. Ask a child to 'read the invisible sentence' to identify the word. Ask the child to spell the word aloud and then turn it over to confirm the spelling. Let several children do this with other words.
- Turn all the cards back to the plain side. The children say the sentence again as they 'line out the sentence.' This means that they touch the palms of their hands to the table once for each word, moving their hand a bit from left to right for each word as they say it.
- Next the children write the sentence on their own paper or dry-erase boards.
- Help children correct errors as they write.
- After children finish writing the sentence, each one reads the sentence aloud.

Story Reading

- Reread with the children one of the *Letterland Take-Home Booklets*, *Letterland Vowel Readers*, or any other material that provides appropriate level practice for your children.
- Once children can comfortably read the story have them partner-read in pairs to maximize practice. After they read with one partner, have them read the same story with a different partner.

Preparation and materials
- Larger *Unit Word Cards* and *Tricky Word Cards* including punctuation needed for your sentence, *TG CD 2*
- Writing materials
- Letterland Take-Home Booklets, or other appropriate level reading

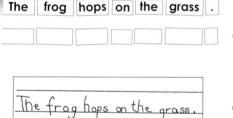

| The | frog | hops | on | the | grass | . |

The frog hops on the grass.

Letterland
Oscar Orange
Fully decodable reader

Clever Cat gets Stuck
A Letterland Take-Home Reader Lesson 148

Section 3: Onsets and Rimes

Unit (Lessons)	Phonic elements	Word Cards	Tricky Words	Sentences
Unit 1 (108-115)	at ap an	cat bat pig hat man pan fan dog cap sun nap map rat tap can	the	The cat is fat. Is the cat fat? The cat is on the mat. Is the cat on the mat?
Unit 2 (116-121)	in ig ip	dig pig wig in pin win lip ship chip dip big fin chin thin	see you	I see a pig. Can you see a pig? Yes, I can see a pig. No, I can see a cat.
Unit 3 (122-127)	op ot ock	mop top hop lock rock sock dot hot pot not	for	This rock is for you. Is this rock for me? Yes, this rock is for you. No, this rock is for [child's name].
Unit 4 (128-132)	ut un ug	bun sun run nut cut shut bug rug hug runs hops	he she to	She runs to the big rock. He hops on the big rock.
Unit 5 (133-137)	et ell eck	neck deck check well bell shell net vet jet get wet let peck yet fell	was now	Clever Cat was on the rock. Now, she is at the well.

Section 4: Consonant Blends

Unit (Lessons)	Phonic elements	Word Cards	Tricky Words	Sentences
Unit 6 (138-141)	sc sk sl sm sn sp st sw	skip spin swing scat skin slip sled smell smog snack snap spill spot stuff stuck swim mud step	we like do and	We like to skip, spin and swing. We do not like to spill stuff.
Unit 7 (142-144)	bl cl fl gl pl	flag class blocks plum clock cliff glass black club flip glad plop plan		Do you see a flag in the class?
Unit 8 (145-148)	br cr dr fr gr pr tr	frog hops grass crab runs truck rolls drip dress trap press grin dress drip crush crack brick brag drop grab		The frog hops on the grass. The crab runs on the grass. The truck rolls on the grass.

Section 5: Long Vowels and Magic e

Unit (Lessons)	Phonic elements	Word Cards	Tricky Words	Sentences
Unit 9 (149-150)	ē, ī, ā, y=ē,	we We go She she he He pool hi no so I my try fly sky		Can we try to fly in the sky? You cannot fly in the sky. But we can try!
Unit 10 (151-154)	ă, a_e	game chase drag gate flat brave wag plate trap safe late made grape hat take lake snake cake shape make long mud did	what	What did you make? I made a <u>snake</u>.
Unit 11 (155-157)	ĭ, i_e	hike pin live nine rid pile wide flip fin five side slip like ride bike take fly kite fish fins smile	for	I like to ride my bike. I like to fly my kite. I like to take a hike. I like to go for a ride.
Unit 12 (158-160)	ō, o_e	hose hop rode clock stop home rod close drop pole cone not those rock bone bike bones clock doze nose snake rope rose stop hot stove	does have	Does a <u>snake</u> have a <u>nose</u>? Does a <u>rope</u> <u>doze</u>? Does a <u>bike</u> <u>stop</u>? Does a <u>home</u> <u>hop</u>? (See more in lesson 159.)
Unit 13 (161-162)	u_e, e_e	tube use cube luck rule mud June pup these		These are cute pups. Did you use the cubes?

Section 6: Vowel Men Out Walking

Unit (Lessons)	Phonic elements	Word Cards	Tricky Words	Sentences
Unit 14 (163-165)	ai ay	train bait wait mail aim chain main trail plain nail waits rain fish trap tray say brat day flag plan way stay play May hay today horse tail may	all	Talking Tess waits for the train in the rain. Firefighter Fred waits with his bait for a fish. May we give hay to the horse today? She will stay and play all day.
Unit 15 (166-167)	ea ee	seat mean teach clean each leaf treat dream feet tree green sleep keep seem free see meet feel sheet shell team sled read neck eat leg Queen needs jeans real reach heat leap deep need feet	some	The Queen needs some clean jeans. I will keep these blue jeans. Did you clean this seat?
Unit 16 (168-172)	oa ie ue	float goat road load soap coat boat die soak tied chip toad goal trip tried shop fried pie drip lie drop tie hope glue blue lies true loan road true clue	they your	Have they tried my pie? I hope your boat will float. The team may not play on the train. The blue boat is not tied up.

Section 7: The Vowel Stealers

Unit (Lessons)	Phonic elements	Word Cards	Tricky Words	Sentences
Unit 17 (173-176)	**ar or**	dark barn park smart bark yard car harm star stars farm horn north card start for short sharp fork born four your more store score door floor oar roar hope goals storm	are going	Are we going to the park in the dark? Yes, we are going to see the stars. Orvil Or was born in the north. These shorts are worn for sports. I hope we can score four more goals.
Unit 18 (177-180)	**er ir ur**	her brother mother ever better winter other summer fur curve burn curb nurse disturb Thursday Saturday bird third thirst girl skirt shirt squirt birthday thirteen hurt stir turn first after		The hurt bird is all better. Jim is my other brother. Her mother is a nurse.

Appendices

Beginning Sound Games

Small Group work

The Beginning Sound Games below are for the last eight letters taught in Section 2. Use them with children who need additional practice in listening for beginning sounds and matching the sounds with these letters. (In earlier lessons, these games are provided under the "Small group/ independent activities" heading in Day 1 for each letter.) For each game you will need the *PCC* for the Letterlander being taught, the six *Beginning Sound Pictures* for the letter (this includes the card with the plain letter), and several other pictures with contrasting beginning sounds.

Jumping Jim

Lay out the six **j** *Beginning Sound Picture* cards mixed in with six or so other pictures beginning with other sounds. Also place Jumping Jim's *PCC* on the table with space around it to surround him with his favorite pictures. Name all the pictures with the children. Each child takes a turn selecting a picture that begins with /**j**/, naming it, and placing it by Jim's *PCC*. As each picture is placed, teach children to say an alliterative phrase for it: **jumbo jet, jiggly Jello, jerky jeep, jars of jam, jeans jacket**. After each picture is placed have all the children repeat these phrases as a child points to each picture. When the plain **j** is placed have everyone say, **"Jumping Jim says /j/"** and do his *Action Trick*.

Red Robot

You will need a bag of some kind to represent Red Robot's sack. If you use a paper bag, you could make lines on it in a net pattern. Display the *PCC* for Red Robot. Let each child in turn hold Red Robot's sack. Lay two *Beginning Sound Pictures* on the table, one beginning with /**r**/, and one beginning with another sound. Have all the children name the two pictures. Then say to the child with the sack, Red Robot, which picture begins with your sound? Let the child name the picture and place it in the sack. Then the child passes the sack to the next child, etc. For the plain **r** have everyone say, **"Red Robot says /rrr/,"** and do his *Action Trick*. After all the cards have been used, take them out of the sack, and have children name them again.

Quarrelsome Queen

Use a Big Capital Picture Code Card of Quarrelsome Queen, or the capital *First Reading Flashcard*. Display the lower case big card as well, along with the six **q** *Beginning Sound Picture* cards. Mix in several pictures beginning with other sounds. Tell children that for her capital letter, Quarrelsome Queen goes into her Quiet Room where she doesn't like to be disturbed. Name all the pictures with the children in whispered voices. Now when it is your turn, look at the pictures and find one that begins with the /**qu**/ sound but don't say it aloud. Instead whisper the word in your neighbor's ear. They will put the picture next to the Queen in her quiet room. Then you can point to all the pictures placed so far, and we will all name them quietly.

Vicky Violet

You will need an empty vase that the *Beginning Sound Pictures* will fit in (a cup will do). Display Vicky Violet's *PCC*. Give two pictures to each child, one beginning with /**v**/, and one with another sound. Explain that Vicky has an extra vase where she likes to keep her favorite pictures. Have the one child be Vicky and hold the vase. The next child says, e.g. **"Vicky Violet, would you like a picture of a volcano or a moose?"** Vicky answers, **"I vote for the volcano."** The child puts the picture in the vase. Then the next child becomes Vicky with the vase, etc. Pull out all of Vicky's pictures at the end and have everyone name them.

Walter Walrus

Make a deck of the six *Beginning Sound Pictures* for **w** mixed randomly with five or six other *Pictures*. Go through the deck first and name all the pictures with the children. Walter Walrus likes to wiggle when he sees something that begins with his sound. When I show you a picture, you name it. If it starts with Walter's /**w**/ sound, then stand up and wiggle. If it doesn't start with his sound, sit down and be still. Do several cards with the whole group. Then you may want some individual responses. For a quieter activity, have children just wiggle their fingers.

Fix-it Max

Make a deck of the six **x** *Beginning Sound Picture* cards mixed randomly with 4 or 5 other pictures. Also display the *Big Capital Picture Code Card* for **X**. Lead the children in naming all the pictures (including the Index card). Tell them that some of these pictures have Fix-it Max's /**x**/ sound at the end of the word, and some in the middle. Each child in turn takes the card on the top of the deck and names it. Everyone repeats the picture name. Everyone makes Fix-it Max's *Action Trick* if the word contains his /**x**/ sound. Elicit from the children where in the word the /**x**/ sound is heard. The child then places the picture on one of the four ends of the capital **X**. The plain **x** goes in the middle of the **X**, and the Index card goes in the middle above the **X**. Each time a new card is played the child placing it points to all the cards around the **X** for all to name. If the word does not contain the /**x**/ sound, it is placed in a discard pile.

Yellow Yo-yo Man

Make a deck combining the six *Beginning Sound Pictures* for **y** and four to six other *Pictures*. Go through the deck and name the pictures with the children. Give each child a small card with **yes** on it, and another with **no**. Show one picture at a time. Have children name the picture. If it begins with /**y**/, the children show you their **yes** cards or if not, their **no** cards. When the plain letter card **y** comes up, everyone stands up and does Yo-yo Man's *Action Trick* (yanking on his yo-yo). Go through the cards a second or third time, going a little quicker each time.

Zig Zag Zebra

Display the five *Beginning Sound Pictures* for **z** (including the plain **z**) mixed randomly with four or five other *Pictures*. Place the plain side of the *Big Capital Picture Code Card* for **Z** on the table, or write a large **Z** that fills a whole sheet of paper. Name the pictures with the children. Each child gets a turn to choose a picture that begins with /**z**/. Zig Zag Zebra likes to zoom very fast in a zigzag pattern wherever she goes. When it is your turn, pick out a picture that begins with her /**zzz**/ sound, then put it at the top left side on the large capital **Z** and slide it along the **Z** across and down "her neck," and across the bottom line. We'll all say **"zzzzzooooommmmm"** as you slide the picture along. Then put your picture right under the **Z** card. We'll all name the pictures that have been placed under the **Z** each time there is a new one.

Decodable Booklets

These decodable booklets (featured in Lessons 98, 107, 115, 120, 127, 131, 137 and at the end of each of Sections 4 and 5) are available on the *Teacher's Guide CD* that accompanies this manual. Also, on the CD you will find Reader's Theater Plays for Sections 6 and 7. You will want to make copies for each child, but to introduce the book you may prefer a larger format.

Options:

1) Project the pages with transparencies on an overhead projector or with an LCD projector;
2) enlarge the pages;
3) Use the booklets in original size and introduce to the whole class or in small groups.

To make individual copies, copy the document *front and back* on the two sides of your copy paper. Cut along the horizontal mid-line. Fold one side of the booklet to fit in a standard stapler and staple in the middle two or three times.

Clear instructions for using each booklet are given in the lessons listed above.

Using the Decodable Booklet in small groups

The booklets are a valuable tool for small group work. Write the sentences, from the booklet that you are working with in the relevant lesson, on sentence strips. Children rebuild the story on the pocket chart. One child could read sentences from the book. The other has to put the sentences in order. Both check it together and then switch roles and begin again. Children could also try to put the sentences in order without looking at the booklet. After placing all the sentences, they can use the book to check.

Handwriting Review

To practice handwriting and consolidate the letter-sound link follow these steps as you do the 'Guess Who?' activity (Volume 1, page 234):

- Hide the *Picture Code Card* and say the sound, e.g. /p/.

- Children repeat the sound.

- Each child writes the letter or letters that stand for the sound. (They could use paper and pencil or dry-eraser markers and boards.)

- Then ask children to name the Letterlander.

- Show the picture side of the *PCC* to confirm the answer.

Teaching Points

- Make sure children begin writing the letter at the correct starting point and write or trace in the correct direction.

- Ask questions to help guide correct letter formation, e.g. What do we do first to make Golden Girl's letter? (**"Go round Golden Girl's head..."**) Where do we go next? (**"Down her golden hair."**) And then we curve to make her... (**"swing"**).

Variations

- Children can write the letters in various ways: air-tracing, tracing on a table or carpet square, writing on dry-erase boards, or writing on paper.w

The Rhyming Words Trick

Objective
● To read words by analogy.

If I can read **can** I can also read **fan**, **man**, **pan** and **than**.

The TRICK
If I can read ___ I can also read ___, ___, ___, and ___.
If I can spell ___ I can also spell___, ___, ___, and ___.

Teaching point
One of the strategies children should consciously use when attempting to read or write a new word is to identify a spelling pattern in a word they already know. (You will need to control the use of this strategy, so that children are not making incorrect analogies.)

Section 3 focuses on developing reading and spelling by analogy, using three main resources:

1 Rhyming Chants

For example:　　**I am happy saying 'ă' in at.**
　　　　　　　　I am happy saying 'ă' in bat.
　　　　　　　　I am happy saying 'ă' in cat.
　　　　　　　　and lots of words like that.

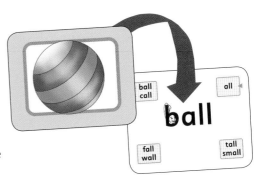

2 Vocabulary Cards

You will find rhyming words on the backs of most of these 78 picture cards. Help children to read these rhyming words by analogy, first using
the *Vocabulary Cards* and then the 6 photocopiable *Rhyming Word Lists* on the insert accompanying the *Vocabulary Cards* pack which contains all 450+ rhyming words.

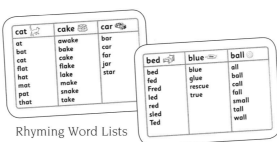

Rhyming Word Lists

3 Character Names

Once children recognize the Letterlanders' names by sight, they will be able to read many more words by analogy. You can help children to deduce certain spelling patterns from these words, for example using the Character Name Flashcards (*TG CD 2*):

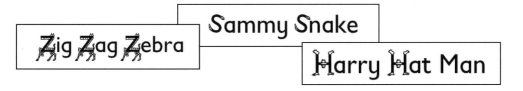

Eyes Shut Riddle Game: Who Am I?

How to Play

Each of the riddles listed below can be introduced on its own just for fun. Or you could select a number of riddles at any time after the Fast Track lessons to present in a quick and lively lesson. Explain the game along these lines.

> "Guess what! Our ears *hear* better when we aren't busy *looking* at things at the same time. We are going to play a *listening* game, and the best way to play it is with our eyes shut!
>
> This game is called 'Who am I?', and it is up to you to come up with the answers! All you have to do is to listen carefully for alliterative words in the question. (That means words that begin with the same sound.) Here's one question for practice.
>
> Shut your eyes and *listen*! Everybody keep eyes shut until the person I call on has answered, but be ready with the answer *yourself* in case I call on *you*! Are your eyes shut? Are your ears ready??? So here's the riddle.
>
> **I rrrun away with other people's rrrulers and rrradios and rrrollerskates!**
>
> **Who am I?"**

Have all the Big Picture Code Cards on the desk, ready to hold up, confirming the right answer. Choose cards in any order.

Ask as many more questions as time allows. Suggestion: When you come to the Walrus riddle, after the children have given the *right* answer to the Walter Walrus question, you could deliberately hold up the *wrong* card: Munching Mike. You could then congratulate the children for catching out your mistake, and ask why Munching Mike might not like wallowing in the water. (You could hint by asking, "What can happen to metal when it gets left in water too long?") Elicit, Munching Mike could get rusty. Confirm this with,

"Yes! Munching Mike might get rusty, and then he couldn't munch on all those metal magnets mixed in mud that his Mom makes for his midday meal. No, you were right, it's Walter Walrus who loves wallowing in water!"

Try more riddles if time allows. Then you may like to finish with the Golden Girl riddle, which instead of asking, ' Who am I ?', changes to 'Guess who I am!' All reply, 'Golden Girl!' Congratulate everyone with, 'You've all been *great* at playing this Eyes Shut Riddle Game!

Later on you could use the riddles again for reading practice by printing them on sentence strips. After going through them together in class, the children could practice reading the riddles independently with one or two partners. When everyone can read at least one fluently, they could visit another class, explain to the new children how all they have to do is to listen carefully with their eyes shut. Then play the game with them.

Some children might like to make up more riddles to share in your class and keep in the Riddle box.

See the **a-z** riddles opposite.

The Riddles

a – I like **a**dding up **a**pples. Who am I?

b – I like to **b**alance my **b**all between my **b**ig **b**rown ears. Who am I?

c – I love eating **c**abbage and **c**ucumbers and **c**arrot **c**ake. Who am I?

d – I think **d**aisies and **d**andelions taste **d**elicious. Who am I?

e – I eat lots of **e**ggs for **e**nergy. Who am I? (You could use a deep voice.)

f – I think it's **f**un to go **f**ishing in my **f**ree time. Who am I?

g – I love playing **g**ames that I'm **g**ood at, like **g**uessing **g**ames. **G**uess who I am!

h – I like playing **h**opscotch and **h**ide-and-seek. Who am I? (You could whisper this one.)

i – **I**f you ask what my favorite color **i**s, it's **i**ndigo. Who am I?

j – I **j**ust love to travel by **j**eep or by **j**et. Who am I?

k – I keep a **k**angaroo and **k**ittens and a **k**ingfisher for pets. Who am I?

l – I **l**ove **l**icking **l**emon-flavored **l**ollipops. Who am I?

m – I love to **m**unch on **m**agnets **m**ixed in **m**ud sauce. Who am I?

n – I like to **n**ibble **n**uts in my **n**ut tree den. Who am I?

o – My best friends are an **o**strich… and an **o**tter. Who am I?

p – I love **p**laying the **p**iano. Who am I?

q – I spend three **qu**arters of my time **qu**arrelling. Who am I?

r – I **r**un off with other people's **r**ulers and **r**adios and **r**ollerskates. Who am I?

s – I'm good at **s**lithering and **s**liding in the **s**and. Who am I?

t – I love playing **t**ennis and jumping on a **t**rampoline. Who am I?

u – I always feel **u**nhappy when I'm **u**pside-down. Who am I?

v – We have lovely **v**elvet petals and **v**elvet leaves. Who looks after us?

w – I like to **w**allow in the **w**ater. Who am I?

x – I have a bo**x** of tools so I can fi**x** things. Who am I?

y – One day I hope to buy a **y**ellow **y**acht. Who am I?

z – I love **z**ipping around and around the Letterland **Z**oo. Who am I?

More Letterland Lore

Some children may surprise you by asking, "Why is this letter silent?" or "What's the story that explains this tricky word?", unaware that they are actually asking for more phonic facts! What better time to tell them than when they really want to know! Use this page, together with the more advanced, matching Picture Code Cards in your pack, to provide the relevant Letterland logic in brief. These vowel and vowel/consonant digraphs are all covered and more in full lessons in the Letterland Step-by-Step Teacher's Guide for Grade One.

 Listen for the '**oo**' sound (as in **put**) which Uppy Umbrella makes when she gets p**u**shed into her letter upside down.
Hear it in words like **pull, push** and cushion.

 Yellow Yo-yo Man works for Mr. E at the <u>end</u> of thousands of words like **rainy, twenty**and **history**, as well as many names, like **Lucy** and **Sammy**.

 Watch out when Walter Walrus is about! When he splashes Annie Apple with salty water she criees out '**Aw**! Don't be so **awful**!'
drawing, seesaw, awkward, yawn

 Wily Walter Walrus knows Uppy Umbrella's letter can hold water. So whenever he fills it and uses it to splash Annie from there, she cries out '**Aw**!' again.
sauce, fault, author, audience

 Eddy Elephant knows Walter Walrus loves to tease. To stop him he squirts water right at him. Walter is so surprised he cries out '**Oo**! **You**!'
'Oo': **flew, threw, jewel**   'You': **few, interview**

 When the boy called Roy plays his 'oy' game with the Yo-yo Man, they both shout '**Oy**!'
annoy, enjoy, tomboy, destroy

 In a few words you will find Roy playing his leapfrog game with Mr. I. Then Mr. I pretends to be annoyed, but they really both enjoy making a big n**oi**se, '**Oi**!'

 When the Boot Twin takes his brother's boots he teases him saying '**oo**, I've got your b**oo**ts!'
food, foolish, rooster, scooter

 When the Boot Twin takes the Foot Twin's boots and the Foot Twin accidentally steps in a puddle, he cries out, '**oo**! Just look at my f**oo**t!'
wooden, crooked, goodness, understood

 Wily Walter Walrus sometimes takes over Uppy Umbrella's letter to tease Oscar. When will you get wiser, Walter? now all we can hear is both of you shouting '**Ou**!' (as in **ou**ch!).
hour, bounce, mountain, surround

 Old Mr. O stops Walter Walrus from teasing Oscar Orange by crying out '**Oh**!' so loudly taht Wlater is too surprised to make any sound at all.
grow, throw, shadow, tomorrow

 Watch out when you see an orange next to Walter Walrus. In many words his teasing gets both Oscar Orange and himself into trouble, so they both h**ow**l '**Ow**!'

 When Mr. I see Golden Girl carefully being completely quiet next to the Hat Man, he call out '**I**' and gives her an ice cream for being so good.
high, sigh, tight, nightclub

Index

Index to Teacher's Guide CD2 Contents

1 Song Lyrics and Verses

Alphabet Song Verses
Alphabet Names Verses
Handwriting Song Verses
Blends & Digraphs
Consonant Blend Songs
Vowel Men Songs
Magic **e** Song
Vowel Men Out Walking Song
Vowel Stealers Songs

2 Plain Letters for Picture-coding

Lowercase (plain **a-z**)
Upper-lowercase (plain **Aa-Zz**)
Rimes for picture-coding (**ap – eck**)

3 Activities

Sentence Completion Poems (26)
Spelling Boxes
Written Word Sort worksheet
Poster with **b d** hands

4 Reading Booklet

My Letterland Reading Booklet (42 pages)

5 Decodable Booklets

The Queen is Sad
What is in the Box?
Is the Hat on the Cat?
Can you See?
Is this for Me?
Fun in the Sun
Did you See Eddy Elephant?
Clever Cat Gets Stuck
Peter Puppy's Presents

6 Plays

Vowel Men Out Walking Play
The Police and the Vowel Stealers Play

7 Assessments and Record Sheets

Section 2 Class Record
Section 2 Individual Record
Beginning Sounds in Words
Word Recognition Fluency
Matching Capital and Lowercase
Section 3 Assessment
Section 3 Class Record
Letter Sound Fluency
Section 4 Assessment
Section 4 Class Record
Sections 3-7 Individual Record
Section 5 Assessment
Section 6 Assessment
Section 7 Assessment

8 Word and Picture Cards

Beginning Sound Pictures (**a-z**)
Character Name Cards (**A-Z**)
Consonant Blend Cards: **s, l, r** blends
Essential Words Phrase Game
Rime Cards (**ap, at, an**, etc.)
Rhyming Pictures
Tricky Word Cards
Unit 1-5 Word Cards
Unit 6-8 Word Cards
Unit 9-13 Word Cards
Unit 14-16 Word Cards
Unit 17-18 Word Cards

9 Lesson Activities

Lesson 109 Sentence Practice
Lesson 111 Sentence Practice
Lesson 112 Onset-Rime Spelling
Lesson 114 Sentence Practice
Lesson 115 Sentence Practice
Lesson 119 Sentence Practice
Lesson 120 Sentence Practice
Lesson 124 Sentence Practice
Lesson 125 Written Word Sort
Lesson 126 Sentence Practice
Lesson 130 Sentence Practice
Lesson 135 Sentence Practice
Lesson 140 Sentence Practice
Lesson 141 Written Word Sort
Lesson 143 Sentence Practice
Lesson 144 Written Word Sort
Lesson 147 Written Word Sort
Lesson 154 Written Word Sort
Lesson 156 Written Word Sort
Lesson 159 Written Word Sort
Lesson 171 Written Word Sort
Lesson 172 Written Word Sort

10 Intervention Next Steps

Next Steps Lesson Log
Fast Sounds
Word Family Houses
Next Steps Word Cards
Next Steps Fluency Word Lists
Reading Robot Racers
Essential Words Phrase Game
Unit 1-5 Word Cards
Unit 6-8 Word Cards
Unit 9-13 Word Cards
Unit 14-16 Word Cards
Unit 17-18 Word Cards
Small Tricky Word Cards
Word Family Race